RELEVANCE LOST

RELEVANCE LOST

The Rise and Fall of Management Accounting

H. THOMAS JOHNSON
Portland State University

and

ROBERT S. KAPLAN
Harvard Business School and
Carnegie-Mellon University

HARVARD BUSINESS SCHOOL PRESS
Boston, Massachusetts

Harvard Business School Press, Boston, Massachusetts 02163
© 1987, 1991 by the President and Fellows of Harvard College.
All rights reserved.
Printed in the United States of America

06 05 04 03 02 01   15 14 13 12 11 10 9 8 7

LIBRARY OF CONGRESS CATALOGING-IN-PUBLICATION DATA
Johnson, H. Thomas, 1938–
    Relevance lost: the rise and fall of management
    accounting / H. Thomas Johnson and Robert S.
    Kaplan.
        p. cm.
    Includes bibliographical references and index.
    ISBN 0-87584-254-2 (paper, acid free paper)
    1. Managerial accounting—History.   2. Managerial
    accounting—United States—History.   I. Kaplan,
    Robert S.
    II. Title.
    HF5605.J64   1991
    658.15′11′09—dc20   90-25035
                                                    CIP

First Published in 1987 by the Harvard
Business School Press

Others apart sat on a hill retir'd,
In thoughts more elevate, and reason'd high . . .
   in wand'ring mazes lost.
                              Milton, *Paradise Lost*

Contents

To Our Editor, Barbara Ankeny

Preface to the Paperback Edition

The publication of the hardcover edition of *Relevance Lost* in March 1987 occurred at a watershed in management accounting theory and practice. Professor William Rotch of the Darden School of Business, University of Virginia, noted:

The book was a major statement about the need for new perspectives and methods of management accounting. It attracted a lot of attention and has even been a bit controversial. It is part of a trend that has made management accounting more important, more interesting and, surprising perhaps to non-accountants, more fun.

Pieces of the picture were described by the authors and others before 1987. A changing environment joined increased data analysis capability to produce both the need and opportunity for change. The authors captured that situation in the book, rooting their analysis in the historical evolution of cost systems, in which they argue that relevance was lost about 50 years earlier.[1]

The book quickly received attention from practitioner and academic communities. Chapter 1 was featured as the cover story in an issue of *Management Accounting*. The book received awards from the American Accounting Association in successive years for its impact on management accounting practice, was translated into several languages, and was widely read and discussed by both scholars and practitioners.

The book's thesis—that the management accounting systems in Western companies were no longer providing relevant information for decision making and control—has become widely accepted, though some academics in the United States and Europe still deny the existence of problems identified in the book. Practitioners seem to have accepted the evidence that management accounting systems, once relevant for the growth of modern enterprises, had atrophied in recent decades. Indeed, so quickly was the book's central theme understood and adopted that we soon found business and professional audiences uninterested in the causes and symptoms of management accounting's decline. They were ready to learn about remedies for their well-documented problems.

During the past few years, there has been an explosion of seminars, professional conferences, corporate programs, and publications on proposed innovations for management accounting systems. We have been pleased that the descriptions and prescriptions for reform contained in chapters 9 through 11 of the book provided a useful road map for discussions of product costing and profitability analysis, per-

1. "Before and After *Relevance Lost*," remarks prepared in presenting the first American Accounting Association-Management Accounting Section award in 1989 for "Notable Contribution to Management Accounting Literature."

formance measurement, and related cost management sub-
jects.

Since the publication of *Relevance Lost*, each of us has
been actively involved in furthering conceptual developments for management accounting. Tom Johnson advanced
the activity management approach as a vital ingredient for
companies pursuing total quality management and just-in-
time operations. The activity management approach is now
part of the continuous improvement activities and operational control systems of many organizations. Bob Kaplan,
together with his Harvard colleague, Robin Cooper, extended the transactions-costing approach described in chapter 10 of the book into comprehensive activity-based cost
(ABC) management systems. The ABC approach has been
adopted by dozens of corporations, has become a part of the
practice of major consulting firms, and has been integrated
into the management accounting teaching of many business
schools. Professional organizations such as CAM-I have further developed several of the themes articulated in *Relevance
Lost*.

As we launch this paperback edition, we remain confident in the validity and value of the messages the book con-
tains. We are also more aware of the debt we owe two individuals whose contributions to the book may not have been
adequately recognized. Professor Robin Cooper of the Harvard Business School helped us identify the failings of existing cost systems and the tremendous opportunities for developing new systems using activity-based costing concepts.
His extensive writings during the past three years have contributed immeasurably to the development and implementation of the approach. For interested readers, the brief
bibliography following this preface lists publications docu-
menting developments in cost management systems over the
past three years.

Our second debt is to Barbara Ankeny, who in 1984, as

the acquisitions editor for the Harvard Business School Press, approached us with the idea for a book on new developments in management accounting. Our initial reaction was lukewarm, but her enthusiasm energized our own interests. Her active participation and support sustained us throughout the project. She, perhaps more than either of us, had the vision of what the book might become. *Relevance Lost* would not have occurred without Barbara Ankeny and to her we dedicate this edition of the book.

Portland, Oregon   H. Thomas Johnson
Boston, Massachusetts   Robert S. Kaplan
December 1990

Selected Bibliography on Management Accounting Systems, 1987–1990

Books

Berliner, Callie, and James A. Brimson. *Cost Management for Today's Advanced Manufacturing: The CAM-I Conceptual Design.* Boston: Harvard Business School Press, 1987.

Brinker, Barry J. *Emerging Practices in Cost Management.*[2] Boston: Warren, Gorham & Lamont, 1990, including:

> Cooper, Robin. "Does Your Company Need a New Cost System?" (Spring 1987), pp. 131–135.

> ———. "Elements of Activity-Based Costing." (Summer 1988, Fall 1988, Winter 1989, and Spring 1989), pp. 3–23.

> ———. "Implementing an Activity-Based Cost System." (Spring 1990), pp. 69–78.

---

2. A compilation of 50 of the best articles published in the *Journal of Cost Management,* Spring 1987 to Fall 1990. The page numbers refer to those in the book.

————. "Cost Classification in Unit-Based and Activity-Based Manufacturing Cost Systems." (Fall 1990), pp. 33–44.

Foster, George, and Charles T. Horngren. "Cost Accounting and Cost Management in a JIT Environment." (Winter 1988), pp. 199–210.

————. "Flexible Manufacturing Systems: Cost Management and Cost Accounting Implications." (Fall 1988), pp. 305–314.

Govindarajan, Vijay, and John K. Shank. "Strategic Cost Analysis: The Crown Cork and Seal Case." (Winter 1989), pp. 469–480.

Johnson, H. T. "The Decline of Cost Management: A Reinterpretation of 20th Century Cost Accounting History." (Spring 1987), pp. 137–144.

————. "Activity Management: Reviewing the Past and Future of Cost Management." (Winter 1990), pp. 145–148.

————. "Beyond Product Costing: A Challenge to Cost Management's Conventional Wisdom." (Fall 1990), pp. 345–354.

Rotch, William. "Activity-Based Costing in Service Industries." (Summer 1990), pp. 55–65.

Sakurai, Michiharu. "Target Costing and How to Use It." (Summer 1989), pp. 249–260.

Shields, Michael D., and S. Mark Young. "A Behavioral Model for Implementing Cost Management Systems." (Winter 1989), pp. 399–410.

Utzig, Larry. "Reconciling the Two Views of Quality." (Spring 1987), pp. 365–368.

Bruns, William J. Jr., and Robert S. Kaplan, eds. *Accounting & Management: Field Study Perspectives*. Boston: Harvard Business School Press, 1987, including:

Cooper, Robin, and Robert S. Kaplan. "How Cost Accounting Systematically Distorts Product Costs," pp. 204–228.

Johnson, H. Thomas. "Organizational Design versus Strategic Information Procedures for Managing Corporate Overhead Cost: Weyerhaeuser Company, 1972–1986, pp. 49–72.

Kaplan, Robert S., ed. *Measures for Manufacturing Excellence*. Boston: Harvard Business School Press, 1990, including:

Johnson, H. Thomas. "Performance Measurement for Competitive Excellence," pp. 63–90.

Kaplan, Robert S. "Limitations of Cost Accounting in Advanced Manufacturing Environments," pp. 15–38.

Kaplan, Robert S., and Anthony A. Atkinson. *Advanced Management Accounting*, 2d ed. Englewood Cliffs, NJ: Prentice-Hall, 1989.

Shank, John K., and Vijay Govindarajan. *Strategic Cost Analysis: The Evolution from Managerial to Strategic Accounting*. Homewood, IL: Dow Jones-Irwin, 1989.

Articles

Cooper, Robin. "You Need a New Cost System When. . ." *Harvard Business Review* (January–February 1989), pp. 77–82.

Cooper, Robin, and Robert S. Kaplan. "Measure Costs Right: Make the Right Decisions." *Harvard Business Review* (September–October 1988), pp. 96–103.

Hiromoto, Toshiro. "Another Hidden Edge—Japanese Management Accounting." *Harvard Business Review* (July–August 1988), pp. 22–26.

Howell, Robert A., and S. R. Soucy. "Cost Accounting in the New Manufacturing Environment." *Management Accounting* (August 1987), pp. 42–48.

Johnson, H. Thomas. "How Weyerhaeuser Manages Corporate Overhead Costs." *Management Accounting* (August 1987), pp. 20–26.

————. "Activity-Based Information: A Blueprint for World-Class Management." *Management Accounting* (June 1988), pp. 23–30.

————. "Managing Costs versus Managing Activities— Which Strategy Works?" *Financial Executive* (January/February 1990), pp. 32–36.

Kaplan, Robert S. "One Cost System Isn't Enough." *Harvard Business Review* (January–February 1988), pp. 61–66.

————. "Management Accounting in Advanced Technological Environments." *Science* (August 25, 1989), pp. 819–823.

————. "The Four-Stage Model of Cost Systems Design." *Management Accounting* (February 1990), pp. 22–26.

Preface

CORPORATE management accounting systems are inadequate for today's environment. In this time of rapid technological change, vigorous global and domestic competition, and enormously expanding information processing capabilities, management accounting systems are not providing useful, timely information for the process control, product costing, and performance evaluation activities of managers. A widespread misconception exists that using accounting information for internal management planning and control activities is a new phenomenon, first suggested by the decision and microeconomic analysis of post–World War II cost accounting textbooks, courses, and research. According to this view, the inadequacy of current systems arises from a lag in replacing prewar cost accounting systems, designed for financial reporting and tax purposes, with modern information and accounting systems.

But it is the decline in relevance of corporate management accounting systems that is the recent phenomenon. Accounting systems for managerial decisions and control can be traced back to the origins of hierarchical enterprises in the early nineteenth century. Unencumbered by any demands for external reporting, management accounting practices developed and flourished in a wide variety of nineteenth- and early twentieth-century corporations. Only in the past sixty to seventy years have external auditing and financial reporting systems come to perform the original function of management accounting systems. The current inadequacy of corporate management accounting systems can therefore be recognized as a relatively recent decline in relevance, not as a lag in adapting older financial accounting systems to modern managerial needs.

We wrote this book to provide the historical context for the current interest in accomplishing major redesign of management accounting systems. By emphasizing the origins of contemporary management accounting practices, we can understand better that attempting to infuse them with decision and control relevance is not a revolutionary idea. It is consistent with the origins of the practices many years ago.

One audience for the book will be the innovative financial and general managers who are contemplating or implementing fundamental changes in their organizations' management accounting systems. We hope they find value in learning the rich historical tradition for their efforts as well as the reasons why so little innovation has occurred during the past half-century. Understanding the reasons behind the obsolescence of existing systems should provide an improved rationale for organizational change.

The book will also prove useful to students and teachers of management accounting. We hope to make them mildly uncomfortable with the isolation of existing courses, textbooks, and research from the interesting and challenging problems of contemporary practice.

The book is more than a retrospective view of the origin and stagnation of management accounting practice. The 1980s provide a critical, perhaps unparalleled, opportunity for major redesign of corporate management accounting systems. The obsolescence of existing systems, combined with extraordinary competitive and technological challenges, requires all organizations to reexamine their existing practices. They must attempt to design entirely new management accounting systems. Not since the development of assembly-line mass production and the multidivisional corporation more than sixty years ago has there been a comparable revolution in the organization and technology of production processes.

We close the book with several chapters identifying paths for major innovations. Not a cookbook of specific procedures, these chapters provide a conceptual framework for the development of managerially relevant procedures to enhance process control, compute product costs, and evaluate periodic performance. We believe these chapters will help guide the efforts of practitioners, researchers, and teachers to improve management accounting practice and theory.

Tacoma, Washington   *H. Thomas Johnson*
Boston, Massachusetts   *Robert S. Kaplan*
September 1986

Acknowledgments

Both authors have benefited greatly from conversations and work with Robin Cooper at the Harvard Business School. His observations on cost accounting practices influenced the writing of chapters 3 and 6 and much of the material in chapters 8 and 10 should be considered joint work with him. Steven Zeff at Rice University and Richard Vangermeersch at the University of Rhode Island provided valuable comments on the historical narrative. Finally, we are grateful for the comments of Richard Brief of New York University, Anthony Hopwood of the London School of Economics, Gary J. Previts of Case Western and Eldon Schafer of Pacific Lutheran University.

RELEVANCE LOST

CHAPTER 1

Introduction

TODAY'S management accounting information, driven by the procedures and cycle of the organization's financial reporting system, is too late, too aggregated, and too distorted to be relevant for managers' planning and control decisions. With increased emphasis on meeting quarterly or annual earnings targets, internal accounting systems focus narrowly on producing a monthly earnings report. And despite the considerable resources devoted to computing a monthly or quarterly income figure, the figure does not measure the actual increase or decrease in economic value that has occurred during the period.

The failings have three important consequences.

Management accounting reports are of little help to operating managers as they attempt to reduce costs and improve productivity. Frequently, the reports decrease productivity because they require operating managers to spend time attempting to understand and explain reported variances that have little to do with the economic and technological reality of their operations. By not providing timely and detailed information on process efficiencies or by focusing on inputs such as direct labor that are relatively insignificant in today's production environment, the management accounting system not only fails to provide relevant information to managers, but it also distracts their attention from factors that are critical for production efficiencies.

The management accounting system also fails to provide accurate product costs. Costs are distributed to products by simplistic and arbitrary measures, usually direct-labor based, that do not represent the demands made by each product on the firm's resources. Although simplistic product costing methods are adequate for financial reporting requirements—the methods yield values for inventory and for cost of goods sold that satisfy external reporting and auditing requirements—the methods systematically bias and distort costs of individual products. The standard product cost systems typical of most organizations usually lead to enormous cross subsidies across products. When such distorted information represents the only available data on "product costs," the danger exists for misguided decisions on product pricing, product sourcing, product mix, and responses to rival products. Many firms seem to be falling victim to the danger.

Finally, managers' horizons contract to the short-term cycle of the monthly profit and loss statement. The financial accounting system treats many cash outlays as expenses of the period in which they are made even though these outlays will benefit future periods. Discretionary cash outlays for new products and improved processes, for preventive maintenance, for long-term marketing positioning, for employee training and morale, and for developing new systems can produce substantial cash inflows for the future. Managers under pressure to meet short-term profit goals can, on occasion, achieve these goals by reducing their expenditures on such discretionary investments. Thus, short-term profit pressures can lead to a decrease in long-term investment. Yet monthly accounting statements using the practices mandated for external reporting can signal increased profits even when the long-term economic health of the firm has been compromised.

Many short-term measures are appropriate for motivating and evaluating managerial performance. It is unlikely, however, that monthly or quarterly profits, especially when based on the practices mandated and used for external constituencies, would be one of them. Today's management accounting systems provide a misleading target for managerial attention and fail to provide the relevant set of measures that appropriately reflect the technology, the products, the processes, and the competitive environment in which the organization operates. Originally designed earlier in this century to help coordinate the diverse activities of emerging vertically integrated enterprises, financial measures such as return on investment (ROI) have become for many organizations the only measure of success. Financial managers, relying exclusively on periodic financial statements for their view of the firm, become isolated from the real value-creating operations of the organization and fail to recognize when the accounting numbers are no longer providing relevant or appropriate measures of the organization's operations.

The Challenge

The contemporary economic environment demands excellence from corporate management accounting systems. With vigorous global competition, rapid progress in product and process technology, and wide fluctuations in currency exchange rates and raw material prices, an organization's management accounting system must provide timely and accurate information to facilitate efforts to control costs, to measure and improve productivity, and to devise improved production processes. The management accounting system must also report accurate product costs so that pricing decisions, introduction of new products, abandonment of obsolete products, and response to rival products can be made with the best possible information on product resource demands. Finally, large decentralized organizations require systems to motivate and evaluate the performance of their managers. The systems should provide appropriate incentives and signals to managers working in different functions, with diverse products and processes, amid globally dispersed operations.

The organization's management accounting system serves as a vital two-way communication link between senior and subordinate managers. It is the means by which senior executives communicate the organization's goals and objectives to subordinate and decentralized managers. In the reverse direction, the management accounting system is the channel by which information about the firm's product performance and production efficiencies is reported to upper levels of management. Further, managerial compensation and promotion decisions are usually based on the numbers reported by the management accounting system.

With these vital roles for planning and control information and for communication, motivation, and evaluation, the organization's management accounting system is a necessary component in the firm's strategy to achieve competitive success. An excellent management accounting system will not by itself guarantee success in today's economy— ultimately, success depends on products that meet customers' needs, on efficient production and distribution systems, and on effective marketing efforts. But an ineffective management accounting system can undermine superior product development, process improvement, and marketing efforts. Where an ineffective management accounting system prevails, the best outcome occurs when managers understand the irrelevance of the system and by-pass it by developing personalized information systems. But managers unwittingly court trouble if they do not recognize an inadequate system and erroneously rely on it for managerial control information and product decisions.

The Opportunity

Fortunately, the increased demands for excellent management accounting systems occur at a time when the costs for collecting, processing, analyzing, and reporting information have been decreasing by orders of magnitude. The enormous expansion in computing capabilities has given today's designers of management accounting systems opportunities that could not have been dreamed about by their predecessors. With many production processes under direct control of digital computers, information can be recorded in real time for analysis of operating performance. In highly automated environments, virtually every transaction can be captured for subsequent analysis. Automated parts recognition and tracking systems combined with local area network technology can provide continuous status reports on work in process. Thus, extensive systems are now feasible to measure and attribute accurately the resource demands made by each product in a diverse line.

Today's designers of management accounting systems can combine such sophisticated electronic technology with improved software technology to devise reporting and control systems that are more accurate, more timely, and, hence, more effective than those designed by their predecessors. Simplified, aggregate procedures, adopted in earlier decades because more relevant and timely procedures would have been too costly or even infeasible, no longer need to be

tolerated. The computing revolution of the past two decades
has so reduced information collection and processing costs
that virtually all technical barriers to the design and implementation of effective management accounting systems have
been removed. The increased complexity of operations in
today's global, technological economy has been matched by
a corresponding increase in the capabilities of systems to
provide relevant and timely information on the operations.

The Background

Historians have demonstrated that accounting reports have been prepared for thousands of years. Bookkeeping records, dating back to ancient civilizations, have been
found engraved on stone tablets. Five hundred years ago, a
Venetian monk, Fra Pacioli, described the basics for a well-
functioning double-entry bookkeeping system. The demand
to record information on commercial transactions has existed for as long as people have traded with one another in
market exchanges.

But the demand for management acounting information—information about transactions occurring within organizations—is a much more recent phenomenon. Before
the early nineteenth century, virtually all exchange transactions occurred between an owner-entrepreneur and individuals who were not part of the organization: raw material
suppliers, labor paid by piecework, and customers. There
were no "levels of management" or long-term salaried employees. Transactions occurred in the market and measures
of success were easily obtained. The owner-entrepreneur
needed to collect more cash from sales to customers than
was paid out to suppliers of the production inputs, primarily
labor and material.

As a consequence of the Industrial Revolution and the
ability to achieve gain through economies of scale, it became

efficient for nineteenth-century enterprise owners to commit significant sums of capital to their production processes. In order to gain maximum efficiency from their capital investment, owners hired workers on a long-term basis, rather than bearing the costs and risks of continual spot contracting. The long-term viability and success of these "managed" organizations revealed the gains that could be earned by managing a hierarchical organization, as opposed to conducting all business through market transactions. Early examples of successful, hierarchical organizations are the textile mills founded in the first half of the nineteenth century, the railroads formed around mid-century, and the steel companies created in the second half of the century.

The emergence more than 150 years ago of such organizations created a new demand for accounting information. As conversion processes that formerly were supplied at a price through market exchanges became performed within organizations, a demand arose for measures to determine the "price" of output from internal operations. Lacking price information on the conversion processes occurring within their organizations, owners devised measures to summarize the efficiency by which labor and material were converted to finished products, measures that also served to motivate and evaluate the managers who supervised the conversion process. The measures were especially important since the factories were frequently located a considerable distance from the central office of the owners. Thus, management accounting developed to support the profit-seeking activities of entrepreneurs for whom multiprocess, hierarchical, managed enterprises were more efficient than conversion processes through continual transactions in the marketplace.

The early management accounting measures were simple but seemed to serve well the needs of owners and managers. They focused on conversion costs and produced summary measures such as cost per hour or cost per pound produced for each process and for each worker. The measured costs included labor and material and involved some attribution of overhead. The goal of the systems was to identify the different costs for the intermediate and final products of the firm and to provide a benchmark to measure the efficiency of the conversion process. The management accounting information was also used to provide incentives for workers to achieve productivity goals.

By the middle of the nineteenth century, great advances in transportation and communication, especially the invention of the railroad and the telegraph, provided further opportunities for gain to large, hierarchical organizations. The enterprises could now coordinate the acquisition of raw materials and the distribution of final products over much larger geographical areas. But without a corresponding increase in the quantity and quality of management accounting information, these organizations would not have been able to capture the full potential gains from increased scale of operations. In fact, effective management accounting systems were necessary to coordinate efficiently the logistical, conversion, and distribution activities of these enterprises and to provide summary measures of performance for decentralized and dispersed managers.

The railroads offer perhaps the best examples of such effective management accounting systems. To oversee the diverse and dispersed operations of these enormous enterprises, new procedures were invented to control the receipt and disbursement of cash. In addition to these significant financial recording or bookkeeping innovations, however, the railroads also developed extensive summaries of their internal operations and performance. Measures such as cost per ton-mile were created and reported for each major segment of operations. The operating ratio, the ratio of revenues to operating costs, was developed both to measure the profitability of various segments of business—passenger versus freight, region by region—and to evaluate the performance of managers.

Improved transportation and communication combined with economies of scale permitted the growth of large distribution enterprises, particularly retail store chains such as Marshall Field, Sears, and Woolworth. These retailers developed their own measures of internal performance to support their managerial planning and control activities. Obviously, measures of conversion cost, such as cost per hour or cost per pound, or the operating measures of the railroads, the cost per ton-mile, were not relevant for these distribution enterprises. The organizations required information on the effectiveness and efficiency of their purchasing, pricing, and retailing activities. For these activities, measures such as gross margin by department—selling revenues less purchases and operating costs—and inventory stockturn were created.

These examples reveal that management accounting information developed to facilitate the management of process-type industries: textile and steel conversion, transportation, and distribution. The management accounting measures were designed to motivate and evaluate the efficiency of internal processes, not to measure the overall "profit" of the enterprise. These organizations really had to do only one activity well: convert raw materials into a single final product such as cloth or steel, move passengers or freight, or resell purchased goods. If they performed this basic activity efficiently, the organizations could be confident that they would be profitable in the long run. Thus, the management accounting system was created to promote efficiency in the key operating activity of the organization. There could be a separate transactions-based system that recorded receipts and expenditures and produced periodic, probably annual, financial statements for the owners and creditors of the firm. But the two systems, management and financial, operated independently of each other.

Further advances in the technology of management accounting systems were made in conjunction with the scientific management movement. The movement started in metal fabricating companies during the last two decades of the nineteenth century. The goal of the scientific management engineers, such as Frederick Taylor, was to improve the efficiency and utilization of labor and materials, but the physical standards they developed, such as labor grade and labor hours per unit and material quantities per unit, were easily converted into standards for labor and material costs. Eventually, these labor and material costs, often combined with an allocation of indirect or overhead costs, were aggregated into a finished product unit cost that could be used for pricing decisions. The standards were frequently updated to reflect fluctuations in the price paid for labor and materials. Thus, finished product standard costs were often closer to what we now call replacement cost than to any measure of historic cost. As with the measures of conversion efficiency developed earlier in process industries, finished product unit costs were calculated to aid managerial decisions—pricing in this case—not to produce external financial statements. Therefore, there was little demand for having the unit cost information be "consistent" with the books of transactions used to prepare summary financial statements.

The final developments in management accounting systems occurred in the early decades of the twentieth century to support the growth of multi-activity, diversified corporations. The Du Pont Powder Company, formed in 1903 as a combination of previously separate family-run or independent companies, was a prototype of this new organizational form. The managers of the new Du Pont Company faced the problem of coordinating the diverse activities of a vertically integrated manufacturing and marketing organization and of deciding on the most profitable allocation of capital to these different activities. Before the coming of integrated firms such as Du Pont, organizations engaged in only a single type of activity, and their only important capital choice was whether to expand the scale of one homogeneous operation.

A number of important operating and budgeting activities were devised by the senior managers of Du Pont, but the most important and the most enduring management accounting innovation was the return on investment (ROI) measure. Return on investment provided an overall measure of the commercial success of each operating unit and of the entire organization. Since capital allocation was a central management function in the early Du Pont company, departmental managers were not held responsible for ROI performance. They took their scale of operations as given and concentrated solely on promoting efficiencies in their internally managed processes, just as their nineteenth century counterparts had done. Only top managers used ROI to help direct their allocations of capital and to evaluate the performance of the operating department (which could be different from the performance of the manager of that department). F. Donaldson Brown, the chief financial officer of Du Pont, decomposed ROI into its component parts and demonstrated that the measure could be viewed as a combination of two of the efficiency measures—the operating ratio (return on sales) and stockturn (sales to assets)—used by single-activity organizations.

Use of the ROI measure was expanded in the 1920s as the multidivisional form of organization evolved in the Du Pont and the newly reorganized General Motors corporations. The decentralized, multidivisional corporation developed to capture economies of scope—the gains from sharing common organizational functions across a broad spectrum of products. The enormous diversity in the product markets served by these giant corporations required new systems and measures to coordinate dispersed and decentralized activities. Division managers were made responsible for profitability and return on capital and had authority to make capital requests. It was no longer possible for the corporate-level departments of marketing, purchasing, and finance to have the requisite information to function effectively or efficiently in all the markets served by their organization. Decentralization was necessary, and each operating division required its own staff functions to support its activities. Thus, central managers were now in the position of providing capital to diverse operating units and attempting to co-ordinate, motivate, and evaluate the performance of their divisional managers. The ROI measure played a key role in permitting this internal market for managers and for capital to function.

Lost Relevance

By 1925 virtually all management accounting practices used today had been developed: cost accounts for labor, material, and overhead; budgets for cash, income, and capital; flexible budgets, sales forecasts, standard costs, variance analysis, transfer prices, and divisional performance measures.[1] These practices had evolved to serve the informational and control needs of the managers of increasingly complex and diverse organizations. At that point the pace of innovation seemed to stop. Perhaps there was little incentive to continue to develop innovative management accounting procedures since the corporate organizational forms developed by companies such as Du Pont and General Motors proved to be the model for many corporations for the next half-century.

Even without significant innovations in organizational forms, however, the diversity of products and complexity of manufacturing processes continued to increase in the decades after 1920. Thus, the need for accurate product costs and effective process control should have imposed new demands on organizations' management accounting systems.

The failure of these systems to keep pace with the evolution of product and process technologies eventually led to the problems described at the outset of this chapter: distorted product costs, delayed and overly aggregated process control information, and short-term performance measures that do not reflect the increases or decreases in the organization's economic position.

In part this stagnation can be attributed to the dominance of the external financial accounting statements during the twentieth century. With more widespread public ownership of corporations' securities, and periodic crises in capital markets, the demand for audited financial statements increased. Auditors and regulators, mindful of their responsibility to users of financial statements, preferred conservative accounting practices based on objective, verifiable, and realized financial transactions. When measuring cost of goods sold and valuing inventory, auditors insisted on product costs based on the historical transactions recorded in the firms' ledger accounts. Further, they wanted the financial statements—the income statement and the balance sheet—to be integrated. That is, the two financial statements had to be based on the same transactions and events. It did not matter for the summary financial statements if the inventory costing procedures distorted or cross-subsidized individual product costs as long as the total value recorded in the inventory accounts was derived from transactions recorded in the ledgers. Thus, simple methods were used to assign direct and period costs to products.

In principle, of course, early twentieth-century managers did not have to yield the design of their cost management systems to financial accountants and auditors. They could have maintained separate systems for managerial purposes and for external reporting. But the information technology early in the century may not have made such parallel systems cost effective. Perhaps in the 1920s the product line of organizations was more focused than that of today's organizations so that the distorting effect of simplistic methods to attach costs to products was not as severe as it has become today. Also the cost of collecting data and providing prompt reports to production managers may have been too high to permit the real-time process control that is now possible. Thus, the decision by managers to forego investing in management accounting systems separate from those already mandated by the demands for financial statements may have been the correct economic decision. The benefits from a more accurate and more responsive management accounting system may not have been worth the cost of maintaining it.

In subsequent decades, as product lines expanded, as production technology changed, as product life cycles shortened, as global competitive conditions shifted, and, most important, as great advances in information technology occurred, we would then expect managers to reconsider their decision not to invest in a more relevant and more timely management accounting system. But by the time these events unfolded, the spirit and knowledge of management accounting systems design, developed and sustained throughout the hundred-year period from 1825 to 1925, had disappeared. Organizations became fixated on the cost systems and management reporting methods of the 1920s. When cost systems became automated on digital computers, starting in the mid-1960s, the system designers basically automated the manual systems they found in the factory. Left unquestioned was whether these systems were still sensible given the great expansion in information technology represented by electronic, digital computers and the already changed nature of the organization's operations.

One might wonder why university researchers failed to note the growing obsolescence of organizations' management accounting systems and did not play a more active or more stimulative role to improve the art of management accounting systems design. We believe the academics were led astray by a simplified model of firm behavior. Influenced strongly by economists' one-product, one-production-process model of the firm, management accounting academics found little value in the cost allocations imposed on organizations by financial accounting procedures. Sixty years of literature emerged advocating the separation of costs into fixed and variable components for making good product decisions and for controlling costs. This literature, very persuasive when illustrated in the simple one-product settings used by academic economists and accountants, never fully addressed the question of where fixed costs came from and how these costs needed to be covered by each of the products in the corporations' repertoire. Nor did the academic researchers attempt to implement their ideas in the environment of actual organizations, with hundreds or thousands of products and with complex, multistage production processes. Thus, the academic literature concentrated on increasingly elegant and sophisticated approaches to analyzing costs for single-product, single-process firms while actual organizations attempted to manage with antiquated systems in settings that had little relationship to the simplified model researchers assumed for analytic and teaching convenience.

Ironically, as management accounting systems became less relevant to the organization's operations and strategy, many senior executives began to believe they could run their firms "by the numbers." Early twentieth-century organizations such as Du Pont, General Motors, and General Electric had been created by owners who understood the technology of their products and processes. In succeeding decades, however, chief executives were selected whose entire careers had been spent in staff functions such as accounting, finance, and legal. Lacking knowledge in their organizations' underlying technology, executives increasingly made decisions based upon their projected impact on short-term financial measures, especially earnings per share and return on investment. But as product life cycles shorten and as more costs must be incurred before production begins—for research and development, product and process design, capital investment, software development, and education and training—so that directly traceable product costs become a much lower fraction of total costs, traditional financial measures such as periodic earnings and accounting ROI become less useful measures of corporate performance.

In some respects, this is not a new phenomenon. If we go back five hundred years to the publication of perhaps the original accounting book by Fra Pacioli, we can ask what kinds of events were occurring in fifteenth-century Venice that led to a demand for accounting information. Undoubtedly, merchants were trading goods with other countries. Consider a group of investors who acquired goods produced in northern Italy and chartered an expedition to sell them in India. With the proceeds the traders purchased tea, traveled back to Venice, and then sold the tea. At the end of the expedition, the accountant subtracted the costs of the caravan and of acquiring the initial load of merchandise from the revenues received from the sale of tea in Italy to compute a profit for the entire trip, a profit to be distributed among the investors in the venture.

To compute overall profitability of the venture and to distribute the net proceeds (the retained earnings) among the initial investors was a worthwhile role for accounting. One has to wonder, however, whether the investors or the Venetian version of the Securities and Exchange Commission or Financial Accounting Standards Board, also asked the accountant to compute the expedition's profits during the third quarter of 1487 when the caravan was traversing the Persian desert en route to India. Probably not. Because even five hundred years ago, investors likely understood that allocating the total profits of expeditions to periods as short as three months was not a meaningful exercise. Yet is not the value of preparing monthly income statements for many of today's organizations not unlike an attempt to allocate the profits of a long venture to every month within that venture?

Arguing that it is meaningless to allocate project profitability to short periods within the life of a project does not imply that we believe it fruitless to obtain indicators of short-term progress. Returning to our Venetian expedition, there were probably many measures of the caravan's performance during the third quarter of 1487 that the investors would have been interested in knowing. For example, what distance did the caravan cover and in what direction? How many provisions were left? What was the condition of the inventory being transported? Were the workers content or rebellious? There were many potentially useful indicators of the caravan manager's performance during the third quarter, 1487. But quarterly profits was not one of them!

Likewise, given the current competitive, technological environment, there are probably many better indicators of a company's short-term performance than its quarterly earnings. Certainly, cash flow is important; we would want to know the pattern and structure of a company's cash receipts and cash expenditures. But knowing sources and uses of cash is very different from working hard every month and every quarter to produce complete income statements and balance sheets, complete with amortizations, capitalizations, and many other accruals.

The challenge and the opportunity for contemporary organizations we outlined at the beginning of this chapter are clear. Management accounting systems can and should be designed to support the operations and the strategy of the organization. The technology exists to implement systems radically different from those being used today. What is lacking is knowledge. But this knowledge can emerge from experimentation and communication. The innovative spirit evident one hundred years ago at the outset of the scientific management movement can be recaptured by innovative managers and academic researchers who are committed to developing new concepts for designing relevant management accounting systems. This book traces the history, development, and stagnation of management accounting systems, but closes with a vision of what the future can bring.

Note

1. Anthony Hopwood has pointed out to us that significant innovations for project management were made in the 1950s and 1960s in the aerospace and defense industries. These innovations include project accounting, cost-benefit analysis, program budgeting, Zero Base Budgeting, and accounting for matrix organizations. These procedures, however, have had limited impact outside the aerospace and defense industries and virtually none of them are described in contemporary management accounting textbooks.

CHAPTER 2

Nineteenth-Century Cost Management Systems

M ANAGEMENT accounting first appeared in the United States when business organizations, instead of relying on external markets to direct economic exchange, began conducting economic exchange internally. These developments occurred during the nineteenth century in industries involved in textile making, railroading, the manufacture of iron and steel, and retail distribution. Firms in these industries specialized in a single economic activity—manufacturing, transportation, or distribution—whereby they converted resources into products or services. By linking many separable processes, complex and extensive organizations evolved to handle each of the activities.

Entrepreneurs linked processes in the new single-activity organizations because they believed that greater value could be achieved by managing the processes in a centrally controlled organization than by exchanging outputs

from the processes in the market. Outputs of separate processes to make textiles, such as sheep shearing, spinning,
weaving, and finishing, for instance, were traditionally exchanged in markets, often by merchants. By 1800, however,
merchant-entrepreneurs in parts of Britain and America had
undertaken to control the output of two or more of these
processes (especially spinning, weaving, and finishing) in
centrally managed enterprises. The owners of early textile-
making firms and of other types of manufacturing firms that
followed in their wake after 1800 hoped to achieve greater
value by controlling the time that others spent in productive
processes. At first the owners probably hoped that centralized control of the work force would enhance profit by sta-
bilizing and increasing the flow of salable output. Very
quickly, however, they also began to pay attention to the
opportunity for increased profit that lay in reducing costs
and increasing productive efficiency.

The owners of nineteenth-century, single-activity businesses created entirely new managerial accounting procedures to monitor and evaluate the output of internally directed processes. Of course, these businesses continued to
rely on market price information to guide their external exchanges with suppliers or customers. They recorded these
external exchanges using age-old bookkeeping methods,
usually in double-entry. In their accounts of external exchanges, the firms kept track of what they owned and owed
and, occasionally, of the profit on their exchanges with the
outside world. These objectives were altered and new management accounting developments emerged, however, as a
consequence of the firms' internally directed processes.

Historians often err in associating the origins of managerial accounting with the coming of "big business," especially railroading. Actually, management accounting pre-
ceded the railroads and had no connection with "big business" as such. It did not arise because vast organizations
required it.[1] On the contrary, management accounting itself

may have facilitated the growth of large-scale firms. It could do so by reversing Adam Smith's famous proposition that the division of labor is limited by the extent of the market.[2] Management accounting undoubtedly widened the extent of the market—the quasi-market for exchanges inside a business firm—by rationalizing new internally directed opportunities for specialization and division of labor. Management accounting focused people's attention on the potential gains from *internal* coordination of economic exchange, thereby encouraging manager-entrepreneurs to increase the size of their firms. That this was the case will be confirmed by examining the development of management accounting in the nineteenth century. Such a study properly begins with scrutiny of representative firms engaged in manufacturing, transportation, and distribution. We first consider manufacturing by examining two firms: an antebellum New England textile-making firm and a late nineteenth-century giant steel-making firm.

Cost Management in Early New England Textile Mills

The first American business organizations to develop management accounting systems were the mechanized, integrated cotton textile factories that appeared after 1812.[3] They used cost accounts to ascertain the direct labor and overhead costs of converting raw material into finished yarn and fabric. The double-entry cost accounts, among the earliest discovered anywhere, differed radically from any accounting records used previously. A perceptive description of that difference was provided over fifty years ago by D R Scott.

Before the industrial revolution, accounting was mainly a record of the external relations of one business unit with other business units, a record of relations determined in the market. But with the advent of large scale productive operations . . . necessity arose for more emphasis upon the accounting for interests within the competitive unit and upon the use of accounting records as a means of administrative control over the enterprise. . . . The appearance of cost accounts in manufacturing . . . is [an] example.[4]

Scott recognized that before the advent of the modern factory, businesses used accounts primarily to record the results of market exchanges. He perceived that the development of a new kind of accounting activity accompanied the new mode of production.

The appearance of new accounting techniques in early textile factories was inextricably connected with management's desire to control the rate at which resources (raw materials, labor, and overhead) were converted into intermediate output. The managerial accounting that appeared in American textile-making firms after the early 1800s would have been inconceivable before the introduction of centralized control over production processes. Early managerial accounts do devote some attention to an organization's total costs and profit. They give primary attention, however, to the outlay on internally controlled resources per unit of intermediate output.

The accounts are particularly concerned with the "cost" of labor. The concern emanated, of course, from the wage system, in which workers surrender control over their labor time. Arguments about the causes, costs, and possible benefits to workers of surrendering control over their labor in return for a fixed income have abounded since Ricardo and Marx. Our concern, however, is with the implications for accounting of the complications that factory managers faced once workers were employed at a wage.

Before the coming of the factory, all intermediate components going into a manufactured product were market-priced outputs. In the pre-factory domestic system, for instance, a market-based price—a piece rate—was paid for the output of independent artisans or subcontractors who carried out almost every process involved in the manufacture of a product. In textile making under the domestic system, spinners were paid per pound for yarn, weavers were paid per yard for cloth, and assemblers were paid per unit. Although merchant-entrepreneurs coordinated the flow of this intermediate output from raw fiber to finished fabric or garment, they did not assume the task of controlling the time spent by artisans in each process. Hence, they kept accounts only to record past exchanges and to keep track of widely scattered inventories. They would not have required information from those accounts to rationalize their undertakings. Indeed, market prices supplied every conceivable bit of information for decision making and control.[5] The market supplied the merchant not only with prices for raw materials and finished goods, but also with prices for all intermediate outputs used in domestic-style production.

Market prices stopped supplying all conceivable information for decision making and control when merchant-entrepreneurs contrived to administer the work of laborers by gathering them together into a centralized workplace.[6] In the factory, wage contracts were substituted for market piece-rate contracts, and overhead items such as hauling and repair work also began to be supplied internally, not subcontracted. No automatic market signals existed to allow one to evaluate internal intermediate output. The market wage paid to factory workers, for instance, contained only partial information about the price of the intermediate output produced by the worker, the missing information being, of course, the worker's productivity during the time he earned his wage. Whereas market piece rates automatically assigned an unambiguous value to intermediate output in the market-mediated domestic system, managers devised procedures to synthesize these values in the administratively organized factory system. In fact, we find that early textile factory cost accounts match the wages paid to workers with the output produced. These "accounted" cost per unit figures were analogous to, if not the same as, the prices paid for intermediate outputs in the market. Most important, they provided a rational basis to evaluate internal conversion costs and to compare these costs with external market prices.

Among the earliest manufacturing cost records known to American historians are those from integrated, multiprocess cotton textile mills founded in New England during the first half of the nineteenth century. The earliest of these records comes from the Boston Manufacturing Company in Waltham, Massachusetts. Boston Manufacturing was the first mechanized textile mill to integrate in a single plant the processes of spinning and weaving. Company records from as early as 1815 reveal that the Waltham firm used a remarkably sophisticated set of cost accounts.[7] Indeed, these accounting procedures were adopted by the founders of other New England textile companies that used production methods similar to those of Boston Manufacturing's famous "Waltham system."[8] One such company for which particularly complete records still exist is the Lyman Mills Corporation. Lyman Mills operated a water-powered, integrated cotton textile mill built during the late 1840s in Holyoke, a town in western Massachusetts.

The accounting records of Lyman Mills, which survive from the early 1850s, are extraordinarily revealing.[9] They include double-entry general ledgers and subledgers kept by the treasurer at the home office in Boston, as well as double-entry factory ledgers with related inventory, payroll, and production subledgers kept by the Holyoke mill agent. Reciprocal entries in the home office and factory ledgers were kept current by means of daily correspondence between the treasurer and the agent. The Holyoke factory ledgers include accounts for current assets, current liabilities, and all operating expenses. The factory ledgers also include two accounts, referred to as "mill" accounts, in which charges were entered for all direct and indirect manufacturing costs incurred at the Holyoke site. One of the mill accounts was charged with manufacturing costs related to coarse goods production and the other with manufacturing costs related to fine goods production. The Boston general ledgers include not only all the accounts kept in the Holyoke factory ledger, but also additional accounts for plant and equipment, capital stock, long-term liabilities, and profit and loss. Sales and nonmanufacturing expense figures were entered only in the home office general ledgers, where they appear in the appropriate mill account. Every six months, all books were closed to determine profit and loss.

The two mill accounts kept in the Holyoke factory ledger (see Figure 2-1) apprised management of the *total* manufacturing costs incurred for both grades of final output. Every accounting period, each mill account, one for coarse goods and the other for fine goods, was charged with its respective share of cotton, factory labor, and factory overhead expense. Charges to the mill accounts were transferred from separate control accounts kept in Holyoke. Cotton, the largest single item of expense, was charged to the mill accounts at the end of each six-month accounting period at the cost of raw material that had been used in production through the weaving stage. "Cost" was based on the contract price of cotton, including freight and insurance charges, and was calculated semiannually (after inventory taking) on a first-in, first-out basis. Factory payroll, the next largest item of manufacturing expense, was distributed to the mill accounts monthly in accordance with daily records from each mill that showed employee hours for every process (for example, picking, carding, spinning, warp weaving, weaving). Factory overhead, including costs of repairs, fuel, starch, teaming, supplies, and the Holyoke office, was distributed to each mill account semiannually according to several criteria such as floor space, number of looms, and the rated horse power of water turbines.

Figure 2-1 Lyman Mills Corporation, Basic Ledger Cost Accounts, Mill No. 1[1]
(Six months ending December 31, 18xx)
A. Accounts in home office ledger

BOSTON General Ledger   Cotton No. 1

18xx			18xx		
June 30	Balance	92,093	Dec. 31	Freight, adjustments, sale of waste cotton, etc.	11,843
July–Dec.	Cotton ordered	365,768	Dec. 31	Balance	176,908[2]
Dec. 31	Freight charges, adjustments, etc.	27,840	Dec. 31	Cotton used (to Mill No. 1)	296,950
		485,701			485,701
18xy					
Jan. 1	Balance	176,908			

BOSTON General Ledger   Mill No. 1

18xx			18xx		
June 30	Balance	1,904	July–Dec.	Sales	506,899
July–Dec.	Manufacturing payroll	78,361	July–Dec.	Other credits	590
July–Dec.	Nonmanufacturing payroll, etc.	27,989	Dec. 31	Balance	14,655[3]
Dec. 31	Cotton used (from Cotton No. 1)	296,950			
Dec. 31	Plant and equipment, manufacturing overhead, sales discounts, etc.	50,585			
Dec. 31	Manufacturing overhead	42,855			
Dec. 31	To Profit and Loss	23,500			
		522,144			522,144
18xy					
Jan. 1	Balance	14,655			

Figure 2-1 (cont.)

B. Accounts in factory ledger

HOLYOKE Plant Ledger	Cotton No. 1
(Same as home office ledger account)	

HOLYOKE Plant Ledger		Mill No. 1	
18xx			
July–Dec.	78,361	Dec. 31	418,166
Manufacturing payroll		To Treasurer (reciprocal account)	
Dec. 31	296,950		
Cotton used			
Dec. 31	42,855		
Manufacturing overhead			
	418,166		418,166

1. Similar accounts were kept for Mill No. 2.
2. Based on a physical inventory of raw cotton and yardage in process through the weaving stage. The pounds of cotton in inventory were valued at cost on a first-in, first-out basis.
3. Based on a physical inventory of yardage finished beyond the weaving stage and on hand at the mill or with the selling agent. The pounds of cotton in inventory were valued at an arbitrary amount close to actual cost. No amount included for payroll or overhead costs.

In the Boston general ledgers, the amounts charged to each mill account for cotton, factory labor, and factory overhead are identical to amounts recorded in the same mill account in the Holyoke ledgers. The Boston general ledger mill accounts also contain entries for items such as nonmanufacturing payroll, insurance, and general (presumably Boston office) expenses. Moreover, each Boston general ledger mill account is credited with sales of finished products and ending inventory values every six months. Therefore, the Boston general ledger mill accounts rationally allocated total profit to the separate mills. When combined, the accounts provided profit and loss data useful in determining the semiannual dividend to shareholders. Separately, each account provided top management in Boston with information about the profitability of the respective Holyoke mills. The mill accounts in the Holyoke factory ledgers, however, recorded costs, and only costs, incurred in Holyoke.

It is evident that Lyman Mills did not compile the cost accounting data in their mill accounts in order to attach costs to product inventory for financial reporting purposes. In the balance sheets found in Lyman's unaudited semiannual reports to stockholders, the inventories of raw cotton and goods in process are valued at market prices, or nearly so.[10] And elements of manufacturing cost such as labor and depreciation are not handled in the factory ledger mill accounts as one might expect were the accounts to be used to value inventories. Depreciation expense does not appear at all in the factory ledgers. Instead of depreciation, charges for plant, equipment, and major renovations are charged currently against profit and loss. Moreover, these charges appear *only* in the home office ledgers. They affect not the manufacturing cost data compiled in the factory ledgers, but only the data on total performance in the Boston ledgers. The overhead items that appear in the factory ledger mill accounts are for periodic outlays on common costs such as supervision, repairs, maintenance, bleach, dyes, fuel, and teaming. These allocated overheads are treated as costs of the period; none is capitalized in work-in-process inventory, contrary to the policy required in twentieth-century manufacturing cost accounts.

Besides the mill accounts, Lyman Mills books contain other records about company-made intermediate output. They contain cost reports that were designed to keep careful track of the efficiency with which the company used cotton, labor time, and general overhead. The reports especially emphasize labor time. Registers that record daily both the wages earned by each worker and the pounds of cotton converted in every single process—picking, carding, roving, spinning, warping, weaving, dyeing, and finishing—are included in the company's records, even as far back as the 1850s. By combining data from these two sets of records, it is possible to determine for each process conducted in the mill the daily direct labor cost per unit of output, although the company seems to have compiled such data no more often than monthly. Monthly manufacturing cost statements, prepared separately for each mill, show the average cotton and overhead cost per pound and per yard for total mill output. Similarly, they show average labor cost per pound and per yard of output in each separate process, including picking, carding, spinning, warping, and weaving. The information on labor expense and cotton usage in these monthly cost statements is current, but the unit cost factors for cotton and general overhead come from calculations made only once every six months, at the time of taking a full physical inventory of cotton. Semiannual cost of manufacturing statements show current actual costs, therefore, for labor, cotton, and general overhead (by detailed category). The totals for cotton and overhead in the semiannual statements agree with the charges made every six months to the factory ledger mill accounts. The preceding evidence reveals, then, that the company compiled very accurate information on all manufacturing costs semiannually and accurate information on labor costs at least monthly.

In addition to using information from special cost ac-

counts to discover the costs of internally made intermediate
output, Lyman Mills compiled data about the unit cost of
various styles of finished output. Internal company correspondence suggests that the company treasurer used this
information to evaluate prices in the wholesale market and
to negotiate special prices on large orders. The unit costs
were not used, however, to value inventories. In the early
years when the company had only two mills and a small
variety of finished cloth styles, unit cost data included only
raw material and direct manufacturing labor costs. By the
1880s when the company had five mills producing a multi-
tude of styles, regular reports on unit costs began to include
not only direct production costs, but also overhead. The
costs resembled modern full-absorption unit product costs
(except that no allowance was made for depreciation). It
appears that these unit costs were calculated by allocating
total manufacturing costs among various styles according to
the weight and quantity of yarn used in each style.[11]

When Lyman Mills and many other American textile
mills that copied the Waltham system of the Boston Manufacturing Company began to manage the processes by which
people convert raw material into finished output, cost accounts began to provide managers with vital information.
The data in Lyman Mills manufacturing cost statements are
drawn directly from the company's ordinary double-entry
books of account, and they provide cost information that is
systematically and reliably reconciled with profit and loss.
But Lyman Mills managers did not invest resources in the
compilation of this information in order to prepare their
semiannual financial reports. They needed the information
to make short-run decisions and to achieve control in the
one aspect of their operation not governed by market exchange prices, the conversion of raw materials into finished
goods. Since competitive market prices, beyond the manager's control, dictated the exchange rates for finished goods,
for raw materials, supplies, and the laborers' time, the man-

ager did not need an accounting system to derive those prices. The mill manager, however, could influence the rate at which laborers converted raw cotton into yarn and fabric. Information from accounts about the cost of the conversion activity aided the manager's task of evaluation and control. Such information included the conversion cost per pound of output by department for each worker and for each type of direct overhead expense. Moreover, correspondence between mill foremen and the company treasurer indicates that they made short-run decisions about special-order prices and equipment modifications using contribution margin information that was derived from these direct conversion costs.

The early cost accounts of Lyman Mills also offered incentives and controls to mitigate slack behavior that might otherwise dissipate the productivity gains inherent in mechanized, multiprocess systems. Workers had a natural inclination to use their time efficiently when paid in the market for each unit of output they produced; they had no automatic incentive to pursue the same goal when paid a fixed wage per period. Periodically, Lyman Mills managers used cost information to monitor employee performance. They compared productivity among workers in the same process at the same time. In addition, they compared productivity for one or more workers over several periods of time. All cost information provided by these accounts was designed to focus managers' attention inward on the shop, rather than outward on the industry. The cost information helped managers evaluate internal processes and encourage workers to achieve company productivity goals. It is significant that these accounting procedures emerged at least fifty years before professional accountants became committed to the idea that manufacturing cost accounting exists to value inventories.[12]

Cost Management in a Late
Nineteenth-Century Steel Works

Manufacturing operations conducted by the late
1800s in iron and steel, foodstuffs, petroleum, chemicals,
and machinery making were vastly more complex and
larger than were operations of the early nineteenth-century
New England textile industry. Nevertheless, at the end of the
century most of these large manufacturing organizations
still conducted, as had the early textile firms, only a single
basic activity, the conversion of raw materials into finished
goods.[13] It is not surprising, therefore, that the giant de-
scendants of the first textile mills used refined and elaborate
versions of the very conversion cost systems that had originated in early textile factories. Moreover, these capital-
intensive giants paid no more attention than did early textile firms to the problems that present-day accountants
associate with financial reporting, especially the problem of
valuing inventories and goods sold.

The accounting information used by Andrew Carnegie,
surely one of the shrewdest entrepreneurs of the nineteenth
century, suggests how capital-intensive manufacturers used
management accounting in the late 1800s. Although few persons have ever gained access to the accounting records of
Carnegie Steel Company, those who have agree that Carnegie
made a fetish of using cost statements to manage his giant
steel works from 1872 to 1902. Carnegie's own brief descriptions of cost accounts as well as those provided by his former
associates and by his latest biographer reveal that his system was concerned primarily with continuously gathering
data on all direct costs in every process of the manufacturing
activity, from blast furnace to rolling mill.[14] Using these descriptions, Alfred Chandler has pieced together a vivid picture of Carnegie's cost system.

[Carnegie's general manager developed] statistical data
needed for coordination and control . . . in part by introducing the

voucher system of accounting which, though it had "long been used by railroads, . . . was not [yet] in general use in manufacturing concerns." By this method, each department listed the amount and cost of materials and labor used on each order as it passed through the subunit. Such information [was used to prepare] monthly statements and, in time, even daily ones providing data on the costs of ore, limestone, coal, coke, pig iron (when it was not produced at the plant), spiegel, molds, refractories, repairs, fuel, and labor for each ton of rails produced. . . .

These cost sheets were Carnegie's primary instrument of control. Costs were Carnegie's obsession. One of his favorite dicta was: Watch the costs and the profits will take care of themselves. He was forever asking [department heads] the reasons for changes in unit costs. Carnegie concentrated . . . on the cost side of the operating ratio, comparing current costs of each operating unit with those of previous months and, where possible, with those of other enterprises. Indeed, one reason Carnegie joined the Bessemer pool, which was made up of all steel companies producing Bessemer rails, was to have the opportunity to get a look at the cost figures of his competitors. These controls were effective. . . . "The minutest details of cost of materials and labor in every department appeared from day to day and week to week in the accounts; and soon every man about the place was made to realize it. The men felt and often remarked that the eyes of the company were always on them through the books."

In addition to using their cost sheets to evaluate the performance of department managers, foremen and men, Carnegie [and his general managers] relied on them to check the quality and mix of raw materials. They used them to evaluate improvements in process and in product and to make decisions on developing by-products. In pricing, particularly nonstandardized items like bridges, cost-sheets were invaluable. The company would not accept a contract until its costs were carefully estimated.[15]

An interesting element of the financial information Carnegie relied on to make operating and investment decisions is that which concerned his competitors' direct production costs. Carnegie's operating strategy was to push his own direct costs below his competitors' so that he could charge prices that would always ensure enough demand to keep his plants running at full capacity. The strategy prompted him to require frequent information showing his direct costs in relation to those of his competitors. Possessing that information, and secure in the knowledge that his costs were the lowest in the industry, Carnegie then mercilessly cut prices during economic recessions. While competing firms went under, he still made profits. In periods of prosperity, when customers' demands exceeded the industry's capacity to produce, Carnegie joined others in raising prices.

Andrew Carnegie's actions reveal that during the late 1800s, managers made quite sophisticated use of accounting information to rationalize the operations of large single-activity manufacturing concerns. Nevertheless, managers of these capital-intensive giants often gave inadequate attention either to asset depreciation or to the forecasts and the return-on-investment data that twentieth-century accountants commonly assemble in capital-intensive firms.[16] But Carnegie's case demonstrates that large single-activity organizations, operating in the expansive market environment of late nineteenth-century America, did not absolutely require accounting information to select or to monitor long-lived assets. The weekly data on direct material and conversion costs for each process in his mills apparently was all the accounting information Carnegie required to invest more capital and to earn higher returns than any other steelmaker in the world before 1902. Carnegie's success depended upon good information about direct operating costs. For that, accounting systems mattered. For the rest, faith and intuition sufficed.

Cost Management in Railroads

After the 1840s America's new railroads also presented complex administrative problems—surely the most complex of any businesses in the nineteenth century. The creation of large railroad companies by entrepreneurs wishing to capture the profits made possible by new iron and steam-power technologies marked the advent of "big business."[17] Harnessing the new technologies to reduce transportation costs, the mid-century railroads grew to sizes that dwarfed the scale of the largest textile factories and that surpassed, by the 1880s, even the size of Carnegie's giant steel works. Managing these enormous entities was an unprecedented task, but by 1870 several railroad administrators had devised ingenious solutions that became the core of modern administrative practice. Alfred D. Chandler, Jr.'s important studies of nineteenth-century railroad administration document the leading role of railroads in resolving many problems of management, finance, labor relations, competition, and government regulations that faced giant enterprises in industrial sectors after 1900.[18] Among the solutions achieved by railroads were internal accounting systems designed to provide information and control within large-scale administrative entities.

Unlike early manufacturing firms, railroads devised special recordkeeping systems that recorded enormous numbers of daily transactions and efficiently summarized the consequences of these transactions for frequent internal reporting.[19] Railroads handled a vastly greater number and dollar volume of transactions than had any previous business. The recordkeeping techniques they created to handle and control efficaciously vast flows of dollars are familiar to businesspersons even today. To control and keep account of receipts from passengers and shippers, for instance, they devised systems both for collecting and depositing cash daily at hundreds of different locations spread over a vast geographic area and also for prompt reporting and transfer of funds to headquarter offices. To accomplish this, railroads led the way in developing prenumbered ticket and invoice procedures, in using imprest cash funds, and in using the telegraph to transfer both funds and information. The railroads also devised new accounting systems to control disbursements of cash and to record disbursements in efficient ways that gave management timely and accurate reports on types of expenditures. The companies solved the problems of controlling and recording disbursements by creating what accountants know today as the voucher system of bookkeeping.[20]

The railroads, like manufacturers, devised cost accounting systems to evaluate and control the internal processes by which they converted intermediate inputs into transportation services. Using the ton-mile as a basic unit of output, they created complex internal accounting procedures to calculate the cost per ton-mile. Perhaps the first railroad manager to use cost per ton-mile information, according to Chandler, was Albert Fink, general superintendent and senior vice president of the Louisville & Nashville in the late 1860s.[21] Fink constructed sixty-eight sets of accounts grouped into four categories according to the different ways that costs varied with output.[22] One category included maintenance and overhead costs that did not vary with the volume of traffic; another category included station personnel expenses that varied with the volume of freight, but not with the number of miles run; a third included fuel and other operating expenses that varied with the number of train-miles run; the fourth included fixed charges for interest. In the first three categories, Fink kept track of the operating expenses on a train-mile basis for each subunit of the railroad. With formulas he worked out to convert costs in each category to a ton-mile basis, Fink not only could monitor costs per ton-mile for the entire road and each of its subunits, but he also could pinpoint reasons for cost differences among the subunits.

The great complexity and geographic scale of a railroad organization suggest why managers such as Fink at the Louisville & Nashville felt compelled to develop more elaborate cost accounts than one finds in manufacturing concerns before the 1880s. The railroads did not simply appoint one person to manage the integration of several specialized processes in one physical location, as was the case with factory manufacturing in the early textile industry. In railroads, the division of specialized tasks was carried out on such a vast and complex scale that there also had to be division of management tasks as well. As Chandler points out, American railroads were the first businesses in the world in which there was a hierarchy of managers who managed other salaried managers.[23] Cost accounting in the railroads became, then, more than just a tool for evaluating internal conversion processes; in the hands of Fink and those who followed him, it became a tool for assessing the performance of subordinate managers.

The railroads also went beyond most manufacturing concerns of the nineteenth century in developing accounting information about the impact of the organization's separate parts on its total financial performance. For example, the "operating ratio," a ratio of operating expenses to revenues that railroads studied assiduously, indicated how variations in the business of diverse subunits would affect the railroad's total performance.[24]

As with every other nineteenth-century single-activity business enterprise, the railroads gathered internal accounting information primarily to gauge the efficiency of the processes in which they invested capital, not to gauge the overall efficiency with which they used capital. Hence, they did not use accounting information to judge the efficacy of new investment or to evaluate the performance of old investment.[25] The railroads did not account, for instance, for the total amounts invested in plant and equipment. The cost of equipment originally put into service was kept on the balance sheet, with all subsequent modifications or renewals charged to current income. Only replacements of equipment were capitalized and then only the excess of the new asset's value over the replaced asset's original cost. Nor did the railroads record systematic charges for depreciation.

Railroads apparently did not feel compelled to invest

resources in capital accounting systems for the same reasons that we suggested Carnegie did not monitor the performance of capital in his giant steel works. Once the decision was made to organize a railroad, little else remained but to build the road and to operate it as efficiently as possible. In designing management accounting information systems, therefore, the railroads were content to ask about nothing more than the efficiency of the firm's internally coordinated processes. For that, the cost per ton-mile and the operating ratio statistics seemed sufficient. Nineteenth-century railroads did, however, release public information, often audited, concerning operating ratios and other financial performance.[26] Their unique willingness to issue public reports arose from their heavy reliance on outside financial capital; railroads faced constraints in the capital market that Carnegie and operators of other owner-managed firms did not.

Cost Management in Distribution and Urban Retailing

In addition to manufacturing and railroad transportation, a third type of single-activity enterprise, the large-scale distributor, developed novel management accounting systems during the nineteenth century. In the last quarter of the nineteenth century the American economy witnessed an incredible outpouring of standardized, mass-produced goods for both producers and consumers. Two forces that we have already discussed helped make this possible. One was the widespread development of manufacturing technologies to mass produce all manner of items including iron and steel, petroleum distillates, alcoholic beverages, chemicals, processed foods, farm implements, machine tools, and household tools such as the sewing machine. These technologies used both complex machinery and intense sources of energy to produce unprecedented volumes of output in large-scale, capital-intensive manufacturing establishments. The other force propelling the outpouring of mass-produced goods was the railroad and the telegraph system, which linked all parts of the nation by 1870[27] and provided the rapid, efficient transportation and communication required to move vast quantities of raw materials and output to and from manufacturing sites. A third force, to which we now turn, was the creation of systems for distributing the mass producers' output to the consumer.

The American market system in the last quarter of the nineteenth century did not provide channels through which manufacturers could quickly and efficiently sell their output directly to consumers. Certainly this was true for the makers of unconventional or technically complex products such as sewing machines, dynamite, and frozen beef; manufacturers of those products eventually overcame high costs of reaching the consumer by investing resources in their own internally managed marketing systems.[28] But it was also difficult for the new mass producers of familiar everyday items such as tobacco products, beverages, cereals, textiles, hardware, and many, many more to reach customers. Linking the producers and consumers of these products was a new breed of mass distributors—wholesalers and retailers—that appeared on the American scene after the Civil War.[29] These firms, associated today with names such as Macy, Marshall Field, and Sears, used all the advantages offered by railroads and telegraphy to widen the market available to manufacturers.

The profit opportunity for mass distributors lay in their ability to narrow the gap between prevailing prices charged by small-scale local manufacturers or distributors and the potentially lower prices that were made possible by the scale economies of mass production and distribution. Distributors could force shippers to compete vigorously, could provide manufacturers with accurate and timely market information, could provide credit and service to consumers, and, above all, could give customers easy access to information about the variety of available merchandise. Without the unique services provided by mass distributors, it is difficult to imagine how late nineteenth-century American consumers could otherwise have enjoyed the material benefits of a national transportation and communication network and a regionally specialized system of mass producers.

To operate efficiently and effectively, the mass distributors created systems for internally administering the high volume, high turnover, and low margins on which their success depended. They had to be extremely conscious of costs, especially the cost of acquiring and financing inventories and of granting customer credit. Not surprisingly, they quickly developed internal accounting systems to aid them in evaluating costs, throughput, and working capital. Nor is it surprising that these mass distributors gathered internal accounting information along much the same lines as did earlier single-activity firms in manufacturing and railroading. Mass distributors engaged in the single activity of distribution, but they did so by integrating several distinct processes connected with that activity; therefore, they developed unique accounting measures of process efficiency analogous to the manufacturers' unit costs and the railroaders' cost per ton-mile.

The internal accounting systems devised by big-city retailers, and the wholesale jobbers from which they often evolved, focused primarily on the performance of a firm's various selling departments. This was true, for instance, at Marshall Field's in Chicago. As the Field Company's historian reports, each department "was run as though it were an independent business firm. The department head was a merchant, completely and independently responsible for the profits within his own separate department or 'store.' He purchased, priced, and advertised as he saw fit, and received a contracted-for percent of the profits that his department produced."[30]

To monitor and evaluate these internal department

heads, Field's collected departmental accounting information on both gross margins and inventory turnover (or "stockturn"). The information on gross margins (sales receipts minus cost of goods sold and departmental operating expenses) was not unique to mass distributors; it was analogous to the information collected by railroads to calculate operating ratios. Gross margin information measured each department's performance and provided a means of comparing departments with each other and with the company's overall performance. The information on stockturn, however, was apparently unique to mass distributors; Chandler contends that the concept originated with American marketers after the construction of a national railroad network permitted the rise of the modern wholesaler.[31] Inventory turnover was for the mass distributor a crucial determinant of gross margins and profit. Unlike the traditional merchant, who considered markup on cost as the determinant of gross margin, the new mass distributors were driven to make profit (or gross margin) on volume. Hence, they placed enormous importance on the rates at which departments turned over their stock each period. Marshall Field was monitoring stockturn as early as 1870.[32]

As did the manufacturers and the railroads before them, the mass distributors had one central reason for internal accounting information. They gathered it primarily to monitor the results of conducting internal processes which otherwise would be coordinated directly through the market, or else would not occur at all. They did not compile this information to gauge the efficiency with which they used fixed capital. Their investment of fixed capital in relation to their volume of business was, of course, much smaller than was typical for either manufacturing or railroading firms.[33] That may explain in large measure their lack of concern for depreciation and fixed asset accounting. It is notable, however, that their use of stockturn information, although concerned only with working capital, presaged a method of linking company performance to capital that early twentieth-century businesses would discover. We will refer to this again in chapter 4, when discussing the evolution of return on investment accounting at Du Pont.

Conclusion

The principal circumstance that shaped the accounting practices we observe in nineteenth-century companies is the search for opportunities to gain by internalizing two or more of the conversion processes for a single economic activity. New management accounting practices in manufacturing, rail transportation, and distribution firms had one common purpose: to evaluate a company's internalized processes. Each type of single-activity business identified a unique type of accounting information for this purpose: in manufacturing firms, the direct cost of converting raw or semifinished material from one stage of production to the next; in railroad transportation, the cost per ton-mile; in mass distribution firms, stockturn. In all cases this new accounting information focused on the efficiency with which single-activity firms used resources in their internally managed processes.

Why did late nineteenth-century circumstances not compel company accountants to produce additional information that seems indispensable to accountants in large-scale businesses today? Particularly puzzling to modern accountants is the absence of accounting information with which to plan and control capital investments. We have already noted that capital-intensive industrial giants of the late 1800s kept no systematic track of physical assets, nor did they use accounting information to evaluate returns on investment. And despite the increased uncertainty that accompanies long-term commitments of capital, these firms apparently used no forecasts or capital budgets to coordinate and monitor investment outlays. Perhaps this absence of interest in capital accounting can be explained by the enormous expansion of markets in late nineteenth-century America, which could reduce the uncertainty associated with long-term investment. Another explanation may be that nineteenth-century manufacturing, transportation, and distribution firms engaged only in single activities. Each firm diversified only among the processes required for its respective activity, reducing the firm's investment decision to a series of closely linked make-or-buy decisions. For those decisions, the firm had to know only how new capital investment would affect stockturn, costs per ton-mile, or unit conversion costs. Adequate for that purpose was the information supplied in most nineteenth-century management accounting systems.

As we will show in chapter 4, accounting systems begin to link a company's performance to the capital invested in the company's business when organizations combine two or more separable activities in a single managed enterprise. Known as vertically integrated firms, these businesses appeared for the first time in the United States around 1900. But before we turn to these management accounting developments in multi-activity enterprises, we will examine in the next chapter an additional set of late-nineteenth century developments in manufacturing cost accounting. Known as scientific management and standard product costing, these developments were carried out by mechanical engineers in metal-working firms. The objectives of the engineers, working for the most part between 1880 and 1910 in single-activity manufacturing firms, were to control the efficiency of very complex internal production processes and to trace the sources of a company's overall profits.

Notes

1. Alfred D. Chandler, Jr., points out, quite correctly we believe, that American railroads, not early nineteenth-century factories, provided the first

administrative model for the modern multiunit business enterprise. (See Chandler, *The Visible Hand: The Managerial Revolution in American Business* [Cambridge, Mass.: Harvard University Press, 1977], 75–81.) But conversion cost accounting, the earliest example of management accounting, appeared in textile factories even before the first railroads were built. Although the railroads very quickly developed accounting (and many other administrative tools) far beyond what the textile factories ever accomplished and ultimately had a far greater impact on American management practice, they were not the first economic enterprises that used cost accounting to rationalize internally coordinated processes.

2. George J. Stigler, "The Division of Labor is Limited by the Extent of the Market," *Journal of Political Economy* 59 (1951), 185–193.

3. Chandler, *The Visible Hand*, 67–72.

4. D R Scott, *The Cultural Significance of Accounts* (New York: Henry Holt, 1931), 143.

5. The Medici accounts, housed in the Baker Library at the Harvard Business School, show how a pre-industrial domestic organization could maintain excellent accounts of external financial transactions and of physical inventories but not require, apparently, cost accounts per se. For a succinct discussion of the Medici accounts see S. Paul Garner, *Evolution of Cost Accounting to 1925* (Tuscaloosa, Ala.: University of Alabama Press, 1954), 7–15.

6. In early proto-factories, such as Adam Smith's famous pin factory, multiple processes could be centralized without being coordinated administratively. (See S. D. Chapman, "The Textile Factory before Arkwright: A Typology of Factory Development," *Business History Review* [Winter 1974], 451–478.) Such organizations did not require cost records if all inputs, including labor, were paid at market prices for output produced. In *Allocating Common Costs* (Urbana, Ill.: Center for International Education and Research in Accounting, 1978), 46–47, M. C. Wells cites several examples of accounting in early piece-rate factories that historians mistakenly refer to as "cost accounting." Cost accounts became essential only after administrators assumed the task of coordinating the conversion of inputs into output. The move toward cost accounting is seen in early proto-factories where organizers of partly market-priced and partly managed production processes compiled production statistics—not systematic cost accounts as such—to audit the output of subcontractors or internal artisans. Indeed, Josiah Wedgwood in the early 1770s compiled cost records, with intriguing results, at his Etruria pottery works. A similar use of production statistics, less sophisticated perhaps than Wedgwood's, occurred about fifty years later at Springfield Armory in Massachusetts. For more on these cases see: Neil McKendrick, "Josiah Wedgwood and Cost Accounting in the Industrial Revolution," *Economic History Review*, Vol. 24 (1970), 45–67; Paul Uselding, "An Early Chapter in the Evolution of American Industrial Management," in Louis P. Cain and Paul J. Uselding, eds., *Business Enterprise and Economic Change: Essays in Honor of Harold F. Williamson* (Kent, OH.: Kent State University Press, 1973), 51–84.

7. An excellent discussion of these records is in David M. Porter, "The

Waltham System and Early American Textile Cost Accounting, 1813–1848," *Accounting Historians Journal* (Spring 1980), 1–15.

8. For a comprehensive and insightful discussion of these records see Paul F. McGouldrick, *New England Textiles in the Nineteenth Century: Profits and Investment* (Cambridge, Mass.: Harvard University Press, 1968), 3–6, 219–222.

9. The discussion of Lyman Mills draws material from and substantially revises the conclusions in H. Thomas Johnson, "Early Cost Accounting for Internal Management Control: Lyman Mills in the 1850s," *Business History Review* (Winter 1972), 466–474.

10. McGouldrick, *New England Textiles*, 92; Chandler, *The Visible Hand*, 70.

11. This method of estimating unit costs apparently was not described in published sources until the 1890s. See, for example, William G. Nichols, *Methods of Cost Finding in Cotton Mills* (Waltham, Mass.: E. L. Barry, 1899), 8–18; and James G. Hill, "Various Systems of Computing the Costs of Manufacture," *Transactions of the New England Cotton Manufacturers' Association*, 67 (October 5–6, 1899), 132–137.

12. We discuss the origins of this idea at greater length in chapter 6.

13. Chandler, *The Visible Hand*, chapter 8.

14. Joseph F. Wall, *Andrew Carnegie* (New York: Oxford University Press, 1970), 325–349, 504–506, 583–586; Harold C. Livesay, *Andrew Carnegie and the Rise of Big Business* (Boston: Little, Brown, 1975), 84–90, 102, 109–118, 150–151.

15. Chandler, *The Visible Hand*, 267–268.

16. Richard P. Brief, "Nineteenth Century Accounting Error," *Journal of Accounting Research* (Spring 1965), 21–30; Michael Chatfield, *A History of Accounting Thought* (Hinsdale, Ill.: Dryden Press, 1974), 102, 160; H. Thomas Johnson, "The Role of Accounting History in the Study of Modern Business Enterprise," *Accounting Review* (July 1975), 448–449.

17. Chandler, *The Visible Hand*, 80–89.

18. Glenn Porter, *The Rise of Big Business, 1860–1910* (New York: Thomas Y. Crowell, 1973), 31.

19. Chandler, *The Visible Hand*, 109–120, 186.

20. George W. Wood, *The Voucher System of Book-keeping* (Pittsburgh: G. W. Wood, 1895). See LCNUC, 1943; vol. 165, 348.

21. Chandler, *The Visible Hand*, 116–120.

22. Fink may have learned to group cost accounts according to the way that costs behave by reading *Railway Economy*, the 1850 treatise by Dionysius Larnder, a professor of mathematics in University College, London. See David Solomons, "The Historical Development of Costing," in David Solomons, ed., *Studies in Cost Analysis* (Homewood, Ill.: Richard D. Irwin, 1968), 3–49.

23. Chandler, *The Visible Hand*, 120–121.

24. *Ibid.*, 110.

25. *Ibid.*, 111–112, 115.

26. Richard Vangermeersch, "Comments on Accounting Disclosures in

the Baltimore and Ohio Annual Reports from 1828 through 1850," *Academy of Accounting Historians Working Paper Series*, Vol. II (1979), 318–337.

27. Richard B. Du Boff, "Business Demand and the Development of the Telegraph in the United States, 1844–1860," *Business History Review* (Winter 1980), 459–479.

28. Chandler, *The Visible Hand*, chapters 9 and 10. We discuss the integrated industrial firm in chapter 4.

29. Chandler, *The Visible Hand*, chapter 7.

30. Quoted in Chandler, *The Visible Hand*, 220.

31. *Ibid.*, 223.

32. *Ibid.*

33. *Ibid.*

CHAPTER 3

Efficiency, Profit, and Scientific Management: 1880–1910

IN the last quarter of the nineteenth century, a demand arose for new management information that was not provided by the conversion cost systems described in the previous chapter. The demand originated in firms that mass produced complex machine-made metal goods such as reapers, sewing machines, locks, scales, pumps, typewriters, and the machines used to make such goods. The complex manufacturing processes made it difficult for managers of these firms to gather precise and accurate information about the efficiency of workers engaged in specialized tasks. The search for this information inspired a systematic analysis of factory productivity in late nineteenth-century machine-making firms that came to be known as "scientific management." Furthermore, diverse (often custom-made) product lines also prompted managers to seek information about the

sources of a firm's profitability. The quest triggered a flood
of research—primarily by mechanical engineers who also
worked on scientific management problems—into methods
for compiling accurate information about product costs.
Between 1880 and 1910, engineer-managers in American
metal-working firms developed a host of new cost measurement techniques both to analyze task productivity and to
link profits to products. The techniques had a profound impact on twentieth-century accounting practice, although the
engineers and managers who developed them had no intrin-
sic interest in accounting as such.

Scientific Management and Efficiency

The scientific quest for knowledge about efficiency
originated in metal-working firms whose owners desired
closer control over increasingly complex and specialized
manufacturing tasks.[1] Until the 1880s manufacturers had
concentrated attention on improving high-speed machine
technology used in their factories; day-to-day supervision of
work in the factory was delegated to semi-autonomous department foremen who acted as, and frequently were, inside
contractors. In a study of inside contracting at the Winches-
ter Repeating Arms Company, historian John Buttrick describes the system as follows:

Under the system of inside contracting, the management of a
firm provided floor space and machinery, supplied raw material
and working capital, and arranged for the sale of the finished product. The gap between raw material and finished product, however,
was filled not by paid employees arranged in the descending hierarchy so dear to the hearts of personnel experts but by contractors, to whom the production job was delegated. They hired their
own employees, supervised the work process, and received a piece
rate from the company for completed goods. The income of a contractor consisted of the difference between his wage bill and his

sales to the company, plus the day pay he earned as an employee himself. The company's largest single expense was the amount paid to the contractors for finished goods.[2]

In short, contract foremen hired, fired, and paid their own work force and were responsible for the economic performance of their departments, keeping anything left over as their own profit.

While the system reduced the cost to owners of supervising and controlling a diverse and often highly skilled work force, it meant that owners knew very little about costs and efficiencies in factory departments. Moreover, the immediate beneficiaries of improved efficiency were the contract foremen and their workers, not the firm's owners who supplied the basic machine technology. Goaded by excess capacity during the depressed 1870s, many manufacturers in metal-working industries began to dismantle the inside contracting system. Sharing ideas at annual meetings of the American Society of Mechanical Engineers, they designed recordkeeping systems to track the flow of material and labor costs going into complex machine-made products. To encourage proper reporting, they established plans for workers to share in the gains of improved efficiencies, and they created clerical staffs to collect and record information about shop-floor activities.[3] By the 1880s managers of many complex metal-working firms had information about material and labor costs similar to the conversion cost information that already existed in textile factories and steel mills.

The engineering-minded managers in some of the metalworking firms then went a step further than their peers in other industries. Instead of designing systems merely to accumulate actual material and labor costs, the chief object of manufacturing cost systems up to that time, these "scientific managers" focused their attention on predetermining "standard" rates at which material and labor should be consumed in manufacturing tasks. The methods they devised to determine standards for material and labor inputs included engineering design of bills of material and time-and-motion study.

Engineers and accountants used information about standards for three very different purposes in the two decades preceding World War I. As we have already mentioned, some scientific management engineers developed information about standards in order to gauge the potential efficiency of tasks or processes. Frederick W. Taylor's search for the "one best way" to use labor and material resources typifies this use of standard performance information. For Taylor, standards provided information for planning the flow of work so that waste of material and time was kept to a minimum. Taylor's manufacturing cost systems were designed to monitor physical labor and material efficiencies, not to monitor financial costs.[4] Consequently, Taylor did not view standards as a tool to control financial costs. But management experts who did not share Taylor's indifference to financial outcomes had no aversion to using the standards for cost control. For instance, Percy Longmuir, an American engineer who wrote about foundry cost management around 1900, devised a novel way of using information about material and labor standards to control *actual* costs.[5] According to David Solomons,

[Longmuir] proposes that the labour costs of each class of work undertaken in the foundry should be ascertained, each type of labour, e.g., moulders, labourers, etc., being kept separate. These labour costs are then related to the weight per cwt. "Experience," he says, "will readily give standard factors for each class of work and these standards may be plotted on a chart as a fair curve (straight line), the departure from which of the actual weekly cost line will instantly show the degrees of good or bad working."[6]

It was only a short step from Longmuir's chart to the development of detailed systems for analyzing variances between standard and actual performance. There is ample evidence that manufacturers around 1900 used information on variances between actual and standard costs to control their operations.[7] Credit for writing the first published descriptions of modern systems for analyzing standard cost variances goes to two management consultants, Harrington Emerson and G. Charter Harrison.[8] Harrison followed Emerson and in 1918 became the first person to publish a set of equations for the analysis of cost variances.[9] Emerson was perhaps the first writer, however, to stress that information about standards permits managers to differentiate between variances that are due to controllable conditions and variances that are caused by conditions beyond managements' control,[10] an idea that management accountants many years later would associate with flexible budgeting.

Accountants, not engineers, developed a third purpose for standard cost information, one that differed greatly from the purposes intended by writers such as Taylor, Longmuir, Emerson, and Harrison. Some financial accountants in the early 1900s recognized that standard costs could greatly simplify the task of inventory valuation. Accountants generally did not accept the idea of entering standard cost information into the financial accounting ledgers, however, until after World War II. We will discuss the impact of twentieth-century financial reporting upon cost accounting at greater length in chapter 6. But it is important to note at this point that financial accountants who discussed standard costing during the interwar decades rarely, if ever, considered how managers could use variances between actual and standard costs to control manufacturing operations. Instead, their main concern was how to properly classify variances—in particular, how to dispose of them—in published financial reports.

Strategic Product Costing for Profitability Analysis

Scientific management experts such as Taylor and Emerson devised new cost accounting procedures primarily to assess and control the financial and physical efficiency of processes and tasks in complex machine-making firms. For Taylor and Emerson, the main purpose of collecting cost information was the same as it had always been for managers of nineteenth-century textile and steel firms:[11] to evaluate the efficiency of processes, not to assess the performance of an entire organization. Taylor and his peers simply extended the use of such information to monitor the efficiency of complex machining processes in firms that customarily relied on inside contracting.

Engineers and management experts in similar firms subsequently developed a new goal for cost accounting: to evaluate the overall profitability of the entire enterprise. Alexander Hamilton Church, a contemporary of Taylor's, was particularly interested in developing management methods to ensure that efficient parts added up to a profitable whole. He expressed this concern by contrasting two approaches to management, analytic (*i.e.*, Taylor's) and synthetic.

> The main distinction between synthesis and analysis in this connection is that synthesis is concerned with fashioning means to effect large ends, and analysis is concerned with the correct local use of given means. . . . The view taken by analysis . . . is a narrow and limited one; it concerns itself with the infinitely small. Its task is to say "how to use certain means to the best advantage." . . . But the synthetical side of management demands that every effort of analysis, like every other effort made in the plant, shall have some proportion, some definite economic relation to the purpose for which the business is being run.[12]

One of Church's principal devices for linking "every effort of analysis . . . to the purpose for which the business is being run" was product costing. He advocated using product cost information to trace a firm's overall profitability to the profits earned on individual products.

> . . . if a perfect system of distributing all the . . . charges incurred in production were in use, and a list were to be prepared of all delivered orders showing:—
> 1. their prime cost . . . wages and materials.

2. the indirect shop charges.

3. a due proportion of general and selling expense, then the aggregate of these items for all orders completed and delivered, when set against the sale prices, would show a difference or balance exactly corresponding to the net profit shown by the profit and loss account.[13]

Church justified this "ideal" product costing system on the principle that "the organization of no works can be considered complete until it is able not merely to connect its costs of all classes with its jobs, but also to check its financial position by aggregating its profits on sales item by item."[14]

Calculations of full product costs for the purpose that Church had in mind required methods to link overheads to products. Nineteenth-century manufacturers had virtually ignored the allocation of overhead to products. The issue was first addressed by mechanical engineers in the 1880s. Many historians mistakenly associate the overhead allocation methods of these early mechanical engineers with the overhead application procedures used by twentieth-century financial accountants.[15] But, the engineers and the accountants applied overhead to products for very different reasons. As we show in chapter 6, modern financial accountants required cost accounting to value inventory for financial reporting. Overall profit measurement and inventory valuation did not require accurate information about the cost of individual products; aggregated information about average costs would do. Church understood that aggregated average cost information would do even for management purposes as long as the factory manufactured only a few products and those products used all the factory's resources at about the same rate. But Church railed against using the "commercial accountants'" overhead allocation procedures in situations where a diverse line of products used factory resources at widely varying rates. His insightful evaluation of crude averaging procedures is worth quoting at length.

No one has ever suggested that prime costs should be averaged. No one ever argues that if $200 has been spent on 20 articles, then the cost of each can be safely considered at $10, unless indeed the product is absolutely uniform. Such a suggestion would be treated with ridicule, because obviously the only use of detailed costs is to reveal the *relative* amounts of wages and material that the different orders have absorbed. The incidence of labour-cost and material-cost on orders is too obviously individual and unequal for us to think of averaging prime costs.

When, however, we come to the second [indirect shop] and third [selling and general] elements of cost . . . an entirely different plan is commonly pursued. Notwithstanding that the expenditure under this head frequently equals and sometimes surpasses in value the item of wages which are generally so carefully traced and allocated to individual orders, it is a very usual practice to average this large class of expense, and to express its incidence by a simple percentage either upon wages or upon time.

That this plan is entirely misleading there can be very little doubt, because few of the expenses in the profit and loss account have any relation either to each other or to wages or to time. To rely upon an arbitrary established percentage which may actually be either much over, or much under, the real incidence of a number of varied factors on a particular order, may be a good way of getting rid of figures and giving an air of finality to cost accounts, but it is very little else. As a guide to actual profitableness of particular classes of work it is valueless and even dangerous.[16]

Church gives an example of the absurdity that can result when indirect costs are averaged over products that use factory resources at widely varying rates.

We find that as against $100 direct wages on order, we have an indirect expenditure of $59, or in other terms, our shop establishment charges are 59 percent of direct wages in that shop for the period in question. This is, of course, very simple. It is also as usually worked very inexact. It is true that as regards the output of the shop as a whole a fair idea is obtained of the general cost of the work. . . . And in the case of a shop with machines all of a size and kind, performing practically identical operations by means of a fairly average wages rate, it is not alarmingly incorrect.

If, however, we apply this method to a shop in which large and small machines, highly paid and cheap labour, heavy castings and small parts, are all in operation together, then the result, unless measures are taken to supplement it, is no longer trustworthy.[17]

Church believed that information about a product's cost should reveal the real resources used to make the product. Consequently, a key to commercial success in manufacturing is "a thoroughly comprehensive method of recording shop work, *including the connection of expenditure of all classes with the items of output on which they are incident.*"[18] (Italics added.) It is relatively easy to connect overhead expenditures with the output "on which they are incident" when dealing with simple processes and few products. "The difficulty of dealing adequately with [overheads] in their relation to [causes] is usually in proportion to the heterogeneity of the business carried on."[19] Church argued that overhead, ideally, was the cost of countless factors of production, each of which should be traced separately to products. For practical purposes, however, he advocated dividing the factory into a series of "production centers" through which overheads should be loaded onto products.

Church believed that indirect costs should consist only of an irreducible element of costs that cannot be traced to individual products. He suggested that the distinction between direct and indirect expenses *of a product* ought to be abandoned in order that accountants and managers focus attention on "the *real* incidence [of expense] on particular jobs"—the differences in rates at which products consume resources.[20] Church argued that cost accountants should give separate consideration to factory and selling expenses because widely different conditions affected their real incidence among individual products, not because factory costs "attach" to products and selling costs to periods. Even though he considered selling and general costs separately from factory costs, Church nevertheless included them all when he computed product costs so that overall company profits could be traced to the profitability of individual products.

Engineers in many metal-working firms developed an

interest in product costing around 1900, although none
seems to have developed as sophisticated a view of costing
as Church. The engineers demanded information about
product costs because their firms' commercial success depended on accurately and rationally quoting prices for complex custom-made machine products. Like Church, virtually
all of the engineer "cost accountants" viewed product cost
as consisting of a portion of *all* costs incurred in the firm,
not just shop costs. Product cost included selling, general
and administrative costs and, in many authorities' view, an
allocation for imputed interest on equity. Implicitly, then,
these engineers sought product cost estimates that would
link product profitability with a company's overall profits.

An English textile company executive, G. P. Norton, described in 1889 another procedure for linking the overall
profits of a manufacturing firm with the efficiency of its
parts.[21] Norton's system did not rely on product costing, but
it did make an intriguing use of standard cost information.
Norton presents an accounting method for comparing an
integrated multiprocess textile company's performance with
the profit that would have been earned if the firm's internally
managed processes were coordinated through market exchange. David Solomons provides a succinct description of
Norton's system.

The cost records, which were kept quite separate from the commercial accounts, were designed to allocate costs to departments
and processes in such a way that the costs could be compared with
the prices that would have been charged by outside specialists,
i.e., the trade or "country" prices, as they were called. The results
of the undertaking are summarized in a Manufacturing Account,
the first part of which compares the actual sales with the work
done valued at the trade prices, the difference after stock adjustments being the amount of profit that should have been made if
the work had been carried out at the trade rates. In the second
section of the account the "actual" costs (*i.e.,* the cost arrived at
after allocations of overhead) of each of the processes, spinning,

weaving, dyeing and finishing, are compared with the work valued at trade prices, the difference showing the "profit" or "loss" on each department. The sum of these profits and losses plus the profit from the first section of the Manufacturing Account show the net profit of the business subject to deduction of certain expenses not allocated between the processes.[22]

Two additional features of Norton's system deserve mention. When the disappearance of "country workers" after 1900 made it impossible to secure external market rates for piecework, Norton in later editions of his book recommended the use of standard costs instead of trade prices; also, Norton valued product inventories for balance sheet and income determination purposes at market prices—his cost system was not designed to serve financial reporting purposes. It is indeed unfortunate that modern accounting historians have discussed Norton's ideas in terms of the financial reporting purposes that shape modern product costing instead of the purposes Norton had in mind. To A. C. Littleton, for instance, Norton's system of accounts, while "ingenious," is less than a "modern reader" might hope for because it fails "to show the calculation of the cost of goods manufactured and to furnish the basis for unit cost prices to be used in computing inventory valuation."[23]

Neither Norton's standard cost system nor Church's product costing system has any precedent in the process-oriented conversion cost systems that we discussed in chapter 2. The earlier systems gathered information to help managers evaluate and control the efficiency of internal processes, not to link performance in each process with a firm's overall profitability. With relatively homogeneous lines of products and few processes, achieving efficiency in the processes was probably enough to insure overall profitability. But heterogeneous product lines and complex processes in metal-working firms—the situation encountered by Church—made it important to know the cost differences among products that used underlying processes at widely different rates. In such firms cost information used to monitor efficiency may also be used to evaluate profitability if it is traced carefully to products.

The use of accounting information to assess overall profitability soon becomes the chief object of management accounting systems in complex industrial enterprises that integrate two or more activities. The next chapter describes the development of these systems in vertically integrated industrial firms. Like Norton and Church, the giant integrated industrials were concerned with a company's system-wide performance, a significant departure from the management accounting systems of nineteenth-century single-activity firms. But vertically integrated firms after 1900 did not use either Church's product costing or Norton's standard costing procedures to link information about the company's overall performance to information about the performance of each separate process. Instead, they developed systems to track the performance of the company and its decentralized units by one common denominator: return on investment. The systems required that companies now give attention to the amount of capital invested in the enterprise, a consideration ignored in all management accounting systems that we have observed before 1900.

Notes

1. Alfred D. Chandler, Jr., *The Visible Hand: The Managerial Revolution in American Business* (Cambridge, Mass.: Harvard University Press, 1977), 271–279; Mariann Jelinek, "Toward Systematic Management: Alexander Hamilton Church," *Business History Review* (Spring 1980), 63–79; Joseph A. Litterer, "Systematic Management: The Search for Order and Integration," *Business History Review* (Winter 1961), 461–476.

2. John Buttrick, "The Inside Contract System," *Journal of Economic History* (Summer 1952), 205–206.

3. The major contributors to this literature up to World War I included Henry R. Towne, Harrington Emerson, Percy Longmuir, John Whitmore, Al-

exander H. Church, Frederick W. Taylor, Henry Gantt, Frederick Halsey, G. Charter Harrison, and Frank Gilbreth.

4. A former associate of Taylor's said that for Taylor "[financial] costs, though of course important, are secondary to productive efficiency." See C. B. Thompson, *The Theory and Practice of Scientific Management* (Boston: Houghton Mifflin, 1917), 71.

5. Percy Longmuir, "Recording and Interpreting Foundry Costs," *Engineering Magazine* (September 1902), 887.

6. David Solomons, "The Historical Development of Costing," in David Solomons, ed., *Studies in Cost Analysis* (Homewood, Ill.: Richard D. Irwin, 1968), 3–49. The text quotation is from page 38.

7. See references to John Whitmore in Solomons, "Costing," 37–40.

8. *Ibid.*, 40–42 (on Emerson), 46–47 (on Harrison).

9. *Ibid.*, 47.

10. *Ibid.*, 40.

11. H. Thomas Johnson, "Management Accounting in an Early Integrated Industrial: E. I. du Pont de Nemours Powder Company, 1903–1912," *Business History Review* (Summer 1975), 193–194; Daniel A. Wren, *The Evolution of Management Thought* (New York: John Wiley, 1979), 131–135.

12. Alexander Hamilton Church, *The Science and Practice of Management* (New York: The Engineering Magazine Co., 1914), 24–25, as quoted in Jelinek, "Toward Systematic Management," 73. We are indebted to Richard Vangermeersch for sharing many fascinating insights from his extensive research in the writings of Alexander Church. For a useful compilation of previously unpublished Church manuscripts, see Vangermeersch, *The Contributions of Alexander Hamilton Church to Accounting and Management* (New York: Garland Publishing, 1986).

13. A. Hamilton Church, "Organisation by Production Factors," *Engineering Magazine* (April 1910), 79–80.

14. A. Hamilton Church, *The Proper Distribution of Expense Burden* (New York: The Engineering Magazine Co., 1908), 24.

15. This point is a major theme developed by M. C. Wells in his *Allocating Common Costs* (Urbana, Ill.: Center for International Education and Research in Accounting, 1978).

16. Church, "Organisation by Production Factors," 80–81.

17. Church, *The Proper Distribution*, 28–29.

18. *Ibid.*, 13.

19. *Ibid.*, 11.

20. Church, "Organisation by Production Factors," 80.

21. George P. Norton, *Textile-Manufacturers' Bookkeeping for the Counting House, Mill and Warehouse* (London: Simpkin, Marshall, Hamilton, Kent, 1889).

22. Solomons, "Costing," 36–37.

23. A. C. Littleton, *Accounting Evolution to 1900* (New York: American Institute Publishing Co., 1933), 344.

CHAPTER 4

Controlling the Vertically Integrated Firm: The Du Pont Powder Company to 1914

PRODUCED around 1900 by a great merger wave were mammoth firms whose names have since become household words: International Harvester, Du Pont, General Electric, National Biscuit, American Tobacco, Pittsburgh Plate Glass, U.S. Steel, to name a few. Each firm subsumed within itself several of the activities formerly conducted by individual companies. Manufacturing, purchasing, transportation, and distribution, formerly the isolated activities of independent firms, became integrated in the multi-activity organization.

Integrated firms developed mainly because they provided new opportunities for entrepreneurs to expand profits by combining previously disparate operations. Nineteenth-century entrepreneurs had attained in single-activity firms unprecedented speeds of throughput. Technological developments enabled industries such as steelmaking, petroleum refining, farm implement manufacture, and food processing to achieve astonishingly vast outputs by the late 1800s. They faced the problem, however, of assuring that their outputs earned the highest possible profit. Manufacturers needed aggressive marketing. They discovered that traditional distributors handling a variety of products supplied by many manufacturers were not interested in promoting any particular manufacturer's line and that it was neither profitable nor effective to offer such incentives as discounts to the distributors. Many mass producers, then, in order to control and streamline the distribution of their products, found it essential to create or acquire their own distribution channels. Some firms also found it necessary to create or acquire sources of raw materials and other inputs, especially where their suppliers enjoyed, but did not pass on in the form of lower prices, scale economies derived from supplying large orders to giant manufacturers. In the multi-activity firms that entrepreneurs conceived, joint ownership and control of resources, information, and rewards gave entrepreneurs the confidence to undertake risky, but potentially lucrative, exchanges that would otherwise go unmet in the market.[1]

The complex system of internal exchanges characteristic of the multi-activity firm mitigates the effects of uncertainty in the market. Ironically, this complexity itself poses another source of uncertainty. Because information about its complicated internal processes is difficult to assimilate, an integrated firm can sink in a morass of bureaucratic inefficiency, losing its potential gains. The most successful of the early multi-activity firms tackled this problem by adopting what is known today as the unitary, or centralized, form of organization.[2] The unitary organization breaks the firm's overall operations into separate departments, each with highly specialized activities (for example, distribution, manufacturing, transportation, finance, and purchasing). The central office coordinates the departments and directs their diverse activities toward common goals.

The centralized unitary structure seemed a natural way to arrange the diverse and interdependent activities of the multi-activity firm. The structure allowed managers within each department to concentrate on efficient and effective performance of their specialized activity. At the same time, it permitted top managers to concentrate on coordinating as a unit the performances of the various departments in the firm.[3] Each department was managed by a specialist who used all the techniques of single-activity management, as though the department were a separate, single-activity company. With these techniques, which were highly developed by 1900 and thoroughly publicized by such writers as Frederick W. Taylor,[4] the department manager achieved cost efficiencies and scale economies. Freed from the task of operating separate departments, top management could apply its energies to attaining peak coordination and to achieving "synergies" inherent in the company's integrated activities. The owners intended, of course, that the profit of the whole company would exceed the profits that could be realized by the separate parts of the company were each part organized either through the market or through another competing firm.

The carefully delineated lines of authority and responsibility in a centralized organization did not by themselves assure that the owners of the multi-activity firm achieved the hoped-for gains. There also had to be mechanisms to ensure that each department's individual performance harmonized with the owners' goals for the firm as a whole. Harmony between the activities of the parts and the desired performance of the whole could not be left to chance. Several mechanisms enable social organizations to achieve the necessary harmony; they include, for example, centrally planned mathematical models, decentralized price systems, and culturally ingrained values.[5] In America's late nineteenth-century multi-activity firms, a popular mechanism was the management accounting system.

To cope with their firms' many activities, managers of successful integrated firms in early twentieth-century America designed procedures to ensure a flow of reliable and useful information and instructions through their centralized organizations. They might have adopted procedures that trace the consumption of diverse resources to products, similar to those advocated by Alexander Hamilton Church. As we mentioned in chapter 3, they did not do this, presumably because existing information-processing technology made use of such procedures too costly. Instead, we find managers of vertically integrated firms adopting systems already in use in single-activity firms to coordinate internally the multiple processes involved in a single productive activity. But managers of vertically integrated firms modified these systems to assist them in evaluating and controlling several diverse activities.

In these modified information systems, individual departments in an integrated multi-activity firm relied on the accounting measures of performance developed by single-activity firms. In a multi-activity firm, however, it was virtually impossible to relate these disparate measures of efficiency (for example, cost per unit, operating ratio, stock-turn) directly to overall company profit. Moreover, heads of single-activity departments, simply employees in a multi-activity company, were not necessarily as motivated to achieve company-wide profit as were heads of independent single-activity firms. Top managers of multi-activity firms mitigated these problems of control and motivation with two new developments in management accounting. First, they devised budgets to coordinate and balance the internal resource flows from raw material to final customer. Second, they developed a new measure, return on investment, to compare performance in the firm's diverse parts with performance of the whole.

The budgeting and return on investment mechanisms

were designed to harmonize actions in the departments with the overall goals of the firm. The primary goal in many early integrated firms was to achieve higher-than-average returns by distributing to America's mass market the output from mass production technologies. Management accounting in the multi-activity firms directed managers' attention beyond the efficiencies of economic processes at the shop level, and even beyond the synergies gained from linking multiple activities. For the first time ever, the attention of managers was focused on the productivity and performance of capital itself.

Single-activity firms in the nineteenth century had ignored how well capital was being used. We mentioned in earlier chapters that managers of such firms were content to know how efficiently processes were being run once capital was in place. In multi-activity firms, however, top managers—not the market—must allocate capital among activities. The emphasis placed on capital by budgets and return on investment information, while prompted by the desire to evaluate and control specific internal activities, had an unforeseen consequence. The efficient and effective management of capital itself eventually became a driving force in the firm.[6] Return on investment, initiated as a tool to facilitate the coordination of diverse activities, ultimately became a guiding principle. The full implications of this accounting-driven attention to capital are still being worked out today—as will be discussed subsequently in chapter 8—but the origins of this development can be viewed in the management accounting systems of early American multi-activity firms. We can gain a vivid understanding of this development by observing how one well-known integrated industrial firm, E. I. du Pont de Nemours Powder Company, was influenced by novel management accounting practices designed initially to govern their complex, multi-activity system.

Formation of the Du Pont
Powder Company

The records of the Du Pont Powder Company, an
explosives firm founded in 1903, provide an excellent example of the early uses of management accounting to evaluate opportunities and to achieve control in an integrated,
multi-activity industrial.[7] The Du Pont Powder Company
supplanted the operations of E. I. du Pont de Nemours and
Company, an explosives manufacturer in America since
1804.[8] The Powder Company was founded by three Du Pont
cousins, Alfred, Coleman, and Pierre, who, having worked
during the 1890s for single-activity manufacturing and
transportation firms employing modern management techniques, were certain that advanced administrative methods
could be applied profitably to the old family firm. Seizing
the opportunity created by a succession crisis in the family
firm, the cousins purchased the firm's assets in exchange for
bonds in the newly created E. I. du Pont de Nemours Powder
Company. By this transaction, known today as a leveraged
buy-out, the owners of the old company exchanged their
assets for bonds, the interest on which was to equal the expected earnings of the old firm. The cousins thus gained
control of the old firm's assets and became owners of a new
company whose value would increase only if they could earn
more with the old firm's assets than did the previous owners.

In order to evaluate and control the efficiency and profitability of their newly acquired company, the Du Pont
cousins immediately began to develop a new administrative
structure.[9] The structure had considerable impact not
merely upon the Powder Company, but also upon the organization of the entire explosives industry. Before 1903, the
industry comprised several independently managed firms,
each of which engaged primarily in manufacturing. Distribution to consumers was handled chiefly by wholesalers and
general merchants. The old Du Pont Company and other

major firms in the industry coordinated prices and set output quotas through the Gun Powder Trade Association, a loosely structured, decentralized black blasting powder cartel. After 1903, the cousins rescinded almost all trade agreements in the Gun Powder Trade Association, bought out numerous firms in which the Du Ponts had partial or controlling interest, and consolidated their operations into one centralized, departmentalized enterprise. In short, the Du Pont Powder Company became a centrally managed enterprise coordinating through its own departments most of the manufacturing and distribution activities formerly mediated through the market by scores of specialized firms.

A centralized accounting system facilitated the flow of information through the Du Pont Powder Company's complex departmental structure.[10] The home office requested from the company's mills and branch sales offices, located throughout the United States, daily and weekly data on sales, payroll, and manufacturing costs. The data were then recorded in the basic books of account. The home office accounting department compiled information from the books to rationalize operations and to monitor efficiency. The information assisted top management, the Powder Company's Executive Committee, in formulating plans that would ensure balanced growth among the company's diverse activities. It was also a means of evaluating and controlling the company's ongoing performance in each of the three main operating departments (manufacturing, distribution, and purchasing) and also for the company as a whole. The design of the Du Pont management accounting procedures gave enormous importance to return on investment, a price signal that had been virtually ignored by single-activity industrial firms in earlier times. Du Pont used return on investment as a common measuring rod of performance with which to plan, evaluate, and control for the profits being sought by the owners of the firm's resources.

Information provided by the company's centralized accounting system enabled top management to carry out two capital planning tasks: the allocation of new investment among competing economic activities (including the maintenance of working capital) and the financing of new capital requirements.[11] Capital allocation became one of the chief occupations of the newly integrated industrial firms because the multi-activity firm forced managers to consider choices that previously had been left to capital markets. Governing the Powder Company's decisions to allocate investment funds was the principle that there "be no expenditures for additions to the earning equipment if the same amount of money could be applied to some better purpose in another branch of the company's business."[12] Return on investment was the criterion used to evaluate any investment project.

The Powder Company may have been one of the first industrial enterprises to use return on investment in management accounting. Single-activity firms before 1900 assessed net earnings, if at all, in relation to costs of operations and not in relation to the firm's total investment in assets. The typical nineteenth-century entrepreneur, being chiefly concerned with controlling costs and raising efficiency in a single activity, had little reason to measure return on investment. He took his firm's investment (i.e., the scale of operations) for granted and concentrated on managing short-run costs. The Powder Company's executives also recognized the importance of controlling day-to-day operations costs, but they perceived that "a commodity requiring an inexpensive plant might, when sold only ten per cent above its cost, show a higher rate of return on the investment than another commodity sold at double its cost, but manufactured in an expensive plant." They concluded that "the true test of whether the profit is too great or too small is the rate of return on the money invested in the business and not the percent of profit on the cost."[13]

An asset accounting system was the main innovation that permitted return on investment to be used as a tool of management accounting. Asset accounting in 1900 represented a significant departure from the previous accounting practice that charged off capital expenditures to retained earnings as quickly as possible. Thus, nineteenth-century businesses rarely kept detailed records of investment in plant and equipment. The Powder Company's system of accounting for productive assets was inaugurated in 1903 when the company made a complete inventory of all its plants and equipment and recorded each item in the general ledger account "Permanent Investment." Thereafter, all new construction was charged (and dismantled assets were credited) to this account at cost. The relevant accounting data on construction and dismantling costs were supplied through a comprehensive construction appropriation procedure.[14]

The construction appropriation system, in addition to supplying timely and accurate information on new investment, also provided information useful to top management in planning new long-term financing, the second of the two planning tasks mentioned above. Since spending on new plant and equipment was the major factor determining the company's need for new financing, information on appropriations and expenditures for construction was imperative for planning long-term capital requirements. The construction appropriation system, however, supplied only part of the information needed to plan financing. Since the Powder Company's basic policy was to finance expansion out of cash generated by earnings and the proceeds of stock sales (debt financing was eschewed),[15] a forecast of cash flows was required to determine the maximum amount of new construction to which the firm could commit itself. Cash flows were forecast by multiplying the projected quantity of explosives to be sold each month (based on sales department estimates) by the estimated contribution margin per unit for each product (based on accounting department records).[16] In calculating margins, consideration was given to probable future

trends in both product prices and input costs. The figure for
operating cash flows was then added to projected nonoper-
ating income (income from land sales, earnings on financial
investments) to estimate total cash inflow. When combined
with data on construction appropriations, this information
on cash flows enabled top management to forecast the company's cash position and thus the anticipated need for new
sales of stock.[17] By 1910, the Executive Committee was receiving monthly forecasts of the firm's cash position for a
year ahead; both the cash position projections and the cash
flow forecasts were reconciled regularly with actual results.[18]

The information from the Powder Company's centralized accounting system also served to evaluate and control
operations within and among the firm's various internal departments. Similar information was produced in the late
nineteenth-century accounting systems of specialized firms
connected with the railroad, metal-working, chemical, electrical equipment, and steel industries. But the founders of
the Powder Company originated budgets and return on investment statistics that synthesized the disparate signals
from departmental accounting systems into information regarding company-wide performance. As a consequence of
these accounting refinements, top management did not need
to administer daily operations, a task that had occupied the
time of managers in single-activity firms before 1900. Top
management could now delegate responsibility for operations to departmental supervisors because of the availability
of reliable standardized information on operating performance and the use of routine operating criteria and instructions. The sophistication and availability of this accounting
information clearly increased the Executive Committee's
span of control and prevented the loss of control that otherwise might have accompanied the Powder Company's
growth after 1903. All conclusions about the company's
management accounting procedures may be better assessed,

however, after the accounting systems used in each of the firm's three main departments are described.

The Du Pont Manufacturing Department

Comprising three separate subdepartments (high explosives, smokeless gunpowder, and black blasting powder), manufacturing was Du Pont's largest and most complex department. Accounting information permitted control and assessment of manufacturing activities in the company's more than forty geographically dispersed mills.[19] The accounting system summarized manufacturing information in two monthly reports, the works cost report and the profit and loss sheet. Data for the two reports came in part from mill production control records such as daily time sheets and daily material usage logs.[20] Both sets of reports were distributed to the Executive Committee (on which sat the vice presidents of each manufacturing subdepartment), while only the works cost report went to the mill superintendents. The works cost report contained information pertinent to the mill superintendents' chief area of responsibility, the operating efficiency of production processes.[21] The additional profit and loss sheet, restricted to the Executive Committee, assisted top management in the execution of its primary responsibility: to maximize overall net earnings and return on investment.

The different purposes served by the two sets of reports can be made apparent by describing their respective contents. The works cost report described both the quantities (not dollars) of raw materials and the dollar costs of all other inputs (except administrative overhead) used by each mill in every production process. Raw material usage was compared both with predetermined standards and with consumption in other mills. The costs of nonmaterial inputs, broken down into labor, power, fuel, and supplies, were shown for each process in a mill. The information in the works cost report enabled each superintendent to assess his mill's performance over time and in relation to the performances of other mills in the same subdepartment. The profit and loss sheet that was sent only to the Executive Committee contained additional information on all manufacturing costs, operating income, and return on investment.[22] The information in this sheet and in supplemental reports enabled top management to assess earnings and return on investment by mill and by product line. A report on "operative income from sales," for instance, showed for each product the total and per unit amounts for gross sales, freight expense, selling expense, mill cost, net operating income, administrative expense, and net income. These data were also aggregated by mill and for the enterprise as a whole.[23] The figure for "mill cost" (*i.e.,* cost of goods manufactured) in the report enabled management to analyze both the cost of each product and the manufacturing costs of each mill in relation to overall net earnings. Mill cost was further analyzed in great detail, in a monthly report that showed its components (ingredients, labor, mill repairs, power, supplies, work accident insurance, and depreciation[24]) in total and per unit of output for each mill and for each of the company's sixteen products.

The division of information between mill superintendents and top management suggests that the company intended mill superintendents to think and act as if they managed a typical late nineteenth-century single-activity factory. The information given to superintendents emphasized the physical efficiency of production processes within the mill; it said nothing about the mill's financial profitability, nothing about mill earnings, nothing on return on investment. Like Andrew Carnegie running his giant steel works, the superintendent of a Du Pont explosives mill could take for granted its scale of operations; his chief concern was to operate the existing facilities as efficiently as possible.

This concern is evident in minutes from the annual meetings of superintendents of the company's high explosives mills.[25] At these meetings the superintendents and manufacturing vice presidents discussed the most recent year's mill operating reports and concentrated almost entirely on comparisons of labor productivity and raw material consumption among the mills. Apparently, the superintendents competed vigorously to be low direct cost producers. There was virtually no talk of profits or return on investment.

Consideration of financial profitability was reserved for the Executive Committee. Thus, the founders of the Du Pont Powder Company did not use their new management accounting information about return on investment as an instrument for delegating decisions about prices, profits, or investment. Decisions about raw material purchases, wage rates, costs of other purchased inputs, and investment in plant and equipment remained highly centralized with top management in the home office. Top management used return on investment information to evaluate alternative uses of capital, not to evaluate the performance of managers in profit or investment centers. The centralization of return on investment information required the Executive Committee to devote more attention to operating details, of course, than would have been the case had the mill superintendents been evaluated as managers of investment centers. But it also relieved top management from the concern, familiar to management accounting theorists today, that mill managers, to enhance their local return on investment, might take actions inimical to the company's best interest.

Surely the Powder Company's top management, who were the owners of the company, were not likely to take actions inimical to the company's long-term profitability simply to enhance short-term return on investment. Modern accounting theorists point out the potential for such "gaming" behavior exists whenever the return on investment figures used to evaluate performance are based on earnings and investment net of accounting depreciation (*i.e.*, straight line or accelerated). In such cases management can generate a rising return on investment trend, for many years, simply by withholding new investment. But this behavior is not likely when the managers using the return on investment statistics, such as the Powder Company's early Executive Committee, are also the firm's owners. The gaming behavior will more likely occur when the managers are employees of the company, having less self-interest than owners have in the company's long-term profitability. But one can reduce the likelihood of gaming by nonowner managers simply by measuring their earnings and investment without any deductions for depreciation.[26] It is interesting, therefore, that the Du Pont Company after 1920, when it adopted a decentralized multidivisional structure, began using gross measures of earnings and investment to measure return on investment in the company's divisions.[27]

The Powder Company's new management accounting system did not leave the manufacturing department without practical problems to frustrate managers and accountants. Indeed, the company's founders debated two problems that continue to vex accounting theorists to this day. The first was whether to allocate indirect costs to intermediate and final products to facilitate intelligent make-or-buy decisions. The company manufactured many of the intermediate products used to make its finished products. In debating how to allocate indirect costs, Hamilton Barksdale, vice president of the high explosives manufacturing unit, insisted on loading indirect costs onto the finished product, but not onto any of the intermediate products. Barksdale feared that allocations of overhead to intermediate products would be arbitrary and would therefore vitiate analyses of internal mill efficiency. Russell Dunham, chief accountant for the company, opposed this policy. He argued that failure to allocate indirect costs to intermediate output precluded meaningful comparisons of company costs with outside market prices for the same products.[28] The company's early records do not show how they ultimately resolved this debate.

The second accounting issue debated by the founders of the Powder Company was how to price internal transfers of products. On this issue, the accounting department had its way; internal transfers were priced at fully loaded accounting costs. The dissenting view, held by Barksdale and a majority of the company's operating chiefs, was that internal transfers should be priced at relevant market prices. The underlying reason for this difference of opinion, according to Alfred Chandler and Stephen Salsbury, was a conflicting belief about the ultimate purpose of the company's accounting information. Those who favored pricing internal transfers at market "wanted to use accounting data to appraise the performance of the company's departments," whereas those who favored pricing transfers at cost "saw the information only as useful in determining the profit and loss and the return on investment for the company as a whole."[29] Interestingly, Pierre du Pont, the chief advocate of the latter view—the view that shaped the early Du Pont Company's transfer pricing policy—subsequently changed his mind and advocated market transfer pricing some years later when he was running the decentralized operations of General Motors.

The Du Pont Sales Department

As in the case of manufacturing, marketing also presented a number of difficult administrative problems to be solved by the Powder Company's centralized accounting system. The major administrative tasks of the sales department included coordinating customer orders with mill production schedules, keeping advised of market trends, evaluating prices, controlling customer accounts, and coordinating and evaluating the performance of the sales staff.[30] The sales department's enormous responsibility for the company's products began when goods were finished in the mills and ended when the goods were sold and delivered to customers. Its task was complicated both by the diversity of the company's products and customers and by the wide geographic dispersion of the company's markets. The sales department managed a large network of branch sales offices scattered across the United States; salaried salesmen working out of the offices sold virtually all the company's products. Most of the branch sales offices (and all the mills) maintained inventories of finished goods. The sales accounting system employed to monitor the complex marketing operation was perhaps the most novel and sophisticated part of the Powder Company's management accounting system.

The primary sales accounting records were sales orders and invoices in the branch sales offices and shipping orders in the mills.[31] Copies of these widely dispersed primary records were sent daily to the home office accounting department, which kept all the ledgers for finished goods inventories, sales, and customer balances. The company maintained centralized control over its cash balances by advising customers to remit payment directly to the Wilmington, Delaware, home office. Centralized control was also maintained by having the home office audit staff periodically verify the branch office and mill inventories.

The most important information compiled by the home office accounting department from sales accounting records was in the daily sales report, a listing derived from each day's invoices of the quantity and dollar amount of every product sold by each branch office. The reports provided timely information on market trends, usually with a time lag no longer than four or five days, to the vice president of the sales department and each branch office manager. The information in the daily sales report was compiled from invoices in an unusually advanced way.[32] Data were entered on punch cards and then sorted using a system introduced by the U.S. Bureau of the Census around 1890. Because of its exceptional flexibility, the punch card system permitted the home office accounting department to prepare not only the daily sales report, but also the following sales information: a monthly summary of quantities sold and average unit prices by geographic region, by type of product, and by type of customer; a sales cost sheet comparing, among the branch offices, the net prices received and the selling expenses for each type of product sold; and a trial balance of finished goods inventories that was reconciled each month with the general ledger. All these reports provided the vice president and staff of the sales department with comprehensive information to control and coordinate the Powder Company's entire marketing activity.

The sales accounting system contributed to centralized control; but, unlike the manufacturing accounting system, it also encouraged maximum decentralization of decision making. A pricing procedure and an incentive-compensation scheme for salesmen provided the basis for decentralized decision making and lower-echelon profit incentives.

Although pricing had been a major task of top management among firms in the Gun Powder Trade Association before 1903, evaluating product prices in the Powder Company became a routine undertaking that seldom required the attention of top management.[33] A committee of sales department executives, the Sales Board, reviewed minimum prices for each product, usually once a month. The review was intended to ensure that prices were high enough for each product line to earn a target return on investment. To facilitate pricing decisions, the home office accounting department prepared monthly estimates of the profit per kcg or per pound needed to earn a given return for the investment in each type of product (15 percent for dynamite and 10 percent for black powder).[34] Using data from construction accounting records on the investment in plant and equipment by product line, the home office calculated the desired earn-

ings (for example, 10 percent of the investment in black powder capacity) and divided the expected earnings both by the
normal output and the capacity output of the mills. The
profit needed per unit of output to earn a desired rate of
return (at both normal output and capacity output) could
then be added to the unit cost of production to obtain the
required minimum product price.

The Du Pont Powder Company set minimum prices on
products to preserve existing competition. Convinced that
their size and expertise in the industry would always enable
them to produce at a lower cost than their competitors, the
executives of the Powder Company did not strive ruthlessly
to eliminate existing competition. On the contrary, they believed (as did Andrew Carnegie a generation earlier) that it
was useful to have smaller, higher cost competitors to provide the industry's excess capacity during market recessions.
The presence of these competitors increased the likelihood
that Du Pont could run its mills at full capacity in all phases
of the business cycle.[35] Their cognizance of the value of existing competition partially influenced the Powder Company
executives' decision to keep prices close to those of competing firms. Information on competitors' prices was gathered
regularly by salesmen and forwarded to branch sales managers and to the home office.

Minimum price figures were sent from the home office
to the branch sales managers, who had final responsibility
for setting customer prices. A sales manager was allowed to
sell above the minimum price, but not below it. His strategy
was to set prices as high as he could without risking the
entry of a new firm into the industry. While existing competitors were tolerated, new competitors were certainly not
sought. For example, in late 1906, the assistant treasurer of
the Powder Company, John J. Raskob, noticed that black
blasting powder produced and sold by the company in the
anthracite region of Pennsylvania was earning 22 percent on
investment, whereas the same type of powder produced and

sold by the company in the rest of the country was earning about 2 percent. Since all plants were running at full capacity, he argued that the price of black blasting powder should go up about 5 percent in all districts outside the anthracite region, whereas the price should go down about 8 percent in the anthracite district. "Unless this is done," he said, "the story our Profit and Loss statement tells is that while we are selling powder at lower prices than ever before all over the country with a view to preventing further investment in the business, we are inviting the same competition in the anthracite region by having prices which net us practically four times such income on the capital invested as we net in all other territories."[36]

The sales accounting system also helped sales managers to control and assess the performance of salesmen through an incentive scheme based on routinely collected financial data. The Powder Company's scheme, as described by the director of sales, was designed "to give greater latitude to our men in the field [with] handling the trade, . . . to place upon our men more responsibility for the results obtained, and to provide so that their compensation will be varied as closely as possible in proportion with the results obtained along the lines we desire."[37] Salesmen were paid salaries tied to productivity incentives, rather than more customary commissions. The home office sales department calculated a "normal" volume and a "base" price (not the minimum price) for each product in every branch office. The branch office sales manager allocated his office's "normal" volume among the salesmen assigned to him. If a salesman's actual monthly sales were equal to his "base sales" (the base price times his normal volume), then he received 100 percent of his basic salary. His salary increased proportionately as his actual sales exceeded his basic sales. (It appears, however, that a minimum salary was guaranteed if actual sales were less than base sales.) The procedure encouraged salesmen to weigh both price and volume of their sales. In effect, it encouraged them to maximize total revenue for the company (and themselves) within the constraints imposed by the firm's pricing policy. The incentive procedure also allowed the sales department to direct salesmen's efforts with minimal intervention. For example, the home office sales department could provide a direct incentive to a salesman to push one line harder than another simply by adjusting the base price of a certain product.

The sales accounting system offered still another means for reducing the administrative responsibilities of top management. It provided a decentralized check on the performance of branch office managers and induced them to control inventories and costs in their branches.[38] The sales department estimated a "normal" ratio of sales costs to gross sales for each branch office. Sales costs included general office expenses plus 5 percent each of the average accounts receivable and average inventory balances. When the ratio of actual sales costs to gross sales was less than the normal ratio, 7.5 percent of the savings was added to the branch manager's salary. The manager was given discretion to distribute an additional 5 percent of the savings to his staff. The Executive Committee received a monthly sales cost sheet that compared gross sales and sales costs by branch office. By creating incentive and establishing control, the Powder Company's sales accounting system helped to coordinate the sales department's performance with the organization's overall earnings goal.

The Du Pont Purchasing Department

The Powder Company's founders perceived that great savings could be achieved if the buying of raw materials were carried out by one purchasing department located in the home office rather than separately at individual mills.

The purchasing accounting system helped to control expenditures on raw materials, to assess alternative sources of supply, and to coordinate purchasing with production. Unlike the manufacturing and sales department systems, however, the purchasing department system was not designed to coordinate and appraise the performance of line operatives.

The purchasing accounting system centralized control over the ordering, receiving, and expensing of all purchases by relying upon the well-known accounts payable voucher system used in the home office accounting department.[39] The voucher system, first used by railroad accountants during the mid-nineteenth century,[40] offers convenient control over balances due on account as well as assurance that purchases are charged to the proper accounts in the proper accounting periods. The purchasing department, which initiated all orders for materials with outside suppliers until about 1908 (when the company began to integrate backward into ownership of supply sources), placed all orders on the basis of market price information. The accounts payable division of the home office accounting department entered each order in a voucher register, issued checks for payment, and provided a monthly summary of all expenses for materials. The summary, derived from the voucher register, provided the basis from which ledgers were posted and cost statements were prepared. Each month the audit staff reviewed all voucher entries and payments.

Having centralized the control over purchase transactions, the purchasing department next concentrated upon achieving the lowest possible prices for raw materials. Until 1908, management had purchased most raw materials from outside agents whose terms could easily be compared with market prices. Consequently, very little internal accounting information had been necessary. Indeed, one of the few times that internal accounting information was required took place after 1905 when the Powder Company, which had customarily purchased nitrates through American commission

merchants, established its own agent in Chile to buy nitrates.[41] The internal reporting required by the venture was
minimal. Regular account was kept of the added cost of the
Chilean office, shipping services, and working capital; these
costs per ton of nitrate were compared regularly with prices
charged by outside agents such as W. R. Grace and Co.[42]

The 1907 recession revealed a major problem with the
decentralized purchasing accounting system. In their careful assessment of the effects of the recession upon the policies of the Powder Company, Chandler and Salsbury point
out that the purchasing department's efforts to buy raw materials at minimum price caused a working capital crisis
during 1907.[43] As prices fell during the business cycle down-
turn, the vice president of purchasing accumulated vast supplies of essential raw materials; the payments required for
these purchases fell due, however, just as declining orders
for explosives reduced working capital. After narrowly es-
caping the crisis, management revised its purchasing policy
to permit the purchasing deparment to buy at the lowest
possible prices only up to a prescribed stock level, a level
that varied with each month's sales projections.

While the maximum stock levels imposed by this new
policy reduced the risk of a working capital crisis, they introduced the possibility of supply shortages in the event of
an emergency, such as disruption to shipping in wartime.
Intent on reducing its dependence on outside suppliers, the
company began to acquire ownership of many supply
sources, although it never achieved full ownership of supplies of all its basic raw materials.[44] The earliest steps toward backward integration involved controlling the production of such critical materials as charcoal, blasting caps, and
packing crates. Each of these inputs accounted for only a
small percentage of total purchases. The Powder Company's
major raw material purchases were for nitrate of soda and
crude glycerine. Of these, the company chose to integrate
backward only into nitrates production.

Although many factors, both strategic and economic, impinged on its decisions to integrate backward, the basic criterion used by the Powder Company to evaluate these steps was return on investment. Basically, an investment in outside supply sources was approved only if it was judged likely to earn at least 15 percent per annum, the return the company normally earned in dynamite making, its most profitable production activity. The purchasing department used two procedures to estimate return on investment in integrated supply operations.[45] One procedure was followed when the company proposed to manufacture its own supplies of certain inputs (for example, dynamite packing crates or blasting caps). The estimated return, or "profit," on such a manufacturing process was calculated by deducting the estimated unit cost of production from current market price. This estimated "profit" was then divided by the estimated net investment that would be required to build or buy the necessary production facilities.

The second procedure was followed when the company proposed to control, but not to own, the source of supply of an essential raw material. It entailed first estimating the savings that would result from buying direct rather than buying through a commission agent. In order to determine these savings, the estimated unit cost of direct purchases was deducted from the market price charged by outside suppliers. Next, the purchasing department computed the return on investment by dividing these savings by the additional investment in inventories that direct buying would require. Although the two procedures have been criticized because they did not take into consideration the effect of the Powder Company's projected demand on market prices, it appears that the company did use conservative estimates of market price in order to make these return on investment calculations.[46] On the whole, therefore, these procedures provided useful guidelines for the allocation of Powder Company resources.

The Ascendance of Return on Investment

The management accounting systems in each department of the Powder Company provided a powerful arsenal of statistical tools with which to plan, control, and motivate people in the company's diverse activities. The information from these systems on the efficiency of processes within each specialized department would have been familiar to managers of many nineteenth-century single-activity firms. But the information on the internal efficiency of capital across the three functional departments was unheard of before the coming of the multi-activity enterprise. The imaginative use of return on investment information enabled the Powder Company's top managers to effectively supplant capital markets in deciding how to allocate resources within the American explosives industry.

Indeed, their intense desire to assess every aspect of the company's activities in terms of the price of capital led the founders of the Du Pont Powder Company to devise an ingenious return on investment formula that continues to serve accountants and financial analysts to this day. The formula, shown pictorially in Figure 4-1,[47] factors return on investment into the product of the sales turnover ratio (sales divided by investment) and the operating ratio (net earnings divided by sales). The formula, as depicted in Figure 4-1, shows how return on investment is affected by a change in any element of either the income statement (via the operating ratio) or the balance sheet (via the turnover ratio). Viewed from that perspective, the Du Pont return on investment formula is an ideal tool for controlling, with accounting numbers, any vertically integrated company's operations. And that was the purpose to which the Powder Company's founders applied the formula. Between about 1915 and 1918 the company established a unique system for reporting the information in Figure 4-1 for each product line and each mill; the information was presented to top man-

Figure 4–1.   The Du Pont Return on Investment Formula
Relationship of Factors Affecting Return on Investment

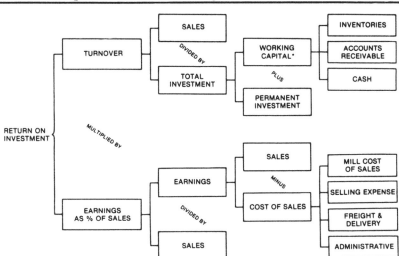

*ALSO INCLUDES SMALL AMOUNTS OF DEFERRED CHARGES
WHICH ARE NOT CHARTED
Source: See Note 47

agement in a series of wall-sized charts—over 350 in fact—
that were updated each month and maintained for easy
viewing in a special Chart Room at the home office in Wilmington.[48]

It would be a mistake, however, to conclude from their
extensive use of formulae and charts that the founders of the
Powder Company "ran the company by the numbers." The
return on investment reports went only to top management
who used the information for planning and company-wide
control. Subordinate managers were not compelled to
achieve return on investment targets; rather, they strove to
achieve economies and efficiencies within their respective
specialized activities. Top management alone assumed responsibility for the investment and allocation decisions that
ultimately determined how effectively the company's integrated activities used capital. There was little chance, there-

fore, that Powder Company operating managers would try to achieve return on investment targets either by under-investing in capital or by curtailing expenses that would raise short-run earnings but diminish the firm's long-run value.

Indeed, it is probable that the Powder Company's founders saw their return on investment formula in terms of its unique historical significance for the multi-activity enterprise. As we have noted, by combining the operations of two or more single-activity firms into one integrated enterprise, the multi-activity firm intends to achieve results superior to those of a collection of single-activity firms acting independently. For a multi-activity firm the logic of combining the operating ratio and the turnover ratio into one index of company-wide performance is impeccable. The Du Pont return on investment formula combines, in effect, the two accounting measures of performance that single-activity firms engaged in manufacturing and distribution had developed separately during the nineteenth century. But the Du Pont formula combined the two distinct measures of performance (the operating ratio and the turnover ratio) in a way that permitted the multi-activity firm to perform as a mini-capital market.

The idea for the Du Pont return on investment formula (and for the Chart Room as well) originated, as far as we know, with F. Donaldson Brown, a college-trained electrical engineer and one-time electrical equipment salesman who joined the Powder Company's sales department in 1909 and became assistant treasurer of the company in 1914.[49] None of Brown's surviving records indicates how he hit upon the idea for his return on investment formula.[50] Interestingly, Brown had no formal training or experience in accounting. His expertise in electrical engineering (at the age of 17 he received the B.S.E.E. degree from Virginia Polytechnic Institute) suggests that he was proficient at mathematics and adept at interpreting relationships among the diverse parts of a complex system. His experience in selling no doubt gave him an appreciation for the effect of turnover and distribution costs on a company's profits. Evidently, his mathematical, engineering, and marketing skills gave Brown a unique perspective on the determinants of company performance that was not understood by most contemporary accountants. Brown's ideas about financial planning and control had a profound impact on the Du Pont organization and later on General Motors. Yet his ideas did not become widely known among professional accountants until the 1950s, when a new generation of management accounting textbooks introduced them into the standard MBA curriculum.

Summary

The need for a uniform financial measuring rod compelled managers of integrated multi-activity firms to push management accounting beyond the cost management systems developed by single-activity enterprises in the nineteenth century. The Du Pont Powder Company discovered one such measuring rod in return on investment, an accounting ratio that helped management determine the price of capital used within the company. The Powder Company's return-on-investment reporting system compared every aspect of the company's diverse internal operations with alternative uses for capital, while preserving the best of single-activity cost management information about each of the company's specialized activities. With no obvious precedent to follow, the Du Pont organization between about 1903 and 1915 created a management accounting system whose essential features remain to this day a model for complex business organizations.

The Du Pont Powder Company's management accounting system mitigated many bureaucratic problems that otherwise might afflict a centrally managed, complex integrated business firm. Left unsolved, these problems would ultimately have limited the size of a vertically integrated enterprise by the cost of coordinating diverse internal activities. The cost increases as a firm grows in size primarily because communication of instructions and information throughout the organization becomes more difficult with larger numbers of people. Communication difficulties that lower the quality of information about opportunities for gain within the firm are analogous to conditions that make prices (*i.e.*, measures of alternative opportunities) less than perfect in product and capital markets. Because of the costs of discovering opportunities for gain both in markets and within firms, we observe economic exchange occurring in both places, and not all in markets or all in firms. To paraphrase the famous theorem that Ronald Coase enunciated over fifty years ago, a firm will grow until the marginal cost of discovering opportunities for gain within the firm exceeds the marginal cost of discovering opportunities for gain in the market.[51] By lowering the cost of discovering opportunities within the firm, management accounting systems such as the one developed by the founders of the Du Pont Powder Company have undoubtedly increased the potential size of complex business organizations.

Notes

1. A discussion of the points summarized in the previous paragraphs is in Alfred D. Chandler, Jr., *The Visible Hand: The Managerial Revolution in American Business* (Cambridge, Mass.: Harvard University Press, 1977), chapters 9–11.

2. Oliver E. Williamson, *Corporate Control and Business Behavior; An Inquiry into the Effects of Organization Form on Enterprise Behavior* (Englewood Cliffs, N.J.: Prentice-Hall, 1970), chapter 2; Alfred D. Chandler, Jr., *Strategy and Structure: Chapters in the History of the American Industrial Enterprise* (Garden City, N.Y.: Anchor Books, 1966; reprint of 1962 ed.), 43–50.

3. Oliver E. Williamson, *Markets and Hierarchies: Analysis and Antitrust Implications* (New York: Free Press, 1975), 133.

4. Joseph A. Litterer, "Systematic Management: Design for Organizational Recoupling in American Manufacturing Firms," *Business History Review* (Winter 1963), 369–391.

5. See H. Thomas Johnson, "Accounting, Organizations and Rules: Toward a Sociology of Price," *Accounting, Organizations and Society* volume 11, No. 4/5 (1986), 341–343.

6. A similar development occurred with the use of conversion cost information in single-activity firms during the nineteenth century. An accounting number such as cost per labor hour also assumed a life of its own by driving the search for labor-saving efficiencies, say, from improved machinery. In the twentieth-century vertically integrated firm, return on investment numbers drove a similar search, this time for more productive opportunities to use capital in general.

7. The records referred to here are described in H. Thomas Johnson, "Management Accounting in an Early Integrated Industrial: E. I. du Pont de Nemours Powder Company 1903–1912," *Business History Review* (Summer 1975), 185, n. 6. The records are cited hereafter as "Hall of Records" with the appropriate box or shelf number.

8. The following account of the Powder Company's early history is drawn from Alfred D. Chandler, Jr., and Stephen Salsbury, *Pierre S. duPont and the Making of the Modern Corporation* (New York: Harper & Row, 1971), 47–120.

9. *Ibid.*, 77–120.

10. *Ibid.*, 144–147. Two papers give a concise description of all facets of the Powder Company's centralized accounting system: R. H. Dunham, "Object of Accounting," paper for the High Explosives Operating Department Superintendents' Meeting No. 33 (New York, April 20–26, 1911), and William G. Ramsay, "Construction Appropriations," paper for the H.E.O.D. Superintendents' Meeting No. 32 (New York, April 12–16, 1910). The papers, on file at the Eleutherian Mills Historical Library, Greenville, Delaware, are reprinted in H. Thomas Johnson, ed., *System and Profits: Early Management Accounting at Du Pont and General Motors* (New York: Arno press, 1980).

11. Chandler and Salsbury, *Pierre S. du Pont*, 158–168, 201–217.

12. Ramsay, "Construction Appropriation," 2.

13. Dunham, "Object of Accounting," 17. The basic figure used by the company for return on investment was net earnings (after deducting depreciation and before deduction of interest on long-term debt) divided by net assests (total assets minus goodwill and other intangibles, current liabilities, and reserves for depreciation).

14. In accordance with this procedure, all proposed investment in plant and equipment was described on standard appropriation forms calling for estimates of expenditure, estimates of the savings in cost or other benefits anticipated from the proposed investment, and evidence of proper authorization. Once an appropriation was approved, a report was presented on the final actual expenditure on the new asset. Proper authorities were then expected to account for any unreasonable variance from the original estimate. See Ramsay, "Construction Appropriation," *passim*.

15. Chandler and Salsbury, *Pierre S. du Pont*, 210–213, 251–254.

16. Examples of the earnings forecasts are found in Hall of Records, boxes 184736–184740, item 43 (about 1907), and shelf area 182701–182712, items 161 and 161A–161D (1910).

17. Chandler and Salsbury, *Pierre S. du Pont*, 251–252.

18. Examples of these monthly cash forecasts (ca. 1910) are in Hall of Records, shelf area 182701–182712, item 173. Reconciliations of cash forecasts to actual cash flows are at item 186. Reconciliations of earnings forecasts to actual earnings are in boxes 184736–184740, item 43.

19. Each mill produced only one type of explosive (smokeless gunpowder, high explosives, or black blasting powder), usually in several varieties, and it also produced many of the intermediate materials (*e.g.*, acids) that were used to make the final products.

20. The company centralized all purchasing and payroll records in the home office accounting department. The mills kept only those records needed to ascertain the quantities of inputs (material and labor) and the quantities of output for each of their processes. Dunham, "Object of Accounting," 7–19.

21. Examples of the reports are in the Minutes of the High Explosives Operating Department Superintendents' Meetings on file at the Eleutherian Mills Historical Library.

22. Chandler and Salsbury, *Pierre S. du Pont*, 146–147. Examples of worksheets used to prepare these reports are in Hall of Records, box 133859.

23. Hall of Records, box 133859.

24. A brief description of the company's depreciation policy is in order. Because the company invested regularly in cost-saving technical improvements, most plant and equipment were replaced long before wearing out. Consequently, the amount charged to depreciation each period was "obsolescence insurance, as it [covered] the replacement or rearrangement of plants or parts of plants, because out of date, or badly laid out according to more recent ideas, or illogically located on account of change in trade conditions, or, in fact, almost any reason other than that the plant is worn out or damaged by accident." (Dunham, "Object of Accounting," 17.) The company also charged an additional amount each period to anticipate the costs of plant and equipment destroyed by fire and explosion (referred to as "work accident insurance"). The monthly rates for depreciation were .5 percent for plant and 1.25 percent for furniture and fixtures; for work accident insurance, 2 cents per keg for powder and 1 cent per pound for dynamite on every unit of explosive manufactured. Current operating expense was therefore regularly charged for all repairs and maintenance to permanent plant and equipment, for the estimated amount of depreciation due to technical obsolescence, and for the estimated loss that would arise from fire and explosions.

25. Minutes of the High Explosives Operating Department Superintendents' Meetings on file at the Eleutherian Mills Historical Library.

26. Theorists will point out that the ideal solution to this problem is to use annuity (or present-value) depreciation in calculating return on investment. For more on the pitfalls of evaluating managers with return on invest-

ment statistics see Robert S. Kaplan, *Advanced Management Accounting* (Englewood Cliffs, N.J.: Prentice-Hall, 1982), 526–534.

27. For more on Du Pont's present-day practice of ignoring depreciation in internal evaluations of return on investment, see David Solomons, *Divisional Performance: Measurement and Control* (Homewood, Ill.: Richard D. Irwin, 1965), 134–135.

28. Dunham, "Object of Accounting," 10–11 and "Discussion," 1–2.

29. Chandler and Salsbury, *Pierre S. du Pont*, 153.

30. *Ibid.*, 140–141.

31. The company's sales accounting records are described in great detail in Dunham, "Object of Accounting," 4–7.

32. *Ibid.*, 5, 19.

33. Chandler and Salsbury, *Pierre S. du Pont*, 163, 141, 155–157. The method described in this paragraph, which the company used to determine minimum product prices, is not discussed by Chandler and Salsbury; it is inferred from worksheets and correspondence in Hall of Records, boxes 184736–184740, items 27 (B. Blasting Powder) and 39 (Dynamite).

34. Company records do not give reasons for the different returns desired on dynamite and black powder. One can surmise that dynamite required a higher return because it was then a relatively new product with riskier market potential.

35. Chandler and Salsbury, *Pierre S. du Pont*, 93, 156.

36. Letter from J. J. Raskob to P. S. du Pont (Wilmington, July 27, 1906), Hall of Records, boxes 184736–184740, item 29. The constraints imposed on sales managers' pricing activities are outlined in the letter from the director of sales cited in note 37.

37. Letter from director of sales dated April 2, 1906, reprinted in Johnson, *System and Profits*.

38. *Ibid.*

39. Dunham, "Object of Accounting," 2–4, 7–13.

40. J. H. Bridge, *Inside History of Carnegie Steel Company* (New York: The Aldine Book Company, 1903), 84; George W. Wood, *The Voucher System of Bookkeeping* (Pittsburgh: G. W. Wood, 1895).

41. Chandler and Salsbury, *Pierre S. du Pont*, 185–186.

42. Hall of Records, shelf area 182701–182712, item 139.

43. Chandler and Salsbury, *Pierre S. du Pont*, 220–228.

44. *Ibid.*, 187, 204, 228.

45. Hall of Records, shelf area 182701–182712, items 116, 137, 138, 139, 145.

46. Chandler and Salsbury, *Pierre S. du Pont*, 245.

47. From T. C. Davis, "How the Du Pont Organization Appraises its Performance," in AMA *Financial Management Series No. 94* (American Management Association: New York, 1950), 7. Reprinted in Johnson, *System and Profits*.

48. *Ibid.* See also F. Donaldson Brown, *Some Reminiscences of an Industrialist* (Easton, Pa.: Hive Publishing, 1977, reprint of 1958 ed.), 27.

49. Brown, *Some Reminiscences*, chapters 1–3 and introduction (by Ernest Dale). For additional interesting background on Brown, see Peter F. Drucker, *Adventures of a Bystander* (New York: Harper & Row, 1978), 263–266.

50. Brown may have read Alfred Marshall's discussion of the relationship between earnings, turnover, and return on capital. See Alfred Marshall, *Principles of Economics* (London: Macmillan, 8th ed., 1920; reprinted in 1969), 260, 511–513.

51. Ronald Coase, "The Nature of the Firm," *Economics*, Vol. IV (1937), 386–405. Reprinted in K. Boulding and G. Stigler, eds., *Readings in Price Theory* (Homewood, Ill.: Richard D. Irwin, 1952), 331–351. An extremely interesting commentary on Coase's article, including a note on its evolution, is in Stephen N. S. Cheung, "The Contractual Nature of the Firm," *Journal of Law and Economics* (April 1983), 1–21.

CHAPTER 5

Controlling the Multidivisional Organization: General Motors in the 1920s

BEFORE World War I, the Du Pont Powder Company was using almost every management accounting procedure for planning and control known today. To monitor and control the intermediate output produced by each single-activity department, Du Pont used accounting systems developed by manufacturing and distribution firms during the nineteenth century. In addition, Du Pont developed new budgeting and return on investment systems to plan and control the use of capital. With its comprehensive accounting systems, the Du Pont Powder Company could assess internalized operations that encompassed every activity in a single industry, from gathering raw materials to serving the final consumer.

The founders of Du Pont and other entrepreneurs created vertically integrated firms because they perceived opportunities for higher profits in a well-managed hierarchy than in unaided market exchange. To search for and manage opportunities for higher profit, vertically integrated firms relied heavily on internal accounting information. Prompt access to such information was no guarantee, however, that top managers would invariably realize sought-after profit.

Two obstacles particularly could jeopardize the success of the integrated firm. One was the complexity of vertically integrated firms; the other was managerial indifference to owners' goals. Growth in the size and variety of firms' activities could overwhelm even the most dedicated owner-managers, but as professional managers replaced owner-managers, a new problem, indifference to owners' goals, arose. As an employee, the manager does not necessarily share to the same degree the owner's interest in attaining profits. Consequently, the public generally believed in the early 1900s that managerial indifference and increased complexity would cause large firms to topple from internal inefficiency or else, by abusing their market power, to pass on to customers, workers, stockholders, and other outsiders the costs of bureaucratic inefficiency.[1]

The Multidivisional Enterprise Emerges

The record of the past eighty years certainly suggests that giant enterprises are capable of efficient and acceptable behavior.[2] Their growth in size and numbers during the volatile and unpredictable course of twentieth-century economic history indicates that they have coped well with the potential loss of management control resulting from complexity and the failure by professional nonowner managers to concentrate on profit-oriented goals. They have overcome these causes of bureaucratic paralysis largely by transforming the unitary, or centralized, organization into a new structure, the multidivisional organization. Referring to the multidivisional structure as "American capitalism's most important single innovation of the 20th century,"[3] Oliver Williamson credits it with preserving the vitality of giant enterprise by permitting "the corporation to limit the degree of control loss and subgoal pursuit that, without innovation, were predictable consequences of large size. Rather than be overcome by what otherwise would have been serious bureaucratic disabilities, the corporation has responded with a demonstrated capacity for self-renewal."[4] The multidivisional enterprise does not abandon "the [unitary] structure; rather, it attempts to harness the [unitary structure's] solution to the division of labor problem within a larger organizing framework. The technical benefits of the [unitary] organization are thereby preserved, while its undesirable control loss and goal pursuit properties are restrained."[5]

The first integrated firms to become multidivisional, such as Du Pont, were owner-managed. The multidivisional organization was created primarily to restrain the loss of control precipitated by inordinately *complex* activities in a unitary firm, not to overcome managers' indifference to owners' goals. Undue complexity of activities threatened the viability of several of the nation's largest and best-run integrated industrial firms (for instance, Du Pont, General Motors, Sears, and Standard Oil[6]) when they expanded into a diverse array of new product lines or new geographic territories after World War I.

At Du Pont, diversification occurred almost by accident. The company's search for ways to use by-products of smokeless gunpowder produced during World War I led to the discovery of several products (among them, plastics, synthetic fibers, and exterior paint additives) that bore no resemblance to the company's traditional line of explosives except for their origins in a common chemical technology. This array of new products multiplied enormously the complexities of managing the company and threatened to unravel the efficient integration of multiple activities the company had achieved before the war with a product line in one industry (explosives). Alfred Chandler gives us a vivid account of the complexities engendered by this product diversification at Du Pont:

> The essential difficulty was that diversification greatly increased the demands on the company's administrative offices. Now [ca. 1919] the different departmental headquarters had to coordinate, appraise, and plan policies and procedures for plants, or sales offices, or purchasing agents, or technical laboratories in a number of quite different industries. The development of plans and the appraisal of activities were made harder because executives with experience primarily in explosives were making decisions about paints, varnishes, dyes, chemicals, and plastic products. Coordination became more complicated because different products called for different types of standards, procedures, and policies. For although the technological and administrative needs of the new lines had many fundamental similarities, there were critical dissimilarities.
>
> The central office was even more overwhelmed than the departments by the increased administrative needs resulting from diversification. Broad goals and policies had to be determined for and resources allocated to functional activities, not in one industry but in several. Appraisal of departments performing in diverse fields became exceedingly complex. Interdepartmental coordination grew comparably more troublesome. The manufacturing personnel and the marketers tended to lose contact with each other and so failed to work out product improvements and modifications to meet changing demands and competitive developments. . . . Each of the three major departments—Purchasing, Manufacturing, and Sales—made its own estimates and set its own schedules.[7]

Companies like Du Pont used the decentralized multidivisional organization to alleviate the chaos and confusion that diversification brought to a centralized, multi-activity organization. Alternatively, they might have managed diversity by designing systems to trace accurately each product line's consumption of resources and profitability. As we showed in chapter 3, this alternative means of managing a diverse line of products was discussed by scientific management advocates in the early 1900s. The high cost of processing information seems, however, to have precluded implementation of strategic product costing systems early in the century. The multidivisional organization offered a less costly means to manage product diversity.

The multidivisional organization assigns to top management the task of planning the company's strategy, while assigning to subordinate managers the task of coordinating and controlling the operating activities for each of the company's different product lines or sales regions. By relieving top managers of responsibility for day-to-day operations, the multidivisional organization extends its span of control to encompass the affairs of several integrated multi-activity organizations. The manager who heads each of the internalized multi-activity organizations, known as divisions, concentrates fully on the operating activities of a single product line or a single geographic region. By separating policy managers from operations managers, the multidivisional firm overcame the main stumbling block to diversification posed by the unitary form of organization: the loss of control that top management faced when asked to administer simultaneously both long-run policy and an impossibly complex array of operating details for several diverse products.

To point these separate management groups toward common firm-wide goals, multidivisional firms relied on management accounting systems for data to evaluate divisional performance, company-wide performance, and future company policy. Understandably, these systems borrowed accounting procedures already used in integrated multi-activity firms; each division of a multidivisional firm resembles a freestanding integrated firm, managing its own business with a centralized organization in which purchasing, manufacturing, and sales managers report to a general divisional manager. However, multidivisional firms had a new use for return on investment information. Whereas unitary, multi-activity firms used return on investment information to centralize the allocation of capital among the firm's varied activities, multidivisional firms used the ROI measure to delegate to division managers the entire responsibility for using capital efficiently. This delegation of responsibility was possible because return on investment information about each division's internalized activities assured top managers that the division managers would give strict attention to top-level profit goals. These relatively unambiguous measures of divisional performance enabled top managers to reward successful division managers with both additional capital and promotions to top management posts. On the other hand, they could withhold capital from, and even dismiss, division managers who failed to perform.

By helping the different management groups, top policy managers and divisional operations managers, work toward common goals, return on investment information enabled early multidivisional firms to perform the same roles as the markets for capital and for managers perform today.[8] In theory at least, these markets can withhold capital from and discipline top managers of integrated firms who fail to perform adequately. In the early 1920s, however, labor and capital markets were relatively undeveloped and inefficient. Multidivisional organizations arose to supplant these markets by internalizing the multi-activity operations of several integrated firms to earn higher asset returns than the market could elicit from the same firms if they operated independently. This argument has been generalized by Williamson in his multidivisional hypothesis:

The organization and operation of the large enterprise along the lines of the [multidivision form] favors goal pursuit and least-cost behavior more nearly associated with the neoclassical profit maximization hypothesis than does the [unitary form] organizational alternative.[9]

Researchers in the past ten or fifteen years have marshalled an impressive array of empirical evidence that supports this hypothesis, although the results are undoubtedly driven by the relative efficiency of markets in the periods studied and should not, therefore, be generalized beyond those periods.[10]

The success of the multidivision organizational form depends on the management accounting system to perform three particular tasks better than the markets for capital or for managers:[11] provide strong incentives for managers to seek profit-oriented goals; increase the power of incentives through internal audits by linking performance to probable causes in a discriminating way; and develop monitoring and measuring procedures that help to allocate cash flows to high-yield uses in a sequential, adaptive manner. By providing an internal quasi-capital market to monitor and discipline top managers of vertically integrated organizations,[12] the management accounting system of the multidivisional firm undoubtedly did much to avert Adolph Berle and Gardiner Means's dire prophecies about professionally managed giant enterprise.[13] The system was able to stimulate in the multidivisional firm a market for professional general managers, a market that virtually did not exist before the 1920s.[14] It provided, in other words, a mechanism not only to evaluate general managers, but also to channel their self-interest toward the owners' interest in profits.

Executives of large American corporations did not quickly recognize and understand the unique properties of either the multidivisional firm or its management accounting systems. Substantial numbers of vertically integrated firms did not adopt the multidivisional structure before World War II. The academic and general business public did not become familiar with this remarkable innovation until the 1950s. It is all the more intriguing, then, to examine the ideas about management accounting that leaders of one of the first multidivisional industrial organizations, General

Motors Corporation, expressed in the 1920s. Their management accounting procedures reflected a profound understanding of the gains from having the multidivision firm
internalize the markets for capital and for managers.

General Motors

Founded in 1912 by the visionary William C. Durant, General Motors combined into one organization several
integrated units, each of which manufactured and sold a
unique line of autos or parts.[15] Each unit performed all the
operating functions, such as marketing, manufacturing, and
purchasing, that an independent manufacturing company
performs, and each unit's administrative system resembled
a unitary form of organization. Durant, in consolidating
these autonomous auto and parts manufacturing units into
one giant firm, hoped to achieve economies in areas such as
manufacturing, finance, and management. He originally en-
visioned, in other words, a consolidated enterprise whose
total profits would exceed the combined profits that would
have been earned by the individual units operating as separate companies.

Despite this noble goal, Durant's practice at GM nevertheless failed, primarily because he was unable to resolve
the problems entailed in administering a diversified company. He did not have an administrative system that could
direct the activities of each operating unit toward common
goals. His unwieldy management procedures immersed
Durant in the detailed activities of each operating unit. Thus
embroiled, Durant could not give his attention to general
policy making and could not achieve the savings that coordinated operations can produce. Durant's special style of
management even prevented many of GM's operating units
from performing as efficiently as they might have done as
independent companies.

Durant's inability to control GM's diverse operating

units precipitated an inventory crisis in 1920 that led to
Pierre du Pont succeeding Durant as company president.
The Du Pont Company had invested heavily during the war
in Durant's forward-looking enterprise. With their substantial investment threatened by Durant's unanticipated mis-
management, the Du Ponts were drawn inexorably into
managing the auto company's affairs after the Armistice.
Already known for their prowess as managers, the Du Pont
Company officials took over from Durant with the blessings
of GM's creditors and other stockholders.

Pierre du Pont's leadership, coupled with the brilliant
insights of Alfred P. Sloan, Jr., one of Durant's executives, led
to developing GM's well-known multidivisional structure in
which top management coordinates, appraises, and plans
GM's diversified activities without having to supervise its
day-to-day operations. This structure places full responsibility for operating performance on the general managers of
each division, freeing top management to concentrate on
policy making and to coordinate divisional performance
with company policies. Not surprisingly, a key component
of this Du Pont-designed organization was a sophisticated
set of management accounting procedures introduced by
Donaldson Brown, who applied to GM the Du Pont Company's advanced and sophisticated financial control techniques.

GM's management accounting system performed three
tasks to permit what Brown described as "centralized control with decentralized responsibility." First, it provided an
annual operating forecast to compare each division's *ex ante*
operating goals with top management's financial goals. Top
management used the operating forecast to coordinate each
division's expected performance with company-wide financial policy. Second, the system provided sales reports and
flexible budgets that indicated promptly if actual results
were deviating from planned results. They further specified
the adjustments to current operations that division managers should make to achieve their expected performance

goals. The sales reports and the advanced flexible budget system provided the control for each division's actual performance. Third, the management accounting system allowed top management to allocate both resources and managerial compensation among divisions on the basis of uniform performance criteria. This encouraged both a high degree of automatic compliance with company-wide financial goals and, also, divisional managers' autonomy. We shall describe in some detail, how this innovative management accounting system facilitated coordination, control, and compliance at GM in the twenties.[16]

GM's fundamental goal was to secure "the permanent welfare of the owners of the business."[17] Brown said that "a business owes its existence to its owners" and therefore is "expected to operate for their benefit." The basic financial policy that guided GM's top management after 1921 was to earn the highest long-run return on investment "consistent with a sound growth of the business."[18] The policy did not mean that the company should strive to earn, in Brown's words, "the highest attainable rate of return on capital, but rather the highest return consistent with attainable volume, care being exercised to assure profit with each increment of volume that will at least equal the economic cost of additional capital required."[19] In practice, top management stipulated that the corporation over the long run should earn average after-tax profits equal to 20 percent of investment while operating on average at 80 percent of rated capacity (the so-called "standard volume").

It was extremely difficult, however, to coordinate the company's actual operations in the short run with these long-run rate of return and standard volume goals. At GM, or any automaker for that matter, sales and profits in the 1920s fluctuated enormously over seasonal and cyclical trends that were difficult to predict. Contributing to these fluctuations were the volatile demand for automobiles, a durable capital good whose purchase or replacement consumers could postpone for long periods of time; the practice, industry-wide by the 1920s, by which automakers announced retail prices at the beginning of a model year and adhered to those prices during the year, even when market demand changed; and the typical automaker's high fixed costs. Rigid annual prices and high fixed costs meant that an automaker's profits and return on investment varied greatly, depending upon annual fluctuations in the ratio of output to average annual capacity. These largely unpredictable short-run variations made it difficult to coordinate short-run operating plans with long-term financial goals.[20]

Responding to this difficulty, Brown designed a unique annual "Price Study" that enabled GM's top management to coordinate each division's annual operating plan with the company's long-term return on investment and standard volume policies. Each division manager prepared a Price Study every December for the coming model year (August 1–July 31).[21] Albert Bradley, Brown's protégé at GM, provided a succinct description of the Price Study.

[The Price Study] embodies the Division's estimates of sales in units and in dollars, cost, profits, capital requirements, and return on investment, both at Standard Volume and at the forecast rate of operations for the new sales year, all on the basis of proposed price. The Price Study, in addition to serving as an annual forecast, also develops the standard price of each product; that is, the price which, with the plant operating at standard volume, would produce the adjudged normal average rate of return on capital which has been referred to as the economic return attainable. Proposed prices can therefore be directly compared with the standard prices which express the Corporation's fundamental policy, and a means is thereby provided for the measurement of departures from the policy. . . .[22]

A division's Price Study consisted of three basic elements: a forecast of operations calculated at the coming year's expected volume, a forecast of operations calculated at the standard volume, and a determination of each product's standard price. Top management used two of the elements, the forecast at expected volume and the standard price data, to coordinate each division's *ex ante* operating plan with the company's long-run financial policy. These two elements of the Price Study provided, in Bradley's words, "a means of gauging an operating program in terms of the fundamental policy of the Corporation regarding the rate of return on capital investment, as related to the pricing of the product, and the conditions under which additional capital will be provided for expansion." The third element of the Price Study, the forecast at standard volume, provided top management with "a tool for the control of current operations."[23]

A division manager's initial task in preparing the annual Price Study was to forecast the coming year's expected revenue, costs, and return on investment. First he estimated the two components of total revenue: proposed selling price and expected sales volume. Between the two components, price was presumably the least difficult to predict. The company's policy after 1921 was to restrict the products of each division to a distinct price range. Moreover, the coming year's price had to correspond to the current year's prices and to competitors' expected prices. Next, the manager estimated sales volume. Each division manager had sole responsibility for establishing the number of vehicles the division would sell and for seeing to it that his division's ultimate sales goal was met. Considerable help with making sales estimates was available, however, from top management's advisory staff. In fact, by 1925 the corporate central office assisted the divisions in making their sales forecasts by estimating GM's share of national automobile demand in each division's price range. The central office derived these estimates from data on expected consumer disposable income, sales trends of the past three years, and the expected impact of style, quality, and price on GM's share of each division's market.[24]

After arriving at an estimate of the coming year's total revenue, the division manager estimated operating costs, capital requirements, and return on investment. Division managers used data on past ratios of costs to output and investment to output, tempering these data, of course, with information concerning expected changes in both factory prices and productive efficiency. Presumably it was not difficult to estimate unit variable operating costs. An estimate of new fixed investment was probably more difficult to make. The only available indication, found in a published source, of how the company planned its capital expansion suggests that management geared new investment both to estimated future output and to the company's standard volume policy that annual output should average 80 percent of practical annual capacity over the long run. It may be, as several authorities believe, that the company's standard volume policy provided a means of estimating long-run capital requirements.[25] Certainly the forecast did predict the actual investment expected during the coming year. With that investment figure, and the net profit calculated from the revenue and cost estimates, the coming year's actual return on investment could be forecast.

A divisional manager's expected return on investment and his proposed selling prices for a coming year did not inevitably meet the basic long-run goal formulated by top management. For example, when the projected operating rate exceeded 80 percent of capacity, proposed selling prices could be high enough to ensure a divisional return on investment forecast that was at or above 20 percent for the coming year but too low to ensure an average return of 20 percent in subsequent years, when operating rates might fall below 80 percent. To avoid unintentional cases in which proposed prices and expected return on investment rates did not meet the corporation's long-run goals, top management compared the proposed selling prices in each division's forecast with the so-called "standard price." Standard prices, as Bradley said, expressed "the Corporation's fundamental policies [and they provide a means] for the measurement of departures from the policy."[26]

The standard price was the factory-delivered price that

a division had to charge at standard volume (80 percent of capacity) in order to earn the standard return on investment (20 percent). Standard price ratios, the markup rate over factory production costs, were apparently calculated from Price Study data. The ratio remained unaltered until a permanent change occurred either in capital turnover rates, factory operating efficiency, or the division's return on investment target.

Because the company applied fixed factory production costs at the standard volume rate to all units produced, unit factory production costs, by which the standard price ratio was multiplied, varied during the model year only if changes occurred in variable material or labor costs.[27] Consequently, the dollar equivalent of the standard price ratio (unit factory costs at standard volume multiplied by the standard price ratio) yielded just enough total revenue to cover all costs and return 20 percent on investment at standard volume.

If the factory-delivered price charged to dealers always equalled the standard price, then total profits would yield a return on investment in excess of 20 percent when the operating rate exceeded 80 percent and conversely a return below 20 percent when the operating rate was less than 80 percent. The company expected that the high profits earned at high operating rates and the low profits earned during low operating rates would average out to a long-run 20 percent on investment. Given its standard price data, top management felt reasonably certain that *if* the actual selling prices proposed for the coming model year were in line with the standard price, *then* the operating forecast in a division's annual Price Study would conform to the company's long-run policies regarding return on investment and standard volume.[28]

It should be emphasized that GM did not use standard price data to determine the actual prices to be charged during any given model year. Rather, the apparent purpose of the standard price policy was to determine the minimum markup needed to make the planned operations of a division comply with the corporation's long-run financial policy. Top management assumed that the proposed selling price for any particular year was determined in the competitive marketplace. The divisional manager's main responsibility was to adjust costs and capital turnover ratios in order to assure that his return on investment corresponded to long-run objectives. In other words, if the proposed selling price for any model fell below the standard price, and if the gap between the two prices could not be attributed to short-run competitive pressures, then top management requested a division manager to reduce proposed operating costs.[29] Were top management to accept selling prices that fell for a prolonged time below prices dictated by the standard price, it would be violating its acknowledged obligation to protect the owners' "permanent welfare." Top management would also request changes in a forecast in which the proposed selling price *exceeded* the standard price; such action was implicit in its commitment to long-run policies. Clearly, the standard price formula provided top management with a compact and powerful means of coordinating a division's forecast operating plan with company-wide financial policy.

After top management had reviewed and approved the annual forecast, the division manager proceeded to recast the annual figures into monthly estimates, using for this purpose indices of seasonal output trends prepared by top management's advisory staff. These monthly forecasts were submitted to top management for approval. Submission was expected no later than four months before the operating date; by the twenty-fifth day of each month in other words, the divisional manager had to provide, not only for the current month but also for the coming three months, a forecast including data on plant investment, working capital, inventory, purchase commitments, sales, production costs, and earnings. When top management gave its final approval, the four-month forecast established the division manager's authority to make commitments for production labor, purchases, and other acquisitions. Having reviewed the division's forecasts, top management was assured that, assuming actual operations went according to plan, the division's performance would conform to corporate financial policy. Thereafter, the divisional manager had complete freedom to implement the operating plans in the forecast, and he assumed responsibility for his division's final performance.

If their management accounting system had consisted only of the *ex ante* forecasts that coordinated the decentralized operations of various divisions with company-wide policy, Durant's successors at GM would not have achieved their astonishing success. Perhaps even more important than the operating forecast were management accounting procedures that permitted top management to evaluate the division's actual performance throughout the year. A division's actual operating conditions could deviate from the forecast for a given year in two important ways, either one requiring prompt adjustment if the planned return on investment was to be achieved. In one case, sales to consumers could differ from the forecast plan. In the other, the division's production could depart from the forecast. GM developed two management accounting procedures, sales reports and a flexible budget system, to deal with each of these eventualities.

Severe overproduction at several of the company's divisions in 1924 taught GM's top management that it takes more than accurate sales forecasts, annual or seasonal, to ensure smooth coordination of production and sales. This well-known crisis arose simply because the divisions did not compare their monthly production schedules with timely sales and inventory data from dealers. To prevent production from ever again running ahead of actual demand, the company, after 1924, required dealers to submit a detailed sales report to their respective division every ten days. These reports would ensure "a change in [divisional] production schedules the moment actual experience indicates a change in the trend of retail deliveries to the public."[30]

To assist a division manager in adjusting his production plans, the corporate central office advisory staff prepared seasonal sales indices and minimum/maximum working-capital-to-seasonal-sales ratios for each division. In addition, GM received monthly new car registration figures from the R. K. Polk Company, that provided up-to-date information on changes in GM's share of the national automobile market in each division's respective price class. The ten-day sales report system greatly reduced the annual gap between the number of cars sold by GM to its dealers and the number sold by dealers to the public. While the gap amounted to about 10 percent of sales from August 1923 to March 1924, it was kept to about 1 percent in 1925 and subsequent years.[31]

Nevertheless, further data were needed to evaluate the changes in costs, profits, and return on investment that occurred when the output level departed from the planned level. Indeed, if information in the sales reports caused a division manager to change his output level, the actual profits and return on investment for his division would differ from the planned amounts in the original forecast, given the typical automaker's high fixed costs and inflexible prices. Whenever changes occurred, it was important to know if the resulting variance between actual net income and forecast net income was due exclusively to unplanned changes in the level of output or due to unplanned changes in controllable costs, operating efficiency, and other factors unrelated to the level of output. In other words, did actual income differ from forecast income because the division's sales volume did not match the planned level or because the division's operating efficiency was not at planned levels? Modern management accountants use the "flexible budget" to compare forecast results with the results attained at actual levels of output.

The flexible budget distinguishes between variable and fixed costs and thereby forecasts total costs and profits at any level of actual output (within a given amount of fixed capacity).

Accounting and business historians suggest that flexible budgeting was barely discussed in accounting literature before the 1920s. Historian R. H. Parker takes the view that "it was not until the late 1930s that refined techniques for relating cost to size of output in the short-run were developed." Other writers have noted that flexible budgeting systems actually were being used by 1927 at the Gillette Safety Razor Company and by the late 1930s at the Westinghouse Electric Corporation. As early as 1924, however, Donaldson Brown, in a series of three articles on GM's pricing and budgeting procedures, described an ingenious technique for relating cost, net profit, and return on investment to short-run output variations. Nowhere in these articles does Brown refer to his technique as "flexible budgeting;" nevertheless, he does make it clear that his pricing and budgeting procedures were designed primarily so that the large annual and seasonal variations of sales and output that typified GM's operations would not vitiate management's efforts to control costs and profits. His revolutionary procedures gave GM a fully articulated flexible budget at least as early as 1923.[32]

GM's flexible budget was based on the forecast at standard volume contained within each division manager's annual Price Study. The forecast at standard volume, as we mentioned above, projected operations for the coming model year at the proposed selling price and the standard volume (80 percent of planned capacity). The forecast at standard volume established "standard" values for all the major factors such as fixed cost, variable cost, and capital turnover that affect return on investment. Specifically, the forecast showed each of the following items as percentages of total sales (at the proposed selling price and standard volume): variable costs, fixed costs plus net profit, variable working capital, and fixed investment. These ratios (and ratios of these same items to factory cost at standard volume) were frequently used to project the cost and investment figures in the actual operating plan that a division manager incorporated into his annual forecast.[33] Their main purpose, however, was to provide norms so that deviations could be assessed between the division's forecast and its actual operating performance. Using the standard volume ratios in a simple formula, one could calculate what the annual net return on investment *should* be at *any* volume of output (at the coming year's proposed selling price and with total plant capacity given) in order to satisfy top management's basic financial objective. The same standard volume ratios also made it possible, assuming appropriate seasonal adjustments for production and fixed cost factors, to predict each month what the return on investment should be at any relevant volume.[34]

The ratios in the standard volume forecast enabled top management and the division manager to compare easily and rapidly the *ex post* return on investment at any operating level with the desired return dictated by long-run corporate policy. Unless identified and compensated for, a variation between the two rates of return could prevent a division from achieving its long-run financial objective. In the 1920s, GM managers attributed any discrepancy between the actual and desired rate of return to either unanticipated deviations from the projected selling price, unplanned changes in factory price, or unexpected alterations in operating efficiency. Because each division manufactured a relatively homogeneous line of products in the 1920s, a discrepancy between actual and desired rates of return was not likely to be caused by deviations in planned mix of products. As the divisions' product lines became complex and diverse, certainly the case by the 1970s, the standard volume forecast probably became less useful as a management tool. Records indicate, however, that GM managers in the 1920s regarded the standard volume forecast as a useful tool. They monitored deviations between planned and actual return on investment by comparing the actual price, cost, and capital ratios, adjusted for seasonality, to the standard volume ratios. Each division prepared not only monthly, but even daily, reports designed specifically to compare actual results in every aspect of operations with the standard volume results that had been predicated upon GM's top-level goals for return on investment.[35]

That management as a result of its management accounting system effectively handled fluctuations in demand is suggested by the company's extraordinary return on investment and its remarkable expansion after its reorganization in 1921. Capital turnover data reveal, furthermore, that sales reports and flexible budget forecasting also contributed to efficiency. For example, top management's improved forecasting and a leveling of production schedules permitted the company to raise its average annual inventory turnover from a low of 1.5 in 1921 to a high of 6.3 in 1925. We can safely assume that similar improvements occurred in the turnover of cash, receivables, and fixed plant investment. Speaking in 1926 about the consequences of improved turnover, Albert Bradley said, "the corporation, with no increase in capital, has been able to conduct a larger volume of business at a smaller net profit per unit, and to make a very satisfactory return on its capital; and to pass along to the public the savings resulting from increased volume and increases in efficiency."[36]

Aligning Managers' and Owners' Interests

We have seen that particular features of GM's management accounting system helped top management delegate operating decisions to the divisions by clearly establishing financial objectives for division managers. Other features in the system helped motivate division managers to comply with the company-wide financial goals. The mechanisms for compliance not only increased the probability that top management's financial goals would in fact be achieved; they also increased the likelihood that top management's goals would be synonymous with those of the company's owners. Top management is more likely to advocate entrepreneurial goals when assurances of subordinates' compliance remove all pressures to compromise top-level objectives for the sake of smoothly coordinated operations.[37]

We already have mentioned Oliver Williamson's hypothesis that the multidivisional firm has powers to exact stricter compliance with owners' goals from heads of divisions than the capital market can exact from top managers of independent vertically integrated firms. The hypothesis implies that the multidivisional organization does a superior job of solving the problem of getting delegated managers to identify their own self-interest with the firm's top-level goals. It does this in large part because top managers can scan complete and timely information about subordinates' performance. Providing this information is the major contribution of management accounting to the multidivisional firm's superior performance.

But even though top managers in a multidivisional firm receive prompt and accurate information from throughout the firm, certain precautions are needed to ensure that the information does not engender dysfunctional or suboptimal activities. One precaution particularly important in a decentralized organization such as GM is to price interdivisional transfers so that the actions which an autonomous division manager takes to enhance his own subunit's profit do not simultaneously impair company-wide profits. Published evidence suggests that GM's new management team adopted a market-based transfer pricing policy in the early 1920s. Sloan had practiced market-based transfer pricing in his United Motors Company before it was brought into GM by

Durant in 1918.[38] Although Sloan was apparently unsuccess-
ful at selling Durant on the idea of market-based transfer
pricing, his idea was accepted by Pierre du Pont after the
1921 reorganization. Brown described the new GM transfer
pricing policy in a speech delivered to a conference of executives in 1927.

The question of pricing product from one division to another
is of great importance. Unless a true competitive situation is preserved, as to prices, there is no basis upon which the performance
of the divisions can be measured. No division is required absolutely to purchase product from another division. In their interrelation they are encouraged to deal just as they would with outsiders. The independent purchaser buying products from any of
our divisions is assured that prices to it are exactly in line with
prices charged our own car divisions. Where there are no substantial sales outside, such as would establish a competitive basis, the
buying division determines the competitive picture—at times partial requirements are actually purchased from outside sources so
as to perfect the competitive situation.[39]

Other precautions besides attention to transfer pricing
are needed to avert circumstances that impair the usefulness
of return on investment as an indicator either of a division's
contribution to company-wide profits or of the performance
of a division manager. We noted in the previous chapter, for
instance, that return on investment statistics net of depreciation can encourage division managers to underinvest. Although the Du Pont organization itself seems to have met
this problem after 1920 by evaluating division managers
using gross return on investment figures, this was not done
at GM. Instead, the architects of GM's early management
accounting system built alternative safeguards within the
system to assure that return on investment would serve as a
valid criterion of performance.

The annual forecast included plans for expansion that
division managers worked out in collaboration with top
management. The role of the corporate staff in assisting with

sales and capital turnover estimates minimized divisional bias in the plans. The expansion plans, presumably stated in terms of expected unit sales, surely placed a lower bound on each division manager's planned investment. The annual forecast therefore compelled a division manager to achieve return on investment targets without stinting on expansion plans.

Another common difficulty with return on investment data is that comparisons of divisional return on investment results do not always properly indicate the comparative performance of the division managers themselves. A capable manager who takes over a division that already has chronic and deep-rooted troubles might be evaluated unjustly were his return on investment to be compared with that of other divisions rather than his own division's past or potential performance.[40] Because top management in a multidivisional firm allocates resources among the firm's operating units, and because a division manager's search for additional resources encourages him to comply with top-level goals, resources must not be allocated strictly according to differential return on investment results. Indeed, in order to maintain company morale, GM's top management as far back as the 1920s occasionally assessed divisional managers with differing targets for return on investment, the target depending upon the division in question.[41]

GM's return on investment criterion for judging divisional financial performance apparently provided proper motivation, then, for division managers to pursue top management's goals. Further motivation was supplied by the timely and accurate reporting of divisional financial performance to GM's top management. The return on investment data sent to top management related each division's performance directly to top-level goals. The data were prepared in all divisions according to company-wide accounting standards; they were audited by top management staff personnel; they were compiled for top management by cor-

porate staff personnel whose company-wide perspective
freed them from divisional biases; and they were timely.[42]
The data revealed promptly and unambiguously any failure
of a division manager to meet the company's basic financial
objectives. In so doing, they enabled top management to
swiftly remove a division manager who failed to perform as
expected. Obviously, such a reporting system put enormous
pressure on the division manager to remove slack and inefficiency at all levels within his division. The intensity of
pressure on a division manager to comply with top-level
profit goals is an important reason why a departmentalized
division within a multidivisional firm may, according to Williamson's hypothesis, be more profitable than an independent departmentalized firm of similar size.

A final means GM used to align division managers' goals
with corporate goals was a bonus-incentive plan for salaried
executives. Based on divisional performance, bonuses were
awarded in the form of rights to GM common stock. A manager's stock bonus for any given year became vested only if
he stayed with GM for a certain period, usually five years.
Therefore, the value of the bonus to an executive depended
ultimately on the long-run performance of the corporation
as a whole. That GM's top management intended the bonus
plan to check division managers' tendencies to pursue local
goals at the expense of corporate goals is apparent in the
following remarks made by Sloan:

> The Bonus Plan established the concept of corporate profit in
> place of divisional profits. . . .
> Before we had the Bonus Plan in operation throughout the
> corporation, one of the obstacles to integrating the various decen-
> tralized divisions was the fact that key executives had little incen-
> tive to think in terms of welfare of the whole corporation. . . .
> Under the incentive system in operation before 1918, a small num-
> ber of division managers had contracts providing them with a
> stated share of profits of their own divisions, irrespective of how
> much the corporation as a whole earned. Inevitably, this system

exaggerated the self-interest of each division at the expense of the interest of the corporation itself. It was even possible for a division manager to act contrary to the interest of the corporation in his effort to maximize his own division's profits.[43]

Given the remarkable growth in value of GM's common stock during the 1920s, it is reasonable to conclude that GM's bonus plan both intensified a division manager's desire to stay with the company and made him eager to comply with company-wide performance goals.[44]

Summary

The multidivisional structure and management accounting procedures that GM's top management devised in the early 1920s enable giant industrial firms to overcome the inefficiency and bureaucratic disabilities that economists once thought were endemic to large-scale organizations. In large, diversified enterprises, the multidivisional organization sharply reduces the volume of communication between divisional and corporate managers, thus enabling managers to employ resources more efficiently and more effectively than if they used centralized organizations. And internal accounting procedures, such as those used at GM in the 1920s, enabled top management to transmit to operating managers in sharp, unambiguous terms the goals for company-wide profits and growth. While the procedures impelled all operating managers to pursue the same corporate goals, they also permitted them enormous freedom to exercise initiative in deciding how to employ resources most efficiently. The internal accounting procedures were undoubtedly essential to GM's remarkable performance record after 1921, as they also were to the performance of countless large firms in the world that adopted the multidivisional structure after the 1920s.

The multidivisional structure was not the only means of managing product diversity in the 1920s, nor is it always the best way. In chapter 3 we mentioned the approach to managing product diversity that scientific management engineers such as Alexander Church had advocated in the early 1900s. Their procedures for strategic product costing offer a potential means of managing diversity without having to decentralize responsibility for operating decisions. As we indicate in the next chapter, the preference that managers in the 1920s showed for divisional structures rather than strategic product costing undoubtedly reflected the high cost of processing information at that time. Recently, sharp reductions in information processing costs have generated new interest in strategic product costing.[45] Conceivably these advances in information technology have reduced the multidivisional structure's appeal as a means of managing product diversity. Moreover, recent changes in costs of using markets may also have diminished the advantages of diversifying product lines in a single organization. It is too early to tell, but "downsizing" and "unbundling" of large multidivisional conglomerates in the late 1970s and the 1980s may signify that the costs of using markets for capital and managers—so high in the 1920s—are no longer high enough to warrant widespread use of the divisional form of organization in the 1980s.

Notes

1. These views were expressed in Adolph Berle and Gardiner Means, *The Modern Corporation and Private Property* (New York: Macmillan, 1932), and in John K. Galbraith, *The New Industrial State* (Boston: Houghton Mifflin, 1967).

2. Alfred D. Chandler, Jr., *Strategy and Structure: Chapters in the History of the American Industrial Enterprise* (Garden City, N.Y.: Doubleday, 1966; reprint of 1962 ed.), 44; Oliver E. Williamson, *Corporate Control and Business Behavior: An Inquiry into the Effects of Organization Form on Enterprise Behavior* (Englewood Cliffs, N.J.: Prentice-Hall, 1970), 4.

3. Williamson, *Corporate Control*, 175.

4. *Ibid.*, vii.

5. *Ibid.*, 134.

6. This episode in American business history is brilliantly analyzed in Chandler, *Strategy and Structure*.

7. *Ibid.*, 110–111.

8. For more on the market for managers, see E. F. Fama and M. C. Jensen, "Separation of Ownership and Control," *Journal of Law and Economics* (June 1983), 327–349.

9. Williamson, *Corporate Control*, 134.

10. See, for instance, H. O. Armour and D. J. Teece, "Organizational Structure and Economic Performance: A Test of the Multidivisional Hypothesis," *Bell Journal of Economics* (Spring 1978), 106–122; R. M. Burton and B. Obel, "A Computer Simulation Test for the M-form Hypothesis," *Administrative Science Quarterly* (1980), 457–466; J. Cable and M. J. Dirrheimer, "Hierarchies and Markets: An Empirical Test of the Multidivisional Hypothesis in West Germany," *International Journal of Industrial Organisation* (1983), 43–62; P. Steer and J. Cable, "Internal Organisation and Profit: An Empirical Analysis of Large UK Companies," *Journal of Industrial Economics* (September 1978), 13–30; D. J. Teece, "Internal Organization and Economic Performance: An Empirical Analysis of the Profitability of Principal Firms," *Journal of Industrial Economics* (December 1981), 173–199. The multidivisional firm's superior performance properties may exist only when markets for capital and managers are relatively inefficient, as in the United States between World War I and the 1960s. Developments in the 1980s (*e.g.*, spin-offs, leveraged buy-outs, takeovers leading to radical "downsizing," and efforts by incumbent managers to "unbundle" complex multidivisional firms) suggest that today's markets for capital and managers evaluate opportunities for gain more efficiently than internal hierarchy does, at least in some industries.

11. Oliver E. Williamson, *Markets and Hierarchies: Analysis and Antitrust Implications* (New York: Free Press, 1975), 145–148.

12. As we mentioned in note 10, enormous improvements in the ability of the capital market to perform these functions since the mid-1970s may considerably reduce the incentive to internalize unitary divisions within multidivisional organizations. When improvements in markets lower the cost of discovering opportunities for gain, it is reasonable to assume *ceteris paribus* that economic exchange will move at the margin from firms to markets.

13. Oliver E. Williamson, "The Modern Corporation: Origins, Evolution, Attributes," *Journal of Economic Literature* (December 1981), 1559–1560.

14. See Fama and Jensen, "Separation of Ownership and Control."

15. The following discussion of Durant's years at GM and Pierre S. du Pont's arrival at GM are drawn from Alfred D. Chandler, Jr., and Stephen Salsbury, *Pierre S. du Pont and the Making of the Modern Corporation* (New York: Harper & Row, 1971), chapters 16–18; Ernest Dale, "Contributions to Administration by Alfred P. Sloan, Jr., and GM," *Administrative Science Quarterly* 1(1956–1957), 30–62; Alfred P. Sloan, Jr., *My Years with General Motors*

(Garden City, N.Y.: Doubleday, 1963), chapter 2; Bernard A. Weisberger, *The Dream Maker: William C. Durant, Founder of General Motors* (Boston: Little, Brown, 1979), chapter 8.

16. The sources of information used to prepare the following discussion of GM's post-1921 accounting practices are Albert Bradley, "Setting Up a Forecasting Program," *Annual Convention Series No. 41,* (American Management Association: New York, 1926), 3–20; Donaldson Brown, "Pricing Policy in Relation to Financial Control," *Management and Administration* 7 (February 1924), 195–198 and (March 1924), 283–286; Brown, "Pricing Policy Applied to Financial Control," *Management and Administration,* 7 (April 1924), 417–422, Brown, "Centralized Control with Decentralized Responsibilities," *Annual Convention Series No. 57,* (American Management Association: New York, 1927), 3–24; and Brown, "Some Reminiscences of an Industrialist" (unpublished ms., Eleutherian Mills Historical Library, Wilmington, Delaware, 1957; reprinted with introduction by Ernest Dale in 1977 by Hive Publishing Co. of Easton, Pa.); Chandler, *Strategy and Structure,* chapter 3; Chandler and Salsbury, *Pierre S. du Pont,* chapters 17–21; Thomas B. Fordham and Edward S. Tingley, "Control through Organization and Budgets," *Management and Administration* 6 (December 1923), 719–724, 7 (January 1924), 57–62, (February 1924), 205–208, and (March 1924), 291–294; R. C. Mark, "Internal Financial Reporting of General Motors," *Federal Accountant* (November 12, 1952), 31–41; C. S. Mott, "Organizing a Great Industrial," *Management and Administration* 7 (May 1924), 523–527; Sloan, *My Years,* chapter 8; Alfred H. Swayne, "Mobilization of Cash Reserves," *Management and Administration* 7 (January 1924), 21–23; U.S. Senate, Committee on the Judiciary, Subcommittee on Antitrust and Monopoly, *Administered Prices, Report and Hearings,* vols. 6 and 7 (Washington, D.C., 1958); and Karl Wennerlund, "Quantity Control of Inventories," *Management and Administration* 7 (June 1924), 677–682.

17. Brown, "Pricing Policy in Relation to Financial Control," 195–196 and "Some Reminiscences," 59–65.

18. Brown, "Centralized Control with Decentralized Responsibilities," 5; Sloan, *My Years,* 141. Other statements confirming that the sole concern of GM management was profit can be found in Fordham and Tingley, "Control through Organization and Budgets," 719, and Mark, "Internal Financial Reporting," 33.

19. Brown, "Pricing Policy in Relation to Financial Control," 197. Several writers have noted the sophisticated example of "marginalist" economic reasoning in this remark of Brown's.

20. An excellent discussion of the auto industry's interwar pricing policies is in Homer B. Vanderblue, "Pricing Policies in the Automobile Industry," *Harvard Business Review,* 17 (Summer 1939), 385–401.

21. Sloan, *My Years,* 129.

22. Bradley, "Setting Up a Forecasting Program," 7.

23. *Ibid.,* 3.

24. The detailed steps involved in preparing a divisional budget are described in Fordham and Tingley, "Control through Organization and Budgets."

Limiting the sales of each division to a specific price range followed from GM's overall product policy, enunciated in late 1921, to minimize duplication and competition among divisions. See Sloan, *My Years*, 65. Although the company's basic product policy indicated a need for some top-level coordination of divisional sales plans, no such coordination existed before 1924. However, top management took a more serious interest in divisional sales forecasts after the excessive optimism of certain general managers caused a serious overproduction crisis in that year. For information on this famous episode in GM's history, see Sloan, *My Years*, 129–134, and Chandler and Salsbury, *Pierre S. du Pont*, 549–554.

25. Bradley, "Setting Up a Forecasting Program," 7–8; Vanderblue, "Pricing Policies," 397, n.14.

26. Bradley, "Setting Up a Forecasting Program," 7.

27. It should be noted that GM did not have an inventory costing system for financial reporting, notwithstanding the mention here of the company "applying fixed costs to units produced." The full-absorption unit cost calculations mentioned here were used to evaluate prices and to control operations, never to calculate the bookkeeping transfers that one often associates with manufactured product inventory valuation. GM did not need inventory cost accounting systems for the simple reason that they had neither work-in-process nor finished goods inventories. Work-in-process inventories were absent because the assembly lines were empty at the end of a normal 16-hour workday; finished goods were absent because vehicles were "sold" to the GM Acceptance Corporation the moment they rolled off the assembly line.

28. Alfred Sloan remarked once that "an alternative approach to our standard-volume policy would have been to evaluate prices strictly in terms of actual unit costs at actual or anticipated production levels." However, "the use of the actual unit-cost type of evaluation would have been socially and economically unsound," he argued, because of the industry's cyclical demand and the company's high fixed costs. Naturally, "unit costs would drop in times of high volume and increase during periods of low production. Any attempt to raise prices during periods of low volume, even if competition permitted, to recover the higher unit costs could have deflated sales still further, with the result of still lower profits, less employment, and a generally depressive effect on the economy." See Sloan, *My Years*, 147.

29. Brown, "Pricing Policy Applied to Financial Control," 417–422; Sloan, *My Years*, 146–148; Dan Cordtz, "Car Pricing, . . . ," *The Wall Street Journal* (December 10, 1957); Vanderblue, "Pricing Policies," 396–401; and Mark, "Internal Financial Reporting," 34. Homer Vanderblue once suggested that cost does not determine auto price; instead, it determines auto quality. Thus, if division managers regarded the coming year's price as more or less given, they probably coordinated proposed price with standard price by postponing, whenever possible, costly quality (or style) improvements. Vanderblue, "Pricing Policies," 395.

30. Bradley, "Setting Up a Forecasting Program," 13; Sloan, *My Years*, 138.

31. Sloan, *My Years*, 138; Ernest Dale, *The Great Organizers* (New York: McGraw-Hill, 1960), 100.

32. Robert H. Parker, *Management Accounting: An Historical Perspective* (London: Macmillan, 1969), 67–70; David Solomons, "The Historical Development of Costing," in David Solomons, ed., *Studies in Costing* (London: Sweet & Maxwell, Ltd., 1952), 36; on Gillette, see R. H. Raymond, "History of the Flexible Budget," *Management Accounting* (August 1966), 12; on Westinghouse, see Dale, *The Great Organizers*, 151, 165–166, and Brown, "Pricing Policy." "In these annual budgets, fixed and non-variable expenses are treated separately from variable so that the figures can be readily adjusted for changes in volume at any time during the year." (Sloan, *My Years*, 143.) See also Mark, "Internal Financial Reporting," 34.

33. Fordham and Tingley, "Control through Organization and Budgets," 722.

34. For a detailed discussion of this formula and an example of how it was applied to an actual situation, see H. Thomas Johnson, "Management Accounting in an Early Multidivisional Organization: General Motors in the 1920s," *Business History Review* (Winter 1978), 505–510.

35. Examples of these reports are in Mark, "Internal Financial Reporting," 36. Albert Bradley once noted that "on the basis of our forecast we work up a balance sheet and income statement [and] during each month as it develops we make up a daily balance sheet and income account, so that we can tell you this afternoon where we stood at the close of business yesterday." (Bradley, "Setting Up a Forecasting Program," 19).

36. Bradley, "Setting Up a Forecasting Program," 15–18.

37. On this point see Oliver E. Williamson, "Managerial Discretion, Organization Form, and the Multi-division Hypothesis," in Robin Marris and Adrian Wood, eds., *The Corporate Economy: Growth, Competition, and Innovative Potential* (Cambridge, Mass.: Harvard University Press, 1971), 358–359.

38. Sloan, *My Years*, 48.

39. Brown, "Centralized Control with Decentralized Responsibilities," 8.

40. The problem of distinguishing between the division's performance and the division manager's performance is succinctly analyzed in Charles T. Horngren, *Cost Accounting: A Managerial Emphasis* (Englewood Cliffs, N.J.: Prentice-Hall, 1977), 713.

41. Different return on investment targets existed for different products at least since 1910 at the Du Pont Corporation, whose methods provided so many of the basic ideas for GM's post-1921 accounting system. See H. Thomas Johnson, "Management Accounting in an Early Integrated Industrial: E. I. du Pont de Nemours Powder Company, 1903–1912," *Business History Review* (Summer 1975), 198–199.

42. It is notable that division controllers at GM were the only company officials who had dual responsibility; they reported both to the division manager and to the corporate controller. Williamson, *Corporate Control*, chapter 8.

43. Sloan, *My Years*, 409.

44. *32nd Annual Report of the General Motors Corporation, Year Ended*

December 31, 1941, 38–40, 81. Sloan, *My Years*, 407–420. The Bonus Plan provided "the means to attract and to hold in the employ of the Corporation men of proven and potential ability." (Brown, "Centralized Control with Decentralized Responsibilities," 13.)

45. For examples of this new interest see Robin Cooper and Robert S. Kaplan, "How Cost Accounting Systematically Distorts Product Costs," in William J. Bruns and Robert S. Kaplan, eds., *Accounting and Management: Field Study Perspectives* (Boston: Harvard Business School Press, 1987).

CHAPTER 6

From Cost Management to Cost Accounting: Relevance Lost

B Y 1925, American industrial firms had developed virtually every management accounting procedure known today. The procedures were developed in just over one hundred years by managers seeking information about opportunities for gain in hierarchies. From the first hierarchies ever used to manage economic affairs—in America, the integrated textile mills of the early 1800s—to the complex multidivisional hierarchies of the 1920s, managers developed accounting measurement and control procedures to meet a demand for information about the efficiency and profitability of internally administered economic activity.

After 1925 a subtle change occurred in the information used by managers to direct the affairs of complex hierarchies. Until the 1920s, managers invariably relied on information about the underlying processes, transactions, and events that produce financial numbers. By the 1960s and

1970s, however, managers commonly relied on the financial numbers alone. Guided increasingly by data compiled for external financial reports,[1] corporate management—the "visible hand"—has "managed by the numbers" since the 1950s. We wait for future historians to explain fully the complex forces that caused this transition. We can offer a partial explanation by tracing the developments that prompted manufacturing managers to use inappropriately the inventory cost information, prepared for financial statements, for strategic management purposes.

As we discussed in chapter 3, engineer-managers in metal-working firms between 1880 and 1910 had developed procedures for computing managerially relevant product costs. But those procedures disappeared from manufacturing accounting practice and writing after 1914.[2] In their place appeared the costing procedures that twentieth-century accountants developed to value inventories for financial reports. While those procedures yield cost information that apparently aids financial reporting, the same information is generally misleading and irrelevant for strategic product decisions. To explain the events leading to this misuse of financial report information by present-day managers, we briefly review the development of strategic cost information in manufacturing firms during the century that ends in the early 1920s.

Diversity, Economies of Scope, and the Cost of Information

Conversion cost information used before the 1880s was relevant to all managerial decisions affecting efficiency and overall profits of single-activity manufacturing firms. The early manufacturing firms attempted to achieve success through economies of scale—reductions in unit cost from increased output of one product in one facility. To monitor scale economies, managers in manufacturing firms gathered information about conversion costs (efficiencies) in each of the firm's separable processes. Information about the costs of different products was superfluous because the firms had relatively homogeneous lines of products that consumed resources in each of the firm's processes at uniform rates. If the firm's processes were run efficiently, the managers had done virtually all they could do to ensure profitable operations overall.

After 1880, managers of vertically integrated firms and metal-working firms needed more than information about the efficiency of their internal processes. Both types of firms needed additional information to manage unprecedented diversity in processes and in products. Integrated firms made diversity manageable with accounting devices (transfer prices and budgeting are examples) to measure performance in each varied activity with a common yardstick such as net income or return on assets. Managers in the early vertically integrated firms did not seem interested in product costs, probably because they tended to focus on relatively homogeneous lines of products and always in a single industry. In contrast, metal-working firms manufactured diverse lines of products that consumed resources at widely varying rates. Managers in these firms attempted to achieve success through economies of scope—the gains from jointly producing two or more products in one facility. The managers needed information on how decisions about product mix could affect overall profits. To estimate the impact of individual products on a firm's overall profitability, engineer-managers in late nineteenth-century metal-working firms sought to develop accurate product cost information.

By 1910, manufacturing cost systems provided information relevant to a wide range of decisions about economies of scale (efficiency) and opportunities for scope (product differentiation). Of these systems, those designed to trace costs accurately to diverse lines of products disappeared

after 1910, certainly by World War I. Perhaps the main reason for the disappearance was their high cost-to-benefit ratio.[3] Existing information-processing technology made it
costly to trace accurately the resources used to make each
diverse product in a complex manufacturing plant. The
higher profits that one might earn by marketing only the
most profitable products and rejecting losers may not have
been worth the cost of information needed to make such
selections. For instance, the high cost of processing information apparently doomed actual applications of Alexander
Hamilton Church's product costing system. Charles Renold,
referring to an application of Church's system in his father's
company around 1900, said that the system "became quite
unmanageable in its ramifications, elaborations and adjustments. It could never be kept up to date [and] gave no convenient guide to action."[4] We know very little about the specific system that Renold referred to, but systems that Church
described in his writings suggest that the outcome in the
Renold Company might have been different had computers
and electronic measuring instruments been available.

The high cost of collecting and processing accurate information about product costs did not prevent firms from
marketing diverse product lines, at least not in the first half
of this century. This certainly was true of small- and medium-sized firms that manufactured machine-made metal
products such as hardware and machine tools. These firms
were leaders in developing product costing systems in the
1880s and 1890s, but they soon concluded that it was not
worthwhile to gather accurate information about individual
product costs. Articles about actual cost systems in ma-
chine-tool firms after World War I suggest that they used
aggregated overhead pools and direct-labor application of
overhead,[5] scarcely the information one needs to trace firm-
wide profits to the profitability of a diverse line of individual
products. Not finding it cost effective to collect the requisite
information to evaluate the relative profitability of special-

ized market niches, small- and medium-sized firms with diverse product lines still earned tolerable overall profits by becoming full-line producers. The strategy apparently worked for many manufacturers from the 1920s to the 1960s, a period when America's domestic market was relatively isolated from world competition.

Giant integrated organizations that adopted a strategy of product diversification around the time of World War I did not find it any easier than small- or medium-sized firms to compile accurate product cost information. They coped with the problem of product diversity by creating divisions. The multidivisional firm, as discussed in chapter 5, created islands of product specialization within self-contained divisions. The divisions could secure affordable information about efficiency and profitability by using management accounting systems that already were familiar to managers of vertically integrated firms. Information about costs of individual product lines was apparently too expensive for these firms to manage diverse product lines by monitoring precisely each product's consumption of resources.

Cost Accounting Supplants Cost Management after 1900

The virtual disappearance of managerial product costing in manufacturing firms did not mean that accountants abandoned all product costing after 1914. Indeed, a subject known as cost accounting flourished after World War I. But cost accounting did not attempt to trace each product's consumption of resources for cost management purposes; instead, it valued inventory for financial reporting purposes. And the demand for financial reporting after 1900 burgeoned because of new pressures placed on corporate enterprises by capital markets, regulatory bodies, and federal taxation of income. But of all the new demands for corporate financial disclosure after 1900, the demand for financial reports audited by independent public accountants probably had the most profound and lasting influence on managerial cost accounting.

The enormous growth of audited financial reporting and the concomitant rise of the professional public accountant was a powerful new force on the accounting scene after 1900.[6] A few American industrial firms in the nineteenth century had issued periodic financial reports to their stockholders and creditors; virtually none had the reports audited by independent public accountants.[7] After 1900, however, many firms needed to raise funds from increasingly widespread and detached suppliers of capital. To tap these vast reservoirs of outside capital, firms' managers had to supply audited financial reports. And because outside suppliers of capital relied on audited financial statements, independent accountants had a keen interest in establishing well-defined procedures for corporate financial reporting.

The inventory costing procedures adopted by public accountants after the turn of the century had a profound effect on management accounting. Every accounting student of the past sixty years has learned about inventory costing—a bookkeeping procedure that manufacturing accountants follow to separate the production expense of an accounting period from the cost of manufactured product inventories at the end of the period. The separation is achieved by "attaching" total manufacturing costs to the equivalent units of product finished in a period. This "accounted" cost is used to value both units of unsold product at the end of a period (finished and in-process inventories) and units of product sold during the period. Inventory costing therefore provides inventory values to report on the balance sheet and manufacturing expenses to match against revenues on the income statement.

Prior to this development, American manufacturing firms did not use cost accounts to value inventories for financial reporting purposes. As we noted in previous chapters, manufacturing firms developed cost accounts for two purposes: (1) to evaluate internal opportunities for gain from their resources and, (2) to control the internal processes and activities that generated those higher returns. A few early manufacturing firms issued financial reports—some as early as the 1830s[8]—but none required cost accounts to separate period expenses from inventory values. Expenditures were associated either with fixed-value assets (as in railroad replacement accounting) or with periods (current or future [deferred]). And end-of-period inventories of manufactured products were not valued by "flowing" expenditures from asset and period accounts into inventory accounts.[9] Instead, balance sheet inventories were valued at amounts that approximated current replacement costs.[10]

After 1900, public accountants' rules for financial reporting gradually ended the practice of valuing manufactured inventories with dollar amounts that originated outside the books of account. The public accountants demanded that information in audited financial reports come from double-entry books that "integrated" all cost and financial accounts.[11] The term *integration* meant that all amounts reported in financial statements, whether they were period expenses or end-of-period assets, had to be traceable to the original (*i.e.*, historical) costs of recorded transactions. The public accountants' (*i.e.*, auditors') demand for "integration" (later referred to as "articulation") led them to advocate what we know today as inventory costing.[12]

Auditors were less interested in the relevance of product cost information for management decisions than for its impact on reported profits. They insisted that inventories be valued at amounts that were objective, auditable, and "conservative."[13] Public accountants in Britain and the United States were particularly concerned that a client corporation not declare dividends out of capital.[14] Such an action could make a corporation vulnerable to creditors' lawsuits and could also jeopardize the auditors' reputation. By calculating production expenses and inventory costs from original transaction data, inventory costing supposedly precluded "anticipating income" or "declaring dividends out of capital."[15]

Auditors had logical and defensible reasons, therefore, to value inventories by attaching original transaction costs to products.[16] Moreover, they developed *economical* methods to attach costs. For auditors' purposes, the costing methods developed by engineers after 1880 seemed unduly complex, not to mention chaotic and confusing. One scientific management authority, Harrington Emerson, once said that engineers found "'to their sorrow' that without tying-in [inventory values and original costs] they could not 'convince those on whose support they must rely that the methods used are really producing the results promised.'"[17] Auditors were concerned only with separating costs of the period from costs in inventory. One did not need accurate costs of individual products to accomplish the separation; as long as the totals were correct, offsetting errors in the details did not matter.

The difference in accuracy between the engineers' product costing and the auditors' inventory costing procedures arose from the allocation of indirect, or overhead, costs. The engineers took care, often at great cost, to trace indirect costs to the specific activities that caused the cost; in other words, they tried to trace *all* costs of the firm as direct costs of products. That clearly was Church's intent, as we discussed in chapter 3. This approach to tracing indirect costs was described succinctly by John Mann in 1903.

It is clear that if the work is of a uniform class the oncost [*i.e.*, overhead] may be applied according to the weight of metal in the castings. . . . Differential rates should be worked out to ascertain the variation in cost and oncost where the castings vary, say between light and heavy goods, and between different methods, as green-sand, dry-sand, and loam. For instance, loam castings requiring large floor space, and crane power, supervision, etc., may justify an expense rate double that required for simple and small green-sand castings, while dry-sand castings would take an intermediate place.[18]

Auditors, however, did not need to distinguish carefully among products and processes. They commonly apportioned all indirect costs as a whole, allocating them to products according to a common divisor such as labor hours or labor cost (information readily available in any manufacturing shop in 1900). Holden Evans, a naval contractor around the turn of the century, described the adverse consequences of using auditor-style inventory costs to estimate prices:

> In some of the large establishments with numerous shops the expense burden is averaged and applied on the basis of productive labor—notwithstanding the fact that in one shop the shop expense percentage is nearly a hundred while in another it is less than twenty-five. Frequently such establishments are called on to bid for work which is almost exclusively confined to the shops where the expense is low, and by using the higher average rate the bids are high and the work goes to other establishments where costs are more accurately determined. Thus profitable work is often lost.[19]

It seems unlikely, however, that firms would persist in losing profits because of inaccurate costing procedures. Since manufacturers after 1914 seem not to have used the careful overhead tracing procedures described by Mann and Holden, we believe that the profits to be gained must not have been worth the added information-gathering costs.

Therefore, it does not seem legitimate to claim, as some historians have, that managerial product costing disappeared in the early 1900s because it was pushed aside by auditors' methods for inventory costing.[20] Because of high information-collection and processing costs, the careful tracing of resource costs to products advocated by Church and many mechanical engineers probably would have disappeared by 1914 even if audited financial reporting had never existed.

What type of cost information would managers have used if auditors and their "integrated" inventory costing procedures had never appeared? It is possible that audited financial reporting would not have arisen if corporations had not turned after 1900 to capital markets for funds. Even so, the demand for external financial reports still could have increased sharply after 1900 to meet the requirements of governmental regulatory and taxing authorities. And government agencies might have insisted on independent audits had auditing not occurred for other reasons. Therefore, pressure to prepare financial reports for nonmanagerial purposes would likely have led companies after 1900 to maintain nonmanagerial cost accounts, even without encouragement from public accountants. And there is no reason to believe that this nonmanagerial cost information would have been more useful to managers than the inventory cost information that did appear.

The ultimate question, then, is not who developed or required nonmanagerial sources of cost information but what prompted rational managers to voluntarily use such information in settings where it was clearly irrelevant? We believe that university departments of accounting may have been the major force in convincing modern managers to "manage by the numbers." University accounting education has paralleled the development of financial reporting in this country. Accounting was virtually unknown in college curricula before 1900; its subsequent development was shaped largely by the demand to train students for public accounting. The theory and problems of financial reporting has comprised virtually all the required courses. Consequently, people trained in accounting before World War II were invariably trained in modern financial reporting, not in management accounting. Many of these graduates started in public accounting careers, but eventually became the financial, accounting, and even senior executives of American manufacturing companies. That they ultimately used financial accounting data as a major source of information for managerial decision making should not, therefore, be surprising.

Academic Influence on Cost Accounting

The disappearance of managerial product costing at the same time that auditor-oriented inventory costing developed was not without consequence. Filling the vacuum left by the disappearance of managerial product costing, inventory costing became the only form of "cost accounting" in manufacturing establishments. When managers and accountants spoke of "product costs" after World War I, they referred to cost information from the ledger inventory accounts. Gradually, accountants and managers came to define the purpose of cost accounting in terms of valuing cost of goods sold and inventories for financial reports, not for managerial decisions or control. The educational system reinforced the tendency. For all practical purposes, academic accountants writing around 1920 never broached the subject of managerial product costing. Textbooks used in 1920s university accounting courses spoke of cost accounting strictly in terms of inventory costing for financial reporting purposes; only in the post–World War II era did academic writers herald the "birth" of management accounting.

Works by academic writers published in the 1920s show how thoroughly the financial reporting view of inventory costing had absorbed the attention of accounting educators. In a 1922 treatise, one of the century's most influential accounting theorists, William Paton, described what he regarded as the cost accountant's chief activity: "the essential basis for the work of the cost accountant—without it, there could be no costing—is the postulate that the value of any commodity, service, or condition, utilized in production, *passes over into* the object or product for which the original item was expended and *attaches to* the result, giving it its value."[21] (Paton's italics.) Thomas Sanders, an accounting educator and theorist no less influential in the 1920s and 1930s than Paton, argued in his 1923 cost accounting text-book that the act of *attaching costs to products* is what sepa-rates ordinary financial accounting from modern cost acounting. Moreover, the purpose of attaching is to arrive directly and reliably at a cost of goods sold figure for finan-cial reports. In Sanders' words,

If we take it that financial accounting must record the transactions of the business with the outside world, these transactions will consist, on the one hand, of the outlays which are incurred for productive purposes, such as the buying of materials and the pay-ment of wages and expenses; and on the other hand of sales of the finished product to customers. But without cost accounting there is no adequate connection between these two classes of transac-tions; there is no assurance that all the expenditures which were incurred for production have been properly attached to the fin-ished products which were sold. [The traditional] procedure in such cases is to take inventories of the raw materials, work in process, and finished goods which remain on hand, and to assume that all the other expenses which have been incurred applied to the goods which were sold. In the absence of cost accounting, we are reduced to this indirect method of computing cost of sales. But cost accounting occupies the ground between the transactions rep-resenting productive expenditures and the transactions represent-ing the sales of the finished product; a direct connection is thereby established between the two. The outlays which have been made for materials, labor, and manufacturing expenses are taken up and *attached to* the specific product or processes upon which they ap-ply.[22] (Italics added.)

Sanders also emphasized the importance of integrating the cost accounts with the general financial accounts, observing that "in the absence of such a tie-up between the cost and financial accounts, the cost accounts are likely to depart from the financial records and there is no guarantee of their reliability."[23] He pointed out that "preserving an exact balance between debit and credit" is one reason why "production managers, efficiency experts, and 'scientific management' people frequently refer to [inventory] cost accounting as a somewhat useless procedure which, whatever its merits, offers very little advantage to them."[24] Sanders admitted that accountants had an obligation to cooperate with production managers, but he leaves no doubt that the main purpose of cost accounts is to value inventories for the financial reports. Indeed, virtually all textbook writers of the 1920s defined "attaching" and "integration" as the cost accountants' two most important considerations.[25]

Textbook authors would usually observe that inventory costing does not provide all information that managers need for evaluation, control, and decision making. The observations are always brief and never advocate any managerial accounting procedures that might detract from the primacy of inventory costing. Glaringly absent from these textbooks is any mention of actual management accounting practices in contemporary industrial organizations.[26] Some authors mention the possibility of using predetermined standards to evaluate departmental and operational performance. But they ignore the vast literature on managerial product costing that engineers wrote in the early decades of the century. Standard costing is usually mentioned, if at all, as a technique that simplifies the task of attaching burden costs to products.[27]

College-level accounting textbooks were not the only publications that gave early authoritative support to the inventory costing approach to cost accounting. Also influential was the historical writing that appeared after 1930 in works by A. C. Littleton, David Solomons, and S. Paul Garner.[28] Littleton's well-known *Accounting Evolution to 1900*[29] legitimized the financial reporting approach to cost accounting by depicting it as the inevitable accounting consequence of factory manufacturing. For Littleton, accounting's evolution progressed inexorably toward twentieth-century financial reporting. For him, the unique accounting problem that manufacturing activity contributed to the evolution was the need to attach costs to inventory. Littleton believed that manufacturing accountants did not develop modern inventory costing procedures until the late 1800s, well after factory manufacturing began. He conjectured that inventory costing did not appear until the 1880s when fixed costs became large enough to force factory managers to give attention to cost allocation procedures.

The historical records we discussed in chapter 2 refute Littleton's interpretation of cost accounting history. Financial reporting did not provide the motivation for managerial product costing. The late nineteenth-century literature that Littleton believed were the first commentaries on modern inventory costing procedure were, in fact, written by engineers who wanted to develop more accurate product costing methods for estimating and pricing—they had no interest in accounting at all.[30]

Had Littleton studied historical company records, he might have discovered the cost accounting practices of early nineteenth-century factories (see chapter 2). He confined his research, however, to publications written by accountants themselves. He interpreted cost accounting history entirely in terms of the technical record keeping procedures that accountants in his day used to compile information for audited financial reports.

Accountants, by the end of World War II, had wholeheartedly accepted both the role of cost accounting for inventory valuation and Littleton's interpretation of cost accounting history. Academic accountants then proceeded to rediscover "managerial accounting for decision making." Many accounting authorities began to write about the managerial shortcomings of financial accounting information;[31] but the primary concern of this writing was to make *financial* accounting information more useful for management decisions, by strategies such as sorting out fixed and variable costs. The financial reporting view of cost accounting was not challenged. The 1950s debate over "direct costing" shows the continuing dominance of the view.[32] In that literature no one challenged the idea of attaching "integrated" costs to products. The debate merely focused on which costs to attach, full or direct.

To avoid anticipating income, *nonmanufacturing* overheads were never attached to inventory. This policy virtually terminated academic discussion of cost accounting for distribution, research, development, marketing, administration, and capital. Indeed, the public accountants' refusal to countenance capitalization of imputed interest led to a bitter dispute among American accountants that culminated in the formation of the National Association of Cost Accountants in 1919.[33] While the issue remained alive in that organization, it disappeared from writings by public accountants and academics.

Many authorities eventually challenged the prevailing view, none more distinguished than William Paton. As we mentioned previously, Paton in his 1922 treatise was among the earliest authorities to legitimize the "costs attach" idea of costing. He also coauthored with Littleton in 1940 the most influential statement of the "costs attach" idea ever published.[34] Speaking at a conference in 1970, however, Paton disparaged the "costs attach" idea by saying,

The basic difficulty with the idea that cost dollars, as incurred, attach like barnacles to the physical flow of materials and stream of operating activity is that it is at odds with the actual process of valuation in a free competitive market. The customer does not buy a handful of classified and traced cost dollars; he buys a product, at prevailing market price. And the market price may be either above or below any calculated cost figure.[35]

Paton did not offer an alternative to attaching when he made this statement. He might have noted that the common nineteenth-century method of determining periodic income did not require inventory costing.[36] The bookkeepers in early American textile companies used market replacement costs (or close approximations of them) to value ending inventories. They charged off all manufacturing costs—direct, indirect, fixed, and variable—as costs of the period; no cost "flowed" into inventory.[37] Or Paton might have mentioned Church's proposal to attach *all* costs to products. Although never taken seriously by academicians, accountants, or auditors in this century, Church's approach to product costing, which appears to eliminate the concept of period costs, would make product cost a bridge between pre-industrial venture accounting and modern periodic income determination.[38]

Acceptance of the inventory costing view of cost accounting is today so complete that all memory or knowledge of cost and managerial accounting practices in pre-1914 American manufacturing firms seems dead. Nowhere is this absence of memory more evident than in the following quotations from three contemporary and representative cost and managerial accounting textbooks:

Managerial accounting is in its infancy. Historically, it has played a secondary role to financial accounting, and in many organizations it still is little more than a by-product of the financial reporting process. However, events *of the last two decades* have spurred the development of managerial accounting, and it is becoming widely recognized as a field of expertise separate from financial accounting.[39] (Italics added.)

Originally, the label *cost accounting* referred to the ways of accumulating and assigning historical costs to units of product and departments, *primarily for purposes of inventory valuation and income determination.*[40] (Italics added.)

While the *traditional role* of cost accounting to record *full product cost data for external reporting and pricing* remains strong, cost accounting for decision making and performance evaluation has gained importance *in recent decades*.[41] (Italics added.)

The authors of these well-known textbooks are in fact expressing Littleton's questionable version of cost accounting history.

One of the coauthors of this book himself enunciated the same belief about the origins of management accounting in the following passage from a textbook that he published in 1982:

Management accounting is a relatively recent phenomenon, especially when compared to the long historical development of financial reporting for external parties such as owners, creditors, regulators, and tax authorities. Cost accounting was the first manifestation of the current management accounting system. Cost accounting was developed to fill a need generated by the financial reporting process. Costs had to be allocated so that product-related expenditures could be separated between cost of goods sold and inventory. . . .

During the 1950s and 1960s, . . . accountants began devising cost accounting procedures that would be most relevant to particular decisions. Emphasis shifted from external to internal users of cost accounting data. One could now think of recording cost data for internal purposes in a manner different from that used for external purposes.[42]

The historical material found in the preceding four chapters refutes two central ideas in the above quotations: that management accounting is a more recent phenomenon than financial accounting and that "cost accounting was developed to fill a need generated by the financial reporting process."

Cost Accounting and Cost Management Contrasted in the U. S. and the U. K.

Evidence from Victorian England casts additional doubt on the academic accountants' (*e.g.*, Littleton's) version of the historical development of cost accounting in American manufacturing. We know today that management accounting, including cost accounting in the nineteenth century, developed much sooner in the United States than in the United Kingdom.[43] Also, public accountants promoted "integration" of cost and financial accounts soon after establishing their presence in the United States, around 1900. In Britain, however, where auditors had established a professional presence nearly fifty years sooner, they did not evince an interest in integrated accounts until long after World War I.[44] Believers in the Littleton hypothesis would have trouble explaining either observation because for Littleton the motive force behind the evolution of cost accounting is financial reporting and the consequent need to account for industrial fixed costs. Britain's early lead in industrial development would presumably have put British cost and managerial accounting ahead of American practice, at least to the end of the nineteenth century. Yet this did not happen.

The earlier, more sophisticated development of cost and managerial accounting in America than in Britain can be explained by differences in the way that industrial activity was organized in the two economies. British industrial firms, at least to the 1920s, tended to specialize in single processes, whereas American industrial firms tended to integrate several processes within the same organization.[45] In recent studies of this contrasting situation, scholars emphasize that Britain's market system was much more sophisticated and more efficient than America's.[46] A leading business historian describes the British situation as follows:

In the last few decades of the nineteenth century and the first decades of the twentieth Britain was perhaps nearer to the ideal of the free market than any other major country at any stage in history. Transport improvements and the densely packed highly urbanized population provided a uniform national market; levels of industrial concentration were low, monopoly positions were almost unknown, and competitive pressures within the economy were strong; international trade was entirely free of tariffs; migration and capital movements were free of control; market institutions were highly developed within a well-understood legal framework; the currency and financial system were stable.[47]

With such extensive market opportunities, there was little need for British industrialists to coordinate economic exchanges within firms. Relying on market prices, the industrialists coordinated a far higher percentage of their exchanges *among* firms than did their American counterparts.

The accounting implications of these different organizational patterns are by now obvious. British companies, because they tended to specialize in a single process, did not need accounting records to ascertain the cost of intermediate outputs; market prices supplied virtually all the cost information they needed. American companies, because they tended to integrate two or more processes under one management, needed cost accounts to compute the cost of their internally made intermediate outputs. The so-called "failure" of British companies to adopt what often are considered advanced American cost accounting procedures was actually the natural consequence of the higher effectiveness of market institutions in Britain. This effectiveness made it beneficial for British companies to coordinate different production processes through market exchanges, thereby eliminating the need for sophisticated internal cost accounting procedures.[48]

In retrospect, British industrialists paid a high price. Heeding strictly to domestic market signals in the late Victorian era, British manufacturing firms remained specialized at a time when the tide was turning in favor of integrated hierarchy. Eventually the British were swamped by the economies of scale achieved by American and German corporations, whose large-scale industrial hierarchies captured world markets for standardized mass-produced goods.

But how does one explain why nineteenth-century British public accountants were uninterested in the "integration" of cost and financial accounts? Public accountants developed a professional presence earlier in Britain than in America and the British market for securities created a demand for audited financial reports in the second half of the nineteenth century. The much simpler structure of British organizations, however, enabled the information from a company's general ledger to be used directly to compile auditable financial reports. Virtually all of a British manufacturing company's transactions were market transactions, and the ledger accounts fully reflected these transactions. British auditors had no reason to press for integration of cost and financial accounts since the general accounts already provided everything needed to prepare auditable financial reports. For instance, British accountants could ascertain directly from double-entry purchase accounts the "cost of sales" figure that caused so much concern to American authorities such as Sanders. Indeed, British auditors argued for *separating* managerial cost accounts (such as they were) from general financial accounts.

Conclusion: Cost Accounting's Lost Relevance for Cost Management

Our discussion in this chapter suggests that little evidence exists to believe that auditors after 1900 persuaded managers to substitute inventory cost accounting figures for strategic product cost information. That managers were not inclined to compile accurate product costs data in the decades after 1900 likely reflects their judgment on the costs and benefits of such information, not a lost sense of what information is relevant to management decisions. Yet having the accounts used to value inventories for financial reporting purposes be the only source of product cost information undoubtedly has affected how accountants and managers subsequently thought about cost management during the past sixty years. Many accountants and managers have come to believe that inventory cost figures give an accurate guide to product costs, when they do not.

Accounting historians should examine carefully the extent to which the writings and teachings by academic accountants (as distinct from auditors and managers) have contributed to cost accounting's lost relevance for cost management. Academic accountants devoted much energy in the last sixty years to forging managerial relevance out of financial accounting information. The forging used a model of a simple manufacturing firm, producing a homogeneous line of goods—scarcely as complex as an early nineteenth-century textile mill. In such a simple setting, academic writers recast inventory cost information to solve contrived production problems. In more complex real-world settings, however, inventory cost information is irrelevant for actual management decisions. That was, of course, the point made by Church and other early twentieth-century writers. Moreover, academic management accountants tend to characterize management decisions in terms of "decision models" derived from the economists' neoclassical theory of the firm. The models portray situations that grossly oversimplify the decision problems managers face in real life. But the forced simplification permits academic writers to show how inventory cost information from financial reports can be made "relevant" to managerial decisions. Academic cost accountants, more than auditors or managers, may have contributed to accounting's lost relevance for cost management, especially since World War II.

Although financial reporting rules *per se* did not thwart managerial cost accounting after World War I, they did have a deleterious impact on the accounting information used to evaluate subordinates' performance in complex industrial organizations. As we remarked previously, large firms used

accounting measures of efficiency and productivity to evaluate subordinate managers' performance well before multidivisional organizations first appeared around 1920. Critics
of present-day American management practice often note
that successful Japanese and German manufacturing firms
also focus on similar measures of performance. But the
emergence of the multidivisional structure in the 1920s encouraged top managers to entrust divisional heads with responsibility for achieving accounting profit or ROI targets,
not merely efficiency or productivity targets. Using profit
performance targets allowed top managers to delegate a
broad variety of operating responsibilities. It also increased
the risk that subordinate managers' local goals might not
conform to the goals of the organization as a whole.

This risk is a topic of great concern today. The spread of
the multidivisional structure throughout American industry
has catalyzed an enthusiasm for motivating *every* member
of a business organization to meet profit goals. Yet undesirable outcomes can occur when subordinates are asked to
respond to profit signals. This and other consequences of
modern financial reporting will be examined as we next consider the continuing evolution of management accounting in
America after 1925.

Notes

1. Richard A. Elnicki, "The Genesis of Management Accounting," *Management Accounting* (April 1971), 16.
2. This observation is documented extensively in M. C. Wells, *Accounting
for Common Costs* (Urbana, Ill.: Center for International Education and Research in Accounting, 1978).
3. We are indebted to Robin Cooper for making this point and for contributing many other important ideas used in this chapter.
4. Quoted in Richard Vangermeersch, "Alexander Hamilton Church: A
Man for All Seasons" (unpublished ms., Kingston, R.I., n.d.), 43.
5. Numerous articles on the cost systems of metal-working firms are
found in the pages of *Management and Administration* during the 1920s.

6. A profession of public accountants appeared when audited financial reporting became important, first in Britain around the middle of the nineteenth century and then in the United States around 1900. For more details see Gary J. Previts and Barbara D. Merino, *A History of Accounting in America* (New York: John Wiley, a Ronald Press Publication, 1979), chapter 5, Eugene H. Flegm, *Accounting: How to Meet the Challenges of Relevance and Regulation* (New York: John Wiley, 1984), 17–18, and David F. Hawkins, "The Development of Modern Financial Reporting Practices Among American Manufacturing Corporations," *Business History Review* (Autumn 1963), 135–168.

7. Although railroads often had their financial reports audited, the auditors generally were members of the board of directors.

8. Andrew Carnegie's steel company, a partnership, did not issue public reports; New England textile companies and American railroad companies did issue semiannual and annual reports to nonmanaging directors from their earliest days, and by the 1850s were issuing annual reports to stockholders. A brief survey of nineteenth-century American financial reporting appears in Previts and Merino, *A History*, 55–62, 80–89.

9. The method of determining periodic income in early textile companies resembles what railroad accountants later would call "replacement accounting." Replacement accounting bridges the pre-industrial "valuation" approach to income determination and the twentieth-century "matching" approach. It does not allocate fixed asset costs to periods as the matching approach does, but it does report periodic revenues, which the valuation approach does not do. It is essentially a cash-based method of determining income. See Richard P. Brief, "Valuation, Matching, and Earnings: The Continuing Debate," in James F. Gaertner, ed., *Selected Papers from the Charles Waldo Haskins Accounting History Seminars* (Atlanta, Ga.: The Academy of Accounting Historians, 1983), 15–29.

10. There is strong evidence that the textile companies valued ending inventories at approximations of market price until well after 1900 and reasonable grounds to believe that nineteenth-century manufacturers in other industries never considered doing otherwise. On the textile situation, see Paul F. McGouldrick, "Notes on Cotton Textile Records at the Baker Library," (Boston, 1958), on file at the Harvard Business School, Archives Division; and his *New England Textiles in the Nineteenth Century* (Cambridge, Mass.: Harvard University Press, 1968), 92. On other industries see Wells, *Accounting* 38, 47, 138–139, 144.

11. American auditors' insistence on integrated cost and financial accounts around 1900 is extensively documented in S. Paul Garner, *Evolution of Cost Accounting to 1925* (Tuscaloosa, Ala.: University of Alabama Press, 1954), chapters 5–6.

12. R. S. Edwards was an early writer to acknowledge "the enormous drawback to a double-entry costing system 'tied-in' [*i.e.*, integrated] to the financial accounts." See his "The Rationale of Cost Accounting" (1937), reprinted in J. M. Buchanan and G. F. Thirlby, eds., *L.S.E. Essays on Cost* (New York: New York University Press, 1981), 71–94. J. M. Clark also spoke of the

need to develop "systems of cost analysis which shall be separate from the formal books of account, though based on the same data." See his *Studies in the Economics of Overhead Costs* (Chicago: University of Chicago Press, 1923), 68.

13. It was probably good business sense, not the influence of the law, that caused accountants to consider the implications of profit measurement for dividends. According to Basil Yamey, "it was the accounting conventions and not the legal requirements that imposed the real restraints on the calculation of divisible profits in practice." See his "The Development of Company Accounting Conventions," *Three Banks Review* (September 1960), 13. We are grateful to Stephen A. Zeff for supplying this reference.

14. Arthur Lowes Dickinson, "The Profits of a Corporation," *Official Record of the Proceedings of the Congress of Accountants, 1904* (New York: Arno Press reprint, 1978), 171–191; R. Montgomery, *Dicksee's Auditing* (New York: Ronald Press, 1905), 171.

15. By valuing inventories with attached historical costs, one never recognizes unrealized holding gains in unsold units; moreover, unrealized holding losses are easily recognized by following the "lower of cost or market" rule.

16. Auditors pressed companies to maintain inventory accounts by "flowing" transaction-based acquisition costs onto units of product even though most financial reports in the early decades of the century did not disclose amounts of inventory or cost of goods sold. The importance of this issue to accountants and evidence that most companies quickly complied is implicit in the debates over "articulation" and in the accounting textbooks written during and shortly after World War I.

17. David Solomons, "The Historical Development of Costing," in Solomons, *Studies in Costing* (London: Sweet and Maxwell, 1952), 41.

18. John Mann, Jr., "Oncost or Expenses," *Encyclopedia of Accounting, 1903–1904* (London: William Green and Sons, 1903), 220. We are indebted to Richard Brief for this reference.

19. Holden A. Evans, *Cost Keeping and Scientific Management* (New York: McGraw Hill, 1911), 1–54. We are indebted to Richard Vangermeersch for this reference.

20. See Wells, *Accounting*, 129.

21. William A. Paton, *Accounting Theory* (Houston, Tex.: Scholars Book Co., 1973 reprint of 1922 ed.), 490–491.

22. Thomas H. Sanders, *Problems in Industrial Accounting* (Chicago: A. W. Shaw Company, 1923), 14–15.

23. *Ibid.*, 15.

24. *Ibid.*, 14.

25. See, for example, James L. Dohr, *Cost Accounting Theory and Practice* (New York: The Ronald Press, 1924); Charles F. Schlatter, *Cost Accounting* (New York: John Wiley & Sons, 1927).

26. An exception to this generalization would be the company practices articulated in the Harvard Business School cases that appear in Thomas Sanders' books. In these books, however, Sanders emphasizes the inventory cost-

ing purposes of cost accounting. Twentieth-century public accountants (and the educators who write textbooks) rarely show an interest in the internal accounting practices of companies. (This is a recurring theme in Flegm, *Accounting*, 16–18, 167–204, and 255–258. Flegm is a former Big Eight CPA who for many years has directed the comptroller's staff of General Motors.) The lack of interest is not because companies kept their practices secret. Industries in which nineteenth-century American firms published descriptions of their accounting systems include textile making (*e.g., Transactions of the New England Cotton Manufacturers' Association*), railroads (*e.g.,* Alfred D. Chandler, Jr.'s references to annual reports by Albert Fink and to articles by Henry Varnum Poor in the *America Railroad Journal*), and machine making (*e.g.,* references to publications of the A.S.M.E. in Wells, *Accounting*, 66–67). A classic early twentieth-century example of published material on a company's management accounting system is the series of articles by GM executives in the 1920s, cited in chapter 5. Perhaps the real reason for auditors' indifference toward company accounting practices is that "for many years it was assumed that the type of information useful to managers had little significance for external users." (Previts and Merino, *A History*, 274.) Donald J. Kirk, chairman of the FASB, restated the same belief recently in "The Impact of Management Accounting on GAAP," *Management Accounting* (July 1985), 26–30, 59.

27. Public accountants and auditors resisted the application of standard cost concepts to product costing until after World War II. Their aversion to standard costs stemmed, it seems, from a fear that "standard" numbers might compromise the integrity of the original-transaction double-entry ledgers— the same fear that originally caused auditors to advocate "integration" of cost and financial accounts.

28. The major historical writings by these authors are referenced and discussed in H. Thomas Johnson, "Toward a New Understanding of Nineteenth-Century Cost Accounting," *Accounting Review* (July 1981), 510–511, 516.

29. Published in 1933 by the American Institute for Accountants (now the AICPA). Chapters 20–22 contain the material on cost accounting history.

30. Wells, *Accounting*.

31. A few of the countless examples one could cite are: Herbert A. Simon et al., *Centralization vs. Decentralization in Organizing the Controller's Department* (New York: Controllership Foundation, 1954), esp. 56–57, 98–100; Billy E. Goetz, "Tomorrow's Cost System," *Advanced Management* (December 1947); H. Justin Davidson and Robert M. Trueblood, "Accounting for Decision-Making," *Accounting Review* (October 1961), 577–582; Sidney Davidson, "The Day of Reckoning: Managerial Analysis and Accounting Theory," *Journal of Accounting Research* (Autumn 1963), 117–126.

32. An excellent discussion of this controversy is in David Green, Jr., "A Moral to the Direct Costing Controversy," *Journal of Business* (July 1960), 218–226.

33. Stephen A. Zeff, "Some Junctures in the Evolution of the Process of Establishing Accounting Principles in the U.S.A.: 1917–1972," *Accounting Re-*

view (July 1984), 448–450. The twentieth-century history of overhead allocation to inventory is still very unclear. The rules concerning allocation of manufacturing overhead to inventory are vague and often misinterpreted. Textbook writers often erroneously assert that "the accounting profession is committed to the inclusion of all manufacturing overhead costs in the costs of production and then into inventory." Nicholas Dopuch, J. G. Birnberg, and J. S. Demski, *Cost Accounting* (New York: Harcourt Brace Jovanovich, 1982), 220. In truth, practice in this regard has been varied. U. S. Steel, for instance, capitalizes as little manufacturing overhead as possible; other firms absorb all the overhead allowed.

34. W. A. Paton and A. C. Littleton, *An Introduction to Corporate Accounting Standards* (Columbus, OH.: American Accounting Association, 1940).

35. Williard E. Stone, ed., *Foundations of Accounting Theory* (Gainesville, Fla.: University of Florida Press, 1971), x–xi.

36. Robert Hamilton's late eighteenth-century views on this method of income determination are discussed in M. J. Mepham, "Robert Hamilton's Contribution to Accounting," *Accounting Review* (January 1983), 43–57.

37. Examples of this approach to income determination and inventory valuation that have been proposed by modern accounting writers are: Don T. DeCoster and Eldon L. Schafer, *Management Accounting: A Decision Emphasis* (New York: John Wiley, 1979), chapters 5–6; T. A. Lee, "The Simplicity and Complexity of Accounting" in Robert R. Sterling and Arthur L. Thomas, eds., *Accounting for a Simplified Firm Owning Depreciable Assets* (Houston, Tex.: Scholars Book Co., 1979), 35–56; and Wells, *Accounting*, 163–166.

38. Stephen Gilman once viewed inventory costing as a consequence of accountants' adopting the period convention; periodization resulted in "the shift from venture accounting to the treatment of units of inventory as separate ventures." See a review of Gilman's *Accounting Concepts of Profit* (New York: Garland Publishing, 1982 reprint edition) by Carl Devine in *Accounting Review* (October 1985), 760. Also see Green, "A Moral to the Direct Costing Controversy," and L. J. Benninger, "The Traditional vs. the Cost Accounting Concept of Cost," *Accounting Review* (October 1949), 387–391.

39. Ray H. Garrison, *Managerial Accounting: Concepts for Planning, Control, Decision Making* (Plano, Tex.: Business Publications, 1982), 18.

40. Charles T. Horngren, *Cost Accounting: A Managerial Emphasis* (Englewood Cliffs, N.J.: Prentice-Hall, 1982), 4.

41. Edward B. Deakin and Michael W. Maher, *Cost Accounting* (Homewood, Ill.: Richard D. Irwin, 1984), 9.

42. Robert S. Kaplan, *Advanced Management Accounting* (Englewood Cliffs, N.J.: Prentice-Hall, 1982), 1–2.

43. Robert R. Locke, "Cost Accounting: An Institutional Yardstick for Measuring British Entrepreneurial Performance, circa 1914," *Accounting Historians Journal* (Fall 1979), 1–22; Wells, *Accounting*, 64, 66–67. An excellent discussion of British-American differences in nineteenth-century cost accounting is in Edgar Jones, *Accountancy and the British Economy, 1840–1980* (London: B. T. Batsford, 1981), 111–119.

44. Locke, "Cost Accounting," 5.

45. An important new study of this phenomenon as it occurred in the textile industry is William Lazonick, "Industrial Organization and Technological Change: The Decline of the British Cotton Industry," *Business History Review* (Summer 1983), 195–236.

46. See the contributions by Leslie Hannah (on Great Britain) and Jurgen Kocka (on Germany) in Alfred D. Chandler, Jr., and Herman Daems, eds., *Managerial Hierarchies: Comparative Perspectives on the Rise of the Modern Industrial Enterprise* (Cambridge, Mass.: Harvard University Press, 1980) 41–76, 203–224.

47. Leslie Hannah, "New Issues in British Business History," *Business History Review* (Summer 1983), 174.

48. One interesting confirmation of this observation is the sophisticated cost accounting system used in an *integrated* multiprocess English textile company operating at the *very start* of the nineteenth century, *before* the British market system displayed the efficient properties described in the text quotation (by Hannah) cited in note 47. This case is discussed in Williard E. Stone, "An Early English Cotton Mill Cost Accounting System: Charlton Mills, 1810–1889," *Accounting and Business Research* (Winter 1973), 71–78.

CHAPTER 7

Cost Accounting and Decision Making: Academics Strive for Relevance

D URING the 1920s, as cost accounting practice and textbooks became increasingly dominated by the financial accounting mentality, some researchers at business schools and in economics departments argued for developing cost systems that could aid managerial decisions. The financial accounting approach had integrated cost accounts into the double-entry bookkeeping system by "attaching costs" to products as they traveled through the factory. The "costs attach" system accumulated all input costs—material, labor, and indirect expenses—into a single account that represented the "cost" of goods produced. After several stages of such aggregations, it was impossible to recover the portions of total cost represented by various subcomponents since labor and indirect, or overhead, costs at one stage were combined into the cost of material transferred to the next stage. While this flow of costs through the factory and through the cost accountants' records was elegantly simple, the resulting cost figures had no relevance other than to permit an objective, albeit arbitrary, allocation of period expenditures between what was sold in the period and what still remained in inventory. Not knowing the fraction of final product cost represented by labor, material, and overhead, management could not generate even reasonable estimates of variable or fixed costs.

Academic researchers, well grounded in the marginal analysis of microeconomics, understood the importance of distinguishing variable from fixed costs for short-run decisions. J. Maurice Clark, at the University of Chicago, was one of the earliest and most influential writers to advocate distinguishing the portion of expenses that rises and falls in direct proportion to changes in output (that is, the variable costs) from costs that, within the limits of the range of output under study, are unaffected by increases or decreases in production (that is, the fixed costs).[1] Clark's writings on separating fixed and variable costs were especially influential in the railroad industry. Based on extensive statistical studies, procedures to estimate long-run variable costs were employed by the Interstate Commerce Commission in the 1930s, procedures that are still in use today.[2] Clark also recognized that notions of fixed and variable cost were only meaningful when measured with respect to a given time period; that many costs, which appear to be fixed over relatively short periods, are variable with respect to longer decision horizons.

Clark had great insight into many important cost behavior patterns that remain prominently featured in all of today's cost accounting textbooks. Among these cost concepts are "differential costs," costs that will vary with respect to a given decision, versus "sunk costs," costs that represent expenditures already incurred and hence may not be escaped even by going out of business.

Clark was particularly lucid and insightful in his presentation of the relevance of "different costs for different purposes." Clark worked through many different business situations to explicate that "there is no one correct usage, usage being governed by the varying needs of varying business situations and problems."[3] He identified ten important functions for cost accounting.

1. To help determine a normal or satisfactory price for goods sold;

2. To help fix a minimum limit on price-cutting;

3. To determine which goods are most profitable and which are unprofitable;

4. To control inventory;

5. To set a value on inventory;

6. To test the efficiency of different processes;

7. To test the efficiency of different departments;

8. To detect losses, wastes, and pilfering;

9. To separate the cost of idleness from the cost of producing goods; and

10. To tie in with the financial accounts.[4]

To satisfy all these diverse purposes for cost accounting information, Clark believed that

there must be studies and analyses of cost *which are not part of the books of account and need not be bound by any of their standards of procedure.* . . . The writer has little disposition to interpose in accounting controversies or to criticize the prevailing methods of accounting from the point of view of the main purpose of financial accountancy, which he takes to be construction of an income account and a balance sheet. But he would insist strenuously that other conceptions of cost and profit must, somehow and somewhere, find adequate recognition and scientific treatment.[5] (Italics added)

In arguing against having information relevant for cost management become subordinate to the consistency, objectivity, and auditability requirements of financial accounting, Clark concluded,

Undoubtedly the ultimate solution lies in the development of systems of cost analysis which shall be separate from the formal books of account, though based on the same data. This analysis will be free to study differential cost and cost as a normal supply-price, without being tied down by the rules that are legitimate and necessary in financial accounting.[6]

Unfortunately, Clark's eminently sensible plea for separating cost analysis from the rigidities of financial accounting went unheeded at the time and remained unheeded until very recently. Cost accounting had already become subservient to the goals of external reporting and only occasionally emerged to aid managerial decisions and control.

The London School of Economics "Opportunity Cost" Tradition

During the 1930s, a group of economists at the London School of Economics (LSE) produced a number of papers[7] on how cost must be measured relative to alternatives foregone. While apparently written without reference to Clark's contributions, they reinforced his emphasis on computing costs relevant to particular decisions and argued against using cost data arising directly from the books of accounts that were the basis of external financial statements.

The LSE economists recognized that the arbitrary systems accountants used for allocating costs to products made product costs virtually useless for decision making.[8] R. S. Edwards, a practicing accountant before he turned to economic analysis, was particularly concerned about the inability of cost systems to predict variable costs. To an economist, the most important aspect of cost behavior was the extent to which costs changed with output. But the cost accountant's books allocated periodic fixed costs to products so that it became impossible to decide which products were most profitable to produce. Edwards, like other economists, was not impressed with the apparent elegance of double-entry accounting systems, especially when they produced product costs of no managerial significance, "The enormous drawbacks to a double-entry costing system 'tied in' to the financial accounts is that some arbitrary assumptions have to be set up to make it workable."[9]

Edwards' LSE colleague, the prominent economist Ronald Coase, reinforced the relevance of variable costs for economic decisions, but Coase's main contribution was to introduce the opportunity cost concept into accounting thinking. In the opportunity cost framework, the cost of taking any action consists of the income foregone if the particular decision had not been taken. Opportunity costs concentrate on decision alternatives rather than on recording the historic costs of decisions made. Opportunity costs are not measured by a transaction-based double-entry accounting system because they represent the costs of actions not taken.

Coase recognized that cost accountants attempt to measure the payments made for production and then to match these payments against the associated revenues. The decision maker, however, wants to look forward at the alternative decisions that now confront him, and for this purpose historical costs are useless. The relevant concerns are those costs that will be incurred in the future or those revenues that will be foregone as a consequence of the decisions now being made.[10]

Coase commented on the lack of decision relevance of the information produced by the cost accounting systems he saw in practice and in textbooks.

These methods do not give one opportunity costs and do not enable one to calculate avoidable costs. . . .[Therefore] any claims that modern cost accounting enables unprofitable lines to be discovered and eliminated is misleading. It is only possible to discover whether or not a particular activity is profitable by comparing the avoidable costs with the receipts. And this is a task which modern cost-accounting methods do not enable one to perform.[11]

While Coase's "modern cost accounting systems" were those existing in the 1930s, his claims remain relevant even for cost systems in the 1980s as we shall see in subsequent chapters.

Conventional Wisdom in the 1940s

The writings of economists such as Clark, Edwards, and Coase had little cogency for academics, practitioners, and textbook writers. With few exceptions, cost accounting was taught as a series of inventory valuation methods. Costs were allocated to products so that period expenditures could be split between products sold and products still in inventory. Little attention was devoted to whether the product costs obtained for inventory valuation had any relevance for managerial decisions or control.

In part, the financial statement focus of cost accounting could be rationalized by the limited computational power available to organizations during the middle of this century. Special studies advocated by economists, to set marginal cost equal to marginal revenue and to measure opportunity cost, could be easily motivated and illustrated with single product examples. But procedures that seemed simple and sensible for decision making with a handful of products could not be applied to organizations that had grown substantially in size and complexity. It would have been impossible for organizations producing thousands of products through complex multistage production processes to have undertaken the data collection, storage, and processing required for the economists' models. Simple means of accumulating product costs and allocating period expenditures to cost centers and products were necessary if the organizations were not to be drowned in a sea of data and special studies.

It is hardly surprising that practice and teaching emphasized arbitrary but simple procedures to assign costs to products for inventory valuation. Unfortunately, while the simplistic practices developed and flourished, no one remembered why more relevant or more complex procedures had been rejected. Arbitrary allocations, rationalized through the "costs attach" imagery, became accepted as correct, the right way of computing product costs and the main function of cost accounting. Charles Horngren recalled well this era.

As a student, my first course in cost accounting in 1947 was similar to those taught in universities throughout the world. It was a plodding excursion through product costing for the primary purpose of inventory valuation and income determination. The three major topics were job order costing, process costing, and standard costing. The highlight of the course was the reconciling of "total costs to account for" in a process costing problem, involving three departments and spoilage. Indeed, the second course in cost accounting at more than one state university was "Advanced Process Costing."[12]

George Foster reviewed seven cost accounting textbooks published between 1945 and 1950 and found that inventory valuation was the subject of 73 percent of the chapters in these books, cost control in 21 percent, and management decision making in only 6 percent.[13]

An Exception: Vatter's *Managerial Accounting*

Despite this gloomy state of affairs, one author, William Vatter, believed that managerial accounting should provide relevant information for management decision and control. Because of his heretical view, Vatter's textbook,[14] based on his University of Chicago lecture notes developed in the mid-1940s, was issued in a paperback rather than a hardcover edition. The publisher's choice signaled the experimental nature of his approach and the need to test it before producing a more authoritative appearing textbook.

In contrast to the inventory valuation emphasis of most 1940s cost accounting texts, Vatter introduced managerial accounting with six chapters on budgeting and managerial control. He emphasized the managerial, as opposed to the external, use of financial data.

The only reason for collecting financial data about a business, from the managerial viewpoint, is that decisions must be made. . . . For management purposes, the financial data must be related to the use to be made of them. Some costs are "sunk," that is, irrecoverable; while others may be escaped, curtailed, or adjusted by managerial action. Some costs are fixed over relevant ranges of activity, while others vary in pattern with respect to output, scope of operations, levels of quality, area of market coverage, number of salesmen, or any one of a large number of independent variables. Costs may be controllable or noncontrollable, avoidable or unavoidable, linear or nonlinear in statistical behavior, efficient or wasteful; there are almost as many ways of classifying cost data as there are questions that can be raised about them. For this reason, there must be a certain flexibility in . . . procedure . . . to provide for putting together those parts of the financial information which are relevant to a given management decision.[15]

Thus, Vatter strongly advocated "different costs for different purposes," continuing the tradition of his University of Chicago predecessor, J. M. Clark.

Vatter also recognized the important time dimension of managerial accounting information. With a financial accounting, inventory valuation mentality, financial statements are prepared only monthly or quarterly. But for managerial purposes, such as process and cost control, the information must be made available in the time frame of the responsible manager: "For management purposes, it may be necessary to record power as consumed . . . over a short period of time such as a week or a month, even though financial statements are prepared only for quarters and the fiscal year."[16] Vatter pointed out that it may be better to get incomplete, perhaps less precise, data to managers quickly than to provide complete information to them too late to affect any of their decisions or actions: "It may be better to prop the barn shut with a handy fence rail, than to wait for someone to bring a lock from town."[17]

Unfortunately, Vatter's recommendation for two different accounting systems, with different degrees of completeness and timeliness, was not adopted. Even today's organizations, with access to far more computational power than Vatter could have imagined when he was writing in 1950, rarely distinguish between information needed promptly for managerial control and information provided periodically for summary financial statements.

Vatter, in the final chapter, affirmed the necessity to distinguish clearly managerial from external uses of accounting data. He emphasized that accounting for managerial purposes was different from the recording of transactions data to establish the financial history of the firm. That is, the managerial accounting system had to serve management; it could not be justified as a system needed by accountants.

The recording process is not maintained for accounting purposes; it is used because it is necessary to carrying on business operations. . . . [It] is not merely to provide data for financial records and to make sure that all accountable transactions are recorded; rather, the system of internal control is aimed at the more efficient and smooth performance of regular operating activities.[18]

In addition to this important process, control justification, Vatter wanted management accounting information to be relevant for management decision making.

Records are of use to management only because they provide a basis for decision-making. Accounting departments of business concerns cost too much if they are used only to provide historical reports of transactions to measure income or financial position at the end of a year. Management's decisions must be made when they are of consequence; they must be made with reference to future activities; managerial decisions must be made promptly when they are called for, even if the data available for such decisions are incomplete or inconclusive.

[Also] the accounting system is valuable to management not because it answers questions but because it raises them. . . . The deviations from planned performance are question-raising data. From the intelligent raising of questions as to why each deviation occurs may be found better ways of accomplishing the tasks that are to be done in the firm.[19]

Vatter concluded his textbook by reemphasizing that the central purpose of managerial accounting is to support management.

Accounting for management is not management, and it should not be thought of as such. But accounting can be made to serve managerial control; and it can help management to do a better job than could be done without it.[20]

Thus, at the close of the first half of the twentieth century, management accounting thought was well positioned to develop more fully the role of accounting data for managerial decisions and control. During the 1950s, management decision making became the focus of research for academic scholars in business schools. Led by advances in microeconomic theory and by the emerging discipline of operations research, an impressive battery of analytic tools was applied to a broad array of management decisions. Of particular interest to management accountants were advances in capital budgeting, product mix and product profitability analysis, transfer pricing, cost control, and divisional control and evaluation.

Capital Budgeting: Discounted
Cash Flow (DCF) Approach

The adoption of the discounted cash flow approach for evaluating capital investment projects has been the main innovation in management accounting practice during the past sixty years. Gordon Shillinglaw, a prolific writer in management accounting, recalled state-of-the-art project evaluation in the post–World War II era.

When I started my professional career in the early 1950s, the consulting firm I worked with [Joel Dean Associates] played a missionary role in the introduction of discounted cash-flow analysis in industry . . . [T]he older systems, based on pay back period or on some undiscounted form of the return-on-investment ratio, were designed by financial managers, most of them accountants. The engineers had been tinkering with cash-flow discounting for years, but they were not very influential.[21]

The time value of money concept had been used in the actuarial literature since the early nineteenth century and appeared prominently in the political economy literature earlier in the twentieth century. But the discounting of future cash flows as a management tool for evaluating new investment proposals did not emerge until the 1950s.

Two authors contributed early writings that established the basis for this development. Eugene Grant's 1938 book, *Principles of Engineering Economy,*[22] provided definitions and examples of the time value of money concept for evaluating new investment projects. Grant's work was followed by George Terborgh, director of research of the Machinery and Products Institute (MAPI), a federation of trade associations in the industrial equipment field. Terborgh in his 1949 book, *Dynamic Equipment Policy,*[23] developed formulas to encourage businessmen to replace their equipment on a more regular and more scientific basis (not an uninteresting subject for the company membership of MAPI). Terborgh was most concerned with the adverse competitive consequences of technological obsolescence. While Terborgh used present value concepts in his analysis, he framed the equipment replacement problem using complex formulas and confusing jargon—"inferiority gradient," "line of indifference," and "challenger's adverse minimum"—which greatly limited the impact his ideas had on senior managers.

Therefore, credit for introducing modern capital budgeting procedures to corporate managers can be attributed to Joel Dean. His 1951 book, *Capital Budgeting*,[24] provided an excellent summary of the practices of leading corporations in the post–World War II era. Interestingly, however, Dean's book emphasized the process of capital budgeting more than it did particular techniques for evaluating proposed projects. In fact, one can find no mention of discounting cash flows in the book; Dean describes procedures for discounting the stream of earnings, not cash flows, from a project and concludes that for many investments, discounting "frequently may not be worth the cost." Several years later, though, Dean recognized the value of the DCF approach and advocated discounting cash flows in a widely referenced 1954 *Harvard Business Review* article.[25]

Dean's work triggered much academic activity on the discounted cash flow technique.[26] In 1956, a trade journal, *The Engineering Economist*, was founded to encourage the dissemination of ideas on newly developed capital budgeting techniques, and textbooks soon followed[27] to establish the acceptance of discounted cash flow techniques among academic scholars and teachers.

Supporting these academic writings were the parallel efforts of engineers in large oil companies. Dissatisfied with the inability of the accounting ROI procedure to reflect the uneven cash flows expected from investments in the petroleum industry, engineers in the Atlantic Oil Company (now ARCO); Socony-Vacuum Oil Company (now the Mobil Corporation), where Dean had worked as a consultant; and

Standard Oil of Indiana developed present value procedures. Despite initial resistance, they eventually succeeded in getting these procedures accepted in their firms.[28] As an interesting side note, the Du Pont Corporation, where the ROI evaluation tool had been developed in the first decade of this century, was one of the later adopters of modern capital budgeting techniques. Du Pont remained wedded to the ROI accounting technique for project evaluation until the 1970s.[29]

Residual Income

The residual income (RI) extension to the return on investment (ROI) criterion also emerged in the post–World War II period. Development of the RI procedure is generally attributed to the General Electric Company, though the idea of levying an explicit capital charge on investment when computing net income can be found in extensive writing earlier in the century.[30] The residual income concept does not appear in the management accounting literature until the 1960s.[31] The RI approach overcame one of the dysfunctional aspects of the ROI measure in which managers could increase their reported ROI by rejecting investments that yielded returns in excess of their firm's (or division's) cost of capital, but that were below their current average ROI.[32] Despite the conceptual appeal of the RI measure, it failed to generate the same degree of acceptance as the DCF approach or the ROI measure. Surveys continued to show the widespread acceptance of ROI, rather than RI, as the primary financial control measure for divisional performance.[33] Even its corporate innovator, General Electric, abandoned RI and returned to the ROI measure, apparently because ROI was more consistent with the financial data being reported to shareholders.[34]

Management Control

Apart from these innovations in capital budgeting and in evaluating divisional performance, the post–World War II era saw the systematic exploration of management control processes. Previously, academic writers had concentrated on the role of cost accounting for decision making, but had largely ignored overall systems of accountability used in hierarchical organizations. Such systems had been developed by functionally organized, multi-activity firms such as Du Pont (see chapter 4) and by the increasingly popular multidivisional organizations such as Alfred Sloan's General Motors in the 1920s (see chapter 5). The extensive decentralization trend was largely unexplored until such writers as Herbert Simon[35] investigated the motivation and control problems of decentralized organizations.

As another sign of the new interest in studying decentralized organizations, researchers seemed to discover the transfer pricing problem in the mid-1950s.[36] Sloan knew forty years previously the importance of market-based transfer prices for motivating efficient divisional performance. As president and chief operating officer of United Motors, Sloan recalled:

My divisions . . . had sold both to outside customers and to their allied divisions at the market price. When the United Motors group was brought into the General Motors Corporation in late 1918, I found that if I followed the prevailing practice, I would no longer be able to determine the rate of return on investment for these accessory divisions individually, or as a group. . . . At that time, material within General Motors was passing from one operating division to another at cost plus some predetermined percentage.[37]

Sloan recommended to Durant, then president of General Motors, that for exclusively interdepartmental transactions ... the starting point should be cost plus some predetermined rate of return, but only as a guide. To avoid the possibility of protecting a supplying division which might be a high-cost producer, I recommend a number of steps involving analysis of the operation and comparison with outside competitive production where possible.[38]

Sloan was subsequently able to implement his view when he became head of General Motors. We can recall (see page 114) the forceful description by Donaldson Brown, Sloan's chief financial officer, of GM's market-based transfer pricing policy and of the discipline this policy provided to its internal supplying divisions.

No division is required absolutely to purchase products from another division. In their interrelation they are encourged to deal just as they would with outsiders. ... Where there are no substantial sales outside, such as would establish a competitive picture, at times partial requirements are actually purchased from outside sources so as to perfect the competitive situation.[39]

Economists[40] also seemed to discover the transfer pricing problem in the 1950s, at about the same time as management scholars. Economists demonstrated the optimality of using the opportunity cost of the selling division as the appropriate transfer price. In cases where the market for the transferred good is "perfectly competitive" (a convenient construct of great popularity among economists), the opportunity cost of the selling division is the market price since any products transferred internally cause the selling division to lose the sales revenue to an outside customer. With the "perfectly competitive market" assumption, the selling division could sell all of its potential output to outside customers without affecting the market price.

Without the perfect market assumption, the economists' opportunity cost rule recommends that the optimal transfer price is the selling division's marginal cost.[41] Despite the clear demonstration by economists of the optimality of using marginal cost for most transfer pricing situations, companies rarely seem to use this practice.[42] Among the most common transfer pricing rules used by firms is some version of the full cost of the selling division, a practice that has yet to be shown by analytic methods to be optimal or even desirable in any situation. Thus, the transfer price issue remains poorly understood despite extensive studies during the past thirty years.[43]

A further improvement in our understanding of the planning and control functions of decentralized organizations was made by Robert Anthony.[44] Anthony proposed a hierarchical framework for the diverse planning and control activities performed by organizations.

Strategic Planning: the process of deciding on objectives of the organization, on changes in these objectives, on the resources used to attain these objectives, and on the policies that are to govern the acquisition, use, and disposition of these resources.

Management Control: the process by which managers assure that resources are obtained and used effectively and efficiently in the accomplishment of the organization's objectives.

Operational Control: the process of assuring that specific tasks are carried out effectively and efficiently.[45]

Anthony also made the distinction between accounting activities carried out to facilitate management decisions and control and those required to satisfy external constituencies.

Strategic planning, management control, and operational control are internally oriented. . . . There is a certain amount of confusion between these processes and financial accounting which has an entirely different orientation. . . . Society has developed certain financial accounting principles to which all businesses are expected to adhere, whereas no such externally imposed principles govern management control information.[46]

Anthony's framework for management control had been foreshadowed more than a decade earlier by Herbert Simon's investigation of the controllership function in decentralized organizations.[47] As part of understanding the multifaceted role of divisional controllers, Simon also articulated three functions of accounting information for control and decision making: "scorecard keeping," attention directing, and problem solving.

Anthony's interest in the management control practices of decentralized organizations was reinforced by his Harvard Business School colleagues, particularly John Dearden and Richard Vancil. They collectively produced textbooks[48] and a large number of cases that described contemporary management control practice. Also, David Solomons published a study, sponsored by the Financial Executives Institute, to document management control practices—including transfer pricing, budgeting, and the use of profits, return on investment, and residual income—useful for evaluating divisional performance.[49] In addition to surveying current practices, Solomons provided a summary of the economic theory underlying these practices.

The extensive documentation of actual management control practices stands in stark contrast to what is available to document and understand actual cost accounting practices in firms. Cost accounting textbooks and academic research continue to concentrate on highly simplified, frequently abstract representations of cost systems. The imbalance between our fairly good knowledge of firms' management control systems and our ignorance of their cost accounting systems is a curious phenomenon for which we do not have a satisfactory explanation.

Operations Research and Management Accounting

Perhaps cost accounting teaching and research focused more on simple models than on actual practice because of the influence of operations research and economics.

The discipline of operations research started in Great Britain during the late 1930s when analytically trained scientists—principally physicists, mathematicians, and statisticians—formulated mathematical models of real-world decision problems. Originally, the motivation was to improve allocation of resources such as radar and fighter aircraft during the Battle of Britain.[50] The effort expanded throughout the war years as modeling and optimization methods were applied to a broad range of operational and logistics problems. Assisting the operations research analysts were the newly developed electrical computing machines, both analog and digital, that could solve complex systems of equations.

After the war, the analysts turned their attention to modeling industrial problems and to solving the complex optimization problems found in this setting.[51] They were joined by mathematical economists who were expanding their "Theory of the Firm" by introducing more complex optimizing behavior at the firm level.[52] Great advances in both digital computing machines and in mathematical algorithms, such as the simplex method for solving large linear programming problems, led to a flourishing of the operations research (O.R.) discipline during the 1950s. Researchers, consultants, and internal O.R. corporate groups began to apply linear, nonlinear, and integer programming models, dynamic programming models, queuing theory, inventory theory, game theory, and decision theory to a broad array of managerial decision problems. The role of the computer, not just as an advanced and very fast calculating machine, but as an integral part of production and managerial processes, also started to emerge at this time.[53]

Eventually, the influence of O.R. spilled over into the management accounting area. Between 1960 and 1975, a stream (some might describe it as a torrent or flood) of articles appeared showing how operations research techniques could be applied to cost data to provide information relevant to a broad variety of management decisions and control problems. The techniques included mathematical programming techniques for optimizing product mix decisions in the presence of production and sales constraints; the use of probability and decision theory for analyzing cost-volume-profit decisions under uncertainty; computing opportunity costs and losses in the context of optimizations models; decision theory and dynamic programming approaches to determine when to investigate variances reported from the firm's accounting system; mathematical programming models for allocating overhead costs, service department costs, joint and by-product costs, and even capital costs (depreciation); and the use of statistical methods such as regression analysis for estimating fixed and variable costs.[54]

The introduction of these quantitative techniques, however, did not extend the domain of management accounting. The techniques were applied to tactical planning and control decisions firms had been making for the past century: assessing product profitability and determining improved product mixes, aiding make versus buy decisions, allocating costs to departments and to products, and analyzing the sources of deviation between actual and budgeted performance. The operations research literature could therefore be viewed as the successor to the scientific management era of cost accounting (1895–1915) in which careful attention was focused on improving the local efficiency of the workplace, on developing techniques to aid lower-level managerial decisions, and on monitoring operating performance.

Unlike the scientific management era, the major advances of which were made and described by practicing engineers and managers, the O.R. literature was developed almost exclusively by university researchers and communicated primarily to other academics. The researchers paid virtually no attention to working with actual organizations to implement their ideas or even to communicate very effectively with operating managers on the implications of their proposals for practice. In contrast, Wells,[55] reviewing early cost accounting innovations arising out of the scientific management movement, described the extensive communication among the U.S. mechanical engineers responsible for the new managerial technology.

A shop culture developed which had all the hallmarks of a gentlemen's club. Within the club, information was freely shared. The result was a vast mutually owned store of knowledge and experience closely akin to a body of scientific knowledge. . . .

Papers dealing with costing invariably described a system actually in use. They provided intimate detail of the systems installed in well-known machine shops.[56]

Also, we have seen in chapters 2–5 that the major developments in cost management and cost control occurred in the innovative enterprises of each era: the Lyman Mills Textile Corporation, the railroads, mass merchandisers, Carnegie Steel Company, Du Pont, and General Motors.

The contemporary academic literature on applying analytic techniques to management accounting problems was devoid of references to "systems actually in use" or to "systems installed in well-known [organizations]." Instead, the references were to the writings of other university researchers—economists, operations researchers, accountants, and the like. Contemporary researchers' knowledge of managerial issues derived not from studying decisions and procedures of actual firms, but from the stylized models of managerial and firm behavior articulated by "theorists" in other academic disciplines. Thus, the models were not developed for or tested on actual enterprises.

Information Economics: Single Person Decision Theory

During the late 1960s, a new approach developed for analyzing the content and value of accounting systems.

The information economics viewpoint emphasized deriving the demand for accounting information from the utility of the information for decision makers. The information economics approach is, in an important sense, the foundation discipline for understanding and analyzing management accounting systems. As articulated by one of its leading contributors:

Information Economics is the term given to research that analyzes the economic impact of and demand for alternative information systems. If we view accounting systems as information systems, then information economics must be viewed as a fundamental discipline in accounting research.[57]

Information economics achieved this lofty status by attacking the choice of management accounting systems at a fundamental level. It approached the subject not by attempting to understand what "true" costs actually are or by analyzing the information "needs" of managers. Rather, it attempted to derive the value of information from a formal model of how information will affect the beliefs, decisions, and rewards of decision makers as well as the cost of supplying the information to decision makers.

It would be difficult to quarrel with the fundamental assumptions of the information economics viewpoint. How can one disagree with an attempt to evaluate an information system based on its value to decision makers, relative to its cost? The problems arise in making this fundamental concept operational. To date, the information economics approach has been applied only in extremely simplistic settings and under highly restrictive assumptions. It has not been applied either normatively or descriptively to actual organizations. The main impact of information economics has been to elevate the benefit-cost approach as an important issue to be confronted by any cost system designer.[58]

Information Economics: Agency Theory

A recent extension of the information economics approach was made when researchers recognized that accounting systems did more than provide signals to decision makers. The numbers produced by accounting systems are often used as the basis for contracting between economic agents, such as between managers and subordinates or between managers and shareholders. The new approach, called principal/agent or, more simply, agency theory research, explicitly recognized the economic self-interests of the many users of accounting information. Baiman[59] in an excellent survey of the applications of agency theory to management accounting thought described this approach.

Because managerial accounting information is produced and used by individuals within a multiperson organizational setting, the benefit and cost of installing a managerial accounting procedure depend upon how people react to and use its output in that setting. The agency model of the firm is based on a description of individual behavior within a multiperson organization.

In agency theory the firm is viewed not as an individual, but merely as an overlapping set of contracts among principals and agents, each of whom is assumed to be motivated solely by self-interest.[60]

In fact, agency theory provided the analytic framework within which, at least in principle, we could model the demand for management control procedures as firms became more complex and required an increased degree of decentralization. Recall the development of new management control procedures by nineteenth-century organizations as they became more hierarchical and decentralized, with increased separation between owners of capital and managers entrusted with this capital (see material in chapters 2–5). Management accounting information was needed to motivate and evaluate the performance of production workers and lower-level managers in complex organizations. The recent agency theory research provides a mathematical representation of the demand for management accounting information in rudimentary decentralized firms. But mathematical and modeling difficulties have confined the management accounting applications of agency theory research to abstract models that do not represent any interesting managerial setting.[61]

Agency theory research remains a highly exploratory attempt to develop a formal theory of the demand for information to be used for contracting among the diverse interests of the firm. To the extent that it portrays a firm as something other than a monolithic entity, it aids our thinking about organizations. But because of mathematical difficulties and the consequent lack of realism of the models and their assumptions, the potential for agency theory research to inform or even understand managerial accounting practice will likely be realized, if at all, only many years in the future.

Management Accounting Thought by 1980: A Summary

Most of the writing in management accounting thought since 1920 has been contributed by academics, whether the insights on decision making by Clark, Edwards, and Coase or the more recent excursions into operations research, information economics, and agency theory. In order to illustrate their points, the academics have emphasized simple decision-making models in highly simplified firms—those producing one or only a few products, usually in a one-stage production process. The academics developed their ideas by logic and deductive reasoning. They did not attempt to study the problems actually faced by managers of organizations producing hundreds or thousands of products in complex production processes. Thus, it would be easy for

practicing executives to agree in principle with all the recommendations of academic researchers yet still find it difficult to apply the recommendations in their much more
complex organizations. Perhaps, too, the ideas that seem
eminently sensible when illustrated by academics for single-
product, single-activity firms are less powerful and relevant
in multiproduct, multistage processing organizations.

In contrast, the nineteenth- and early twentieth-century
management accounting innovations were made by industrialists and practitioners—the managers of early textile,
railroad, and merchandising companies such as Andrew
Carnegie, Pierre du Pont, Donaldson Brown, Alfred Sloan,
and the engineers of the scientific management movement.
What have management accounting practitioners been
doing for the past sixty years? If there has been much innovation between 1925 and 1980, other than the introduction
of discounted cash flow procedures discussed in this chapter,
the innovating practitioners have managed to keep it mostly
secret. While some innovations in organizations' planning,
budgeting, and control systems may have occurred, virtually
no new ideas have affected the design and use of cost management systems.

During the 1950s, the National Association of Accountants published a series of monographs that adequately summarized existing management accounting practice. Nevertheless, these books, dealing with topics such as breakeven
analysis, cost-volume-profit analysis, direct costing, and
fixed and variable cost estimates, did not represent significant departures from ideas already incorporated in textbooks like Vatter's *Managerial Accounting.* One can not find
examples of monographs written by practitioners describing
interesting innovations in management accounting procedures. A perusal of the journal *Management Accounting,* published for practicing management accountants by the National Association of Accountants, does not reveal any
startling innovations in practice published between 1955
and 1980.[62]

Thus, by 1980 we had arrived at an unfortunate situation. Researchers in universities were busy developing highly sophisticated models for management accounting in simplified, stylized production settings. The research was neither motivated by actual organizational phenomena nor tested nor even testable on the data from contemporary organizations. Meanwhile, practicing management accountants were not writing about either the problems or the innovations in their organizations. Unlike the situation a century before, the practitioner community was uninterested in management accounting research or innovation. Not surprisingly, in this situation actual management accounting systems provided few benefits to organizations. In some instances, the information reported by existing management accounting systems not only inhibited good decision making by managers, it might actually have encouraged bad decisions, a theme we will develop in the subsequent chapters.

Notes

1. J. Maurice Clark, *Studies in the Economics of Overhead Costs* (Chicago: University of Chicago Press, 1923), 51–54.

2. "Explanation of Rail Cost Finding Procedures and Principles Relating to the Use of Costs," in *Interstate Commerce Commission, Bureau of Accounts, Statement No. 7–63* (Washington, D.C.: November 1963).

3. Clark, *Studies*, 175.

4. *Ibid.*, 233–244.

5. *Ibid.*, 256–257.

6. *Ibid.*, 68.

7. These essays have been collected in J. M. Buchanan and G. F. Thirlby, eds., *L.S.E. Essays on Cost* (London: London School of Economics and Political Science, 1973).

8. J. R. Gould, "Opportunity Cost: The London Tradition," in Harold Edey and B. S. Yamey, eds., *Debits, Credits, Finance and Profits* (London: Sweet & Maxwell, 1974), 91–107.

9. R. S. Edwards, "The Rationale of Cost Accounting," in A. Plant, ed., *Some Modern Business Problems* (London: Longman, 1937), and reprinted in Buchanan and Thirlby, *L.S.E. Essays*, 73–92.

10. R. H. Coase, "Business Organization and the Accountant," in Bu-

chanan and Thirlby, *L.S.E. Essays*, 97–132; based on a series of twelve articles published in *Accountant* (October 1 to December 17, 1938).

11. *Ibid.*, 113.

12. Charles T. Horngren, "Cost and Management Accounting: Yesterday and Today," in M. Bromwich and A. Hopwood, eds., *Management Accounting: Current Issues and Research* (London: Pitman Press, 1987).

13. George Foster, "The Decision Making Theme in Expositions of Accounting," (Master's thesis, Sydney, Australia, 1971), as referenced in Horngren, "Cost."

14. William J. Vatter, *Managerial Accounting* (New York: Prentice-Hall, 1950). The preface to the book (page v) begins, "This book is the product of much experimentation, in efforts made at the University of Chicago to determine how the need of present and prospective managers for an understanding of accounting cost best be met. Since the answer to this problem is only tentatively drawn, the book is presented here in preliminary form so that it may be tested in other classrooms and in other circumstances than those in which it developed."

15. *Ibid.*, 102–103.

16. *Ibid.*, 105.

17. *Ibid.*, 106.

18. *Ibid.*, 506.

19. *Ibid.*, 506–507.

20. *Ibid.*, 510.

21. Gordon Shillinglaw, "Old Horizons and New Frontiers: The Future of Management Accounting," in H. P. Holzen, ed., *Management Accounting: 1980* (Urbana: University of Illinois, Department of Accounting, 1980), 6.

22. Eugene Grant, *Principles of Engineering Economy* (New York: Ronald Press, 1938).

23. George Terborgh, *Dynamic Equipment Policy* (New York: McGraw-Hill, 1949).

24. Joel Dean, *Capital Budgeting* (New York: Columbia University Press, 1951).

25. Joel Dean, "Measuring the Productivity of Capital," *Harvard Business Review* (January-February 1954), 120–130.

26. See, for example, the work of Charles Christenson, "Construction of Present Value Tables for Use in Evaluating Capital Investment Opportunities," *Accounting Review* (October 1955), 666–672; James H. Lorie and Leonard J. Savage, "Three Problems in Rationing Capital," *Journal of Business* (October 1955), 229–239; Myron J. Gordon and Eli Shapiro, "Capital Equipment Analysis: The Required Rate of Profit," *Management Science* (October 1956), 102–110; Ezra Solomon, "The Arithmetic of Capital-Budgeting Decisions," *Journal of Business* (April 1956); and J. Hirshleifer, "On the Theory of the Optimal Investment Decision," *Journal of Political Economy* (August 1958).

27. Harold Bierman and Seymour Smidt, *The Capital Budgeting Decision* (New York: Macmillan, 1960), was perhaps the first textbook to feature discounted cash flow for capital investment analysis.

28. See James B. Weaver, "Use of Engineering Economics by the Chemical Industry," *Engineering Economist* (Fall 1956), 19–25; and James B. Weaver and Robert J. Reilly, "Interest Rate of Return for Capital Expenditure Evaluation," *Chemical Engineering Progress* (October 1956), 405–412.

29. Much of the narrative in this paragraph came to our attention through an unpublished manuscript, "Some Aspects of the Development of Modern Capital Budgeting," by Scott H. Dulman. A useful historical perspective on managerial use of discounted cash flow appears in R. H. Parker, "Discounted Cash Flow in Historical Perspective," *Journal of Accounting Research* (Spring 1968), 58–71.

30. See, for example, C. H. Scovell, *Interest as a Cost* (New York: Ronald Press, 1924); A. H. Church, *Manufacturing Costs and Accounts* (New York: McGraw-Hill, 1917), 393–394; and Clark, *Studies*, 65–67, 239–240, 244–245, 255–256.

31. R. N. Anthony, "Accounting for Capital Costs," in R. N. Anthony, J. Dearden, and R. F. Vancil, eds., *Management Control Systems: Cases and Readings* (Homewood, Ill.: Irwin, 1965); and "Evaluating Divisional Performance by Return on Investment and Residual Income," Chapter V in David Solomons, *Divisional Performance: Measurement and Control* (New York: Financial Executives Research Foundation, 1965), 123–159.

32. This issue is discussed in John Dearden, "The Case Against ROI Control," *Harvard Business Review* (May–June 1969), 124–136, and in chapter 15, "Investment Centers: Return on Investment and Residual Income," in Robert S. Kaplan, *Advanced Management Accounting* (Englewood Cliffs, N.J.: Prentice-Hall, 1982), 522–526.

33. J. S. Reece and W. R. Cool, "Measuring Investment Center Performance," *Harvard Business Review* (May–June 1978), 28–46, 174–176.

34. R. F. Vancil, "General Electric Company, Background Note on Management Systems: 1981," 9–181–111 (Boston: Harvard Business School, 1981).

35. H. A. Simon, H. Guetzkow, G. Kozmetsky, and G. Tyndall, *Centralization vs. Decentralization in Organizing the Controller's Department* (New York: Controllership Foundation, 1954).

36. Three articles appeared almost simultaneously and apparently independently: P. W. Cook, "Decentralization and the Transfer-Price Problem," *Journal of Business* (April 1955), 87–94; J. Dean, "Decentralization and Intracompany Pricing," *Harvard Business Review* (July–August 1955), 65–74; and W. Stone, "Intracompany Pricing," *Accounting Review* (October 1956), 625–627.

37. Alfred P. Sloan, Jr., *My Years with General Motors* (Garden City, N.Y.: Doubleday, 1963), 48.

38. *Ibid.*, 49–50.

39. Donaldson Brown, "Centralized Control with Decentralized Responsibilities," *Annual Convention Series: No. 57*, American Management Association (New York, 1927) 3–24; reprinted in H. T. Johnson, ed., *Systems and Profits: Early Management Accounting at Du Pont and General Motors* (New York: Arno Press, 1980).

40. J. Hirshleifer, "On the Economics of Transfer Pricing," *Journal of Busi-*

ness (July 1956), 96–108; and his "Economics of the Divisionalized Firm," *Journal of Business* (April 1957), 96–108.

41. See the two articles by Hirschleifer cited in note 40 and chapter 6 in Solomons, *Divisional Performance.*

42. S. Umapathy, "Transfers between Profit Centers," in R. F. Vancil, *Decentralization: Managerial Ambiguity by Design* (Homewood, Ill.: Dow Jones-Irwin, 1978), 167–183.

43. R. G. Eccles, "Control with Fairness in Transfer Pricing," *Harvard Business Review* (November–December 1983), 149–161; and his *The Transfer Pricing Problem: A Theory for Practice,* (Lexington, Mass.: Lexington Books, 1985).

44. R. N. Anthony, *Planning and Control Systems: A Framework for Analysis,* (Boston: Harvard Business School, Division of Research, 1965).

45. *Ibid.,* 16–18.

46. *Ibid.,* 21.

47. Simon, Guetzkow, Kozmetsky, and Tyndall, *Centralization vs. Decentralization.*

48. Anthony, Dearden, and Vancil, *Management Control Systems.*

49. Solomons, "Evaluating Divisional Performance."

50. H. Larnder, "The Origin of Operational Research," *Operations Research* (March–April 1984), 465–475.

51. Two influential books by leading pioneers in the operations research field are Philip M. Morse and George E. Kimball, *Methods of Operations Research* (New York: John Wiley, 1951); and C. West Churchman, R. L. Ackoff, and E. L. Arnoff, *Introduction to Operations Research* (New York: Wiley, 1957).

52. A highly influential work was Tjalling C. Koopmans, ed., *Activity Analysis of Production and Allocation* (New York: John Wiley, 1951).

53. Herbert Simon was one of the earliest scholars to recognize the powerful impact computers would have on managerial processes; see, for example, his *The New Science of Management Decision* (New York: Prentice-Hall, 1960).

54. This material is surveyed in R. S. Kaplan, "Application of Quantitative Models in Managerial Accounting: A State of the Art Survey," *Management Accounting-State-of-the-Art, Beyer Lecture Series* (Madison: University of Wisconsin 1977), 29–71; and is explicated in his textbook *Advanced Management Accounting* (Englewood Cliffs, N.J.: Prentice-Hall; 1982).

55. M. C. Wells, "Some Influences on the Development of Cost Accounting," *Accounting Historians Journal* (Fall 1977), 47–61.

56. *Ibid.,* 51–52.

57. G. A. Feltham, "Financial Accounting Research: Contributions of Information Economics and Agency Theory," in R. Mattessich, ed., *Modern Accounting Research: History, Survey, and Guide,* Canadian Certified General Accountants' Research Foundation Monograph No. 7 (Vancouver, 1984), 179.

58. This point has been emphasized by Horngren in "Cost and Management Accounting" (cited in note 12), and in Kathy Williams, "Charles T. Horngren: Management Accounting's Renaissance Man," *Management Accounting* (January 1986), 28.

59. Stanley Baiman, "Agency Research in Managerial Accounting: A Survey," *Journal of Accounting Literature* (Spring 1982), 154–213.

60. *Ibid.*, 155.

61. This criticism is explicated in R. S. Kaplan, "The Evolution of Management Accounting," *Accounting Review* (July 1984), 404–407.

62. See R. S. Kaplan, "The Impact of Management Accounting Research on Policy and Practice," in John W. Buckley, ed., *The Impact of Accounting Research on Policy and Practice, 1981 Proceedings of the Arthur Young Professors' Roundtable* (Reston, Va.: Council of Arthur Young Professors, 1981), 57–76.

CHAPTER 8

The 1980s: The Obsolescence of Management Accounting Systems

Visits, contemporary writings, and extensive conversations[1] reveal the following characteristics of typical management accounting systems in the 1980s. For the most part, companies are continuing to use the same cost systems that existed twenty or thirty years ago. While all the systems are installed and running on computers, few show any difference in design philosophy to reflect the increased computational power of digital computers. Perhaps twenty years ago, when Management Information Systems (MIS) personnel or computer types first wandered into the factory, fresh from their success in automating financial systems—payroll, accounts receivable, and accounts payable—they automated, with few changes, the manual or electro-mechanical cost system they found there.

Because the 1950 vintage systems were either operated manually or with the limited processing power of punch card mechanical machines, the cost systems incorporated many simplifying assumptions. Overhead costs were combined into large, frequently plant-wide, overhead pools. The large overhead pools were then allocated to cost centers in different ways. Some factories simply allocated all costs directly to cost centers based on estimated direct labor hours or dollars. Others were somewhat more scientific. For each overhead pool, they chose some measure for allocating the pool to individual cost centers. For example, building expenses such as depreciation, property taxes, insurance, factory utilities (heat, light), and housekeeping would be allocated by floor space (for example, square feet occupied by each cost center); electricity by rated machine capacity; indirect labor by direct labor; equipment maintenance perhaps by machine book value; and so on.

However overhead costs were distributed to cost centers, virtually all companies, in a second allocation step, allocated cost center costs to products based on direct labor. That is, after all overhead costs were allocated to each cost center, the costs were then divided by the direct labor hours expected to be worked in the cost center during the next year—based on a forecast of estimated production—to derive a cost center rate per direct labor hour. Typically, this fully burdened cost center labor rate was at least four times the actual direct labor rate paid to workers. In some highly automated cost centers, it was not unusual for the rate to be ten or even fifteen and twenty times the hourly labor rate.

An Example of a Typical Cost System

Figure 8–1 presents an example of an actual product's standard cost sheet for a company following this procedure. The overhead cost rates for the plant's production departments are shown in Figure 8–2. The cost system has many interesting characteristics. Material and labor costs

Figure 8–1   Standard Cost Report for Valve 60073

	Material Cost	Labor Cost	Overhead Cost	Total Cost
PURCHASED PART	$1.1980			$1.1980
OPERATION				
Drill, face, tap (2)		$0.0438	$0.2404	0.2842
Degrease		0.0031	0.0337	0.0368
Remove burrs		0.0577	0.3241	0.3818
Total Cost, This Item	1.1980	0.1046	0.5982	1.9008
Other subassemblies	0.3253	0.2994	1.8519	2.4766
Total Cost, Subassemblies	1.5233	0.4040	2.4501	4.3773
Assemble and test		0.1469	0.4987	0.6456
Pack without paper		0.0234	0.1349	0.1583
Total Cost, This Item	$1.5233	$0.5743	$3.0837	$5.1813
COST COMPONENT %	29%	11%	60%	100%

Figure 8–2   Overhead Burden Rates Per Direct Labor Hour

Department	Activity	Overhead Burden Rate Per Direct Labor Hour
201	Assembly	$24.21
203	Automatic manufacturing	67.65
205	Plating	84.16
213	Packing	40.51
214	General machining	40.07

are estimated from engineering studies and current prices (for material and labor). The distribution of overhead, which represents 60 percent of the costs attributed to the product, is based on direct labor cost, even though labor is the smallest of the three cost categories. Despite the errors introduced by allocating 60 percent of costs based on a cost category representing only 11 percent of costs, the factory accountants, and their computers, have reported the cost data out to five significant digits. Given the arbitrary allocation of overhead, it is unlikely that the first digit of the five is correct!

Some companies do not even have a cost system as sophisticated as the one that generated the product cost data of Figure 8–1. Note that in the final product cost of Figure 8–1, the amount of material, labor, and overhead is clearly identified:

Material	$1.5233
Labor	.5743
Overhead	3.0837
Total	$5.1813

Many companies, however, combine material, labor, and overhead costs at each stage into a single cost that, when transferred to the next stage, is identified as the material input cost to that stage. Using this approach with the cost data in Figure 8–1, the total cost of $4.3773 for all subassemblies becomes the material cost for the final production stage of assembly, test, and packaging. The final product's cost sheet would appear as shown below.

Material	$4.3773
Labor	.1703
Overhead	.6336
Total	$5.1813

While the final product cost is the same, as it obviously must be, all semblance of cost structure has been destroyed. Because "Material" cost at the final stage includes labor and overhead costs from all previous stages, it is impossible to make any estimate of direct or prime costs, much less to make even a crude separation into fixed or variable costs.

Companies that wished to understand the "value added" of their production process, for pricing or productivity analyses, would have to perform special studies. Their cost accounting system would be useless for such purposes.

How could companies have installed and continued to use such a cost accounting system? There seems only one plausible explanation. The above system is a beautiful example of costs "attaching" to a product as it flows through the factory. It is a system that is illustrated in virtually every introductory cost accounting textbook. Material, labor, and overhead at each stage are added, or attached, to the costs incurred at all previous stages, with the new sum used to transfer accumulated costs to the next stage. All factory costs eventually are attached to products, and the cost accountants can demonstrate a fully absorbed product cost at the end of the production process. Such a system is simple to install, simple to operate, and simple to understand. Only one account is needed to transfer the cost of a component or subassembly from one stage to the next, thereby saving storage and processing time (probably an important consideration when the system was operated manually). The system generates product costs that satisfy all external reporting constituencies—stockholders, tax authorities, regulators, and creditors. That for managers it is at best useless, and more likely misleading, seems less important. After all, when product costs are reported with five and six significant digits, who would suspect that the first digit is wrong?

Apart from the destruction of cost structure induced by the above "cost attaching" system, even the three-account-per-product (material, labor, and overhead) system exhibited in Figure 8–1 has serious shortcomings. Certainly its inability to separate short-term variable from fixed costs would leave scholars from earlier in this century (recall the writings of Clark, Coase, and Vatter we discussed in chapter 7) duly unimpressed.

Adverse Consequences of Direct Labor Allocation Systems

By using direct labor to allocate overhead costs to products, cost center managers and product managers have their cost-reduction attention directed solely to direct labor savings. With overhead burden rates of 400 to 1000 percent, small savings in direct labor time have large impacts on cost distributions and product costs. Enormous amounts of time and effort are committed to the detailed recording and processing of labor time. In one instance, we saw a plant where 65 percent of its general ledger computer code processed direct labor transactions even though direct labor represented only 4 percent of total costs. Consequently, it is not unusual to see thousands of dollars of industrial engineering time devoted to saving tenths of hours of direct labor time. At the end of an accounting period, much management time is spent analyzing unfavorable labor variances of seemingly trivial amounts.

Little attention is focused on the overhead accounts, where costs are actually increasing most rapidly. If a production or product manager succeeds in reducing the growth in some overhead cost category, the benefit is distributed broadly to all cost centers and products in the factory because of the allocation procedure. Therefore, rational managers focus their attention where it does them the most "good." To reduce their allocated costs, they attempt to reduce their direct labor charges since that is the account by which all other costs are attached to their cost centers and products. Consequently, less attention is devoted to escalating overhead costs than to small increments in labor costs. We have even seen instances where managers attempt to have workers in "low-burden" rate departments perform work that is supposed to be done in machining departments because these relatively "unburdened" workers are much cheaper to use. In an extreme example, highly paid engineers, whose fully burdened labor cost was less than a factory worker's (because factory overhead had not been distributed to the engineering department), were pressed into service to perform normal machining operations.

Managers soon discover that any process that requires relatively large amounts of direct labor seems very expensive. In fact, it usually becomes easy to find a supplier that can produce the labor-intense component or subassembly cheaper than the cost center can fabricate it. In such a case, costs are apparently lowered by subcontracting. Companies start to buy rather than make. Increasingly, firms subcontract more of their production activities, and not just to local suppliers. "Low labor cost" suppliers, first in the southern part of the United States and subsequently farther away, in East Asia or Latin America, are used for basic fabrication. Left out of such an analysis, however, is the recognition that much of the factory overhead is not driven by direct labor hours so that outsourcing saves only a relatively small fraction of the component's costs.

Actually, overhead costs tend to rise with increased amounts of subcontracting. Subcontracting imposes additional demands on the purchasing department to generate specifications for the component and to investigate qualified vendors; on the scheduling department to provide delivery schedules to the vendor; on the receiving and inspection department to process incoming items; on materials handling departments to place purchased components into storage and bring them out to production when needed; and on the accounts payable department to pay the vendor. All of these new support activities add to overhead costs. But these newly added costs are not traced to the purchased component because it has zero direct labor content. Instead, the higher overhead costs are shifted to the labor-intense products and processes still remaining in the plant.

The direct labor allocation base also distorts product costs and introduces unintended cross subsidies by shifting costs from less labor-intense products to more labor-intense products. Even when cost centers use a flexible budget, which identifies and separates variable and fixed expenses, the variable portion of costs is assumed to vary with direct labor activity. Although the assumption may be appropriate for some cost categories, other variable costs vary with machine hours, with set-ups, with number of inspections, or with materials movement and handling. Products with relatively low direct labor content—say, low-volume jobs that require special set-ups, handling, and quality control—have their variable overhead costs shifted onto products with high direct labor hours. That is, costs are shifted from small-volume, frequent set-up jobs onto long-running, infrequent set-up standard products that require no special handling or attention. In this situation, the factory starts to take on a broader product line (it is becoming a "full-line producer") that includes more low-volume products requiring frequent set-ups, special expediting, engineering design features, quality assurance, and engineering change orders to fine tune the production process.

The additional costs of these activities, however, are traced not to the products that generate the added activities, but to the products with the large number of direct labor hours. Thus, the mature, high-volume, infrequently set-up, stable products become "more costly" as the firm expands its product line and offers special customer features. The mature products subsidize the firm's product proliferation activities through the aggregation and averaging effects of a direct labor cost allocation system.

In some cases, focused foreign manufacturers introduce products in direct competition with the firm's high-volume mature products, and at significantly lower prices. The firm, believing from its cost system that it can not make money at the lower prices now being offered by foreign manufacturers, takes steps to reduce its dependence on these now "unprofitable" products or else looks to produce the mature, stable products in low-wage countries.

In addition to introducing unintended cross subsidies among products, the direct labor overhead allocation system inhibits cost planning and cost control. Consider the example of a relatively sophisticated cost system in which fixed and variable costs are separated so that a flexible budget can be prepared. In almost all such systems, standard direct labor hours are assumed for the basis of variation. But when actual and budgeted production and mix of production differ, either because of market conditions or because the firm changes its desired product mix based on the "costs" and margins reported by its cost system, then even without any spending or efficiency variances an overhead variance will be reported at the end of the period. The variance occurs because many variable overhead expenses vary not with standard direct labor hours, as assumed by the flexible budget, but with other measures of activity such as those mentioned earlier (machine hours, kilowatt hours, setups, materials). The use of only one activity measure, direct labor hours, reduces the ability of the cost system to predict the variation in cost with changes in the volume and mix of actual production. The variance is essentially impossible for a firm to explain. It becomes one of the unsolved mysteries of the firm's cost accounting system, an unexplained variance that each period is closed to the income statement with mutual suspicion between accountants and operating managers because of the difficulty of tracing its source.

The problems introduced by a direct labor-based overhead allocation scheme have gone largely unnoticed by academic accountants. Textbooks, research, and teaching continue to emphasize product costing and cost control in extremely simplified settings. Usually one product is considered; rarely are more than three treated. It is useful to illustrate basic concepts in simplistic settings, but the problems that arise with direct labor allocation systems can not be illustrated by simple, one-product examples. Such simple examples usually display each overhead account associated with the product including, perhaps, a flexible budget for each cost account. In this situation, all overhead costs are traced directly to each product; there is no rationale for using a system to allocate overhead costs to products indirectly, such as by using a single-activity measure like direct labor hours.

The need for overhead allocation determined by a single-activity measure (direct labor) arises only when firms manufacture many different products—dozens, hundreds, or even thousands. In this case, firms find it too costly to compute the amount of each category of overhead used by each individual product. It is much simpler to allocate each category of overhead to a smaller number of cost centers than to a larger number of products. Also, predicting the aggregate volume of activity in each cost center is usually easier than predicting the amount of production of each product. Finally, it appears easy to find objective bases for allocating plant overhead to cost centers (floor space, machine book value, budgeted labor or machine hours, for example). With all costs traced to the cost-center level, a second stage must be introduced in the allocation process to distribute overhead from cost centers to products. Because information on the direct labor hours in each cost center already exists on the standard cost sheet, the measure is convenient to use for distributing overhead costs from cost centers to products. But the academic examples, dealing with only one to three products at a time, never see the need for this two-stage allocation process. Since it is not considered, it is not studied or taught. Thus, perhaps the most important feature of how overhead costs are allocated to products is absent from virtually all textbooks, teaching, and research.

Timeliness

Typical 1980s cost accounting systems also fail a timeliness criterion. Recall Vatter's emphasis (see chapter 7) on the value of timely managerial accounting data.

It may be more important to make available essential internal control information for managerial purposes than to prepare overall statements. . . . As a result of various time-consuming operations [to prepare periodic financial statements], it is seldom possible to obtain financial statements of the conventional type very soon after the period has closed. . . . Incomplete details of an operation, obtained promptly, may be of more use than complete information that is available only after a considerable lapse of time.[2]

There seems to be a general accounting rule that any accounting report for a period will appear just before the middle of the subsequent period. Therefore, quarterly reports usually appear shortly before the middle of the subsequent quarter, monthly reports in the middle of the following month, and daily reports early the next day. Most cost accounting systems follow a monthly cycle to correspond with the preparation of a complete monthly profit and loss statement for divisional and corporate headquarters. A great deal of attention is devoted to performing "fast closes" so that the monthly P&L can be produced as early in the subsequent month as possible. Special seminars are occasionally held at professional meetings of corporate accountants to facilitate the exchange of information on how to accomplish fast closings. But even with the fastest of closings, the cost information is produced too late, and at too aggregate a level, to help short-term production control.

Monthly data from a few accounts may be relevant for cost control. But most of the production action—for control of labor, materials, machine utilization, quality, inventory levels, utilities, and output—occurs daily. If a problem arises in any of these areas, production managers will need to deal with it immediately; they can not wait until sometime the following month to discover production variances. Also, apart from arriving too late to be of much use for controlling the production system, the information is usually produced at too aggregate a level to be able to pinpoint the source of adverse, or even favorable, production variances.

Of course, production managers, being clever, resourceful people, do not operate without short-term information on their operations. Many production managers have installed their own short-term cost control systems to collect relevant data on a timely basis. Occasionally, these systems are "back-of-an-envelope" collections of hourly or daily data on a few key indicators. Alternatively, some production managers have surreptitiously hired their own accountant to design and operate a completely separate local cost control system, a practice that has recently been greatly facilitated by the increased availability of inexpensive personal computers with powerful spreadsheet languages. The local and unofficial systems are not comprehensive. They can not be used to value inventory or to produce periodic statements with fully absorbed costs. But they serve their masters well. They produce relevant data on a timely basis at the appropriate level in the organization for managerial control.

Thus, the "official" cost accounting system produces information too late and at too aggregate a level to be helpful for operational control. Also, the cost data incorporate allocations that are inconsistent with the actual factory production process and product mix. If the information is not useful for accurately tracing costs to products (as argued earlier in the chapter) and is not used by production managers for their day-to-day operational control decisions, what purpose is being served by these systems? The modal view (at least outside the finance office) is that the "official" cost accounting system has been designed by accountants mainly to satisfy the apparent demand by senior management for a monthly profit and loss statement.

The Financial Accounting
Mentality Triumphs

Typical 1980s cost accounting systems are helpful neither for product costing nor for operational cost control; they do not provide information useful for cost management. The rationalization for their production and existence seems only for the periodic, usually monthly, financial reports prepared for senior management. As we saw in chapters 4 and 5, the preparation of periodic profit and loss statements for senior management had its roots in the decentralization movement earlier in the twentieth century. The periodic return on investment (ROI) measure was developed and used by innovative organizations such as the Du Pont Corporation and General Motors. In order to produce a monthly profit and loss (P&L) statement and ROI measure, the accounting group needed to be able to close the books each month to estimate and record all accruals and to make a reasonable allocation of the period's production expenses between inventory and cost of goods sold. There is no doubt that ROI control and the profit center form of organization were not only greatly useful but likely necessary for the growth and prosperity of large, hierarchical organizations during the past sixty years. Nevertheless, despite the successes, problems associated with short-term performance measures such as ROI have become painfully evident in recent years.

The problems likely arise from an excessive focus on achieving short-term financial performance. Many articles and books[3] have criticized U.S. executives for their narrow, short-term outlook and their overreliance on financial transactions to achieve immediate profitability objectives. Rather than rely on academic criticisms of executives, though, we offer criticism from executives themselves.

Dun's *Business Month* queried the 230 chief executives who are members of its President's Panel. . . . A thumping majority of the

panelists agrees that management in the U.S. is excessively concerned with the short-term, at the expense of longer-range considerations that may be far more important.... Most of the executives differ among themselves only on how much the shortcoming
results from outside pressure for quarter-to-quarter performance,
particularly from Wall Street.[4]

The following quotations are a sampling of comments by
the chief executives:

It behooves U.S. management to look beyond the immediate future. The Japanese, West Germany, and Switzerland [sic] have
taught us the need to address long-term results.

The current trend toward high compensation rewards based on
the immediate year's performance rather than long-range growth
is a serious disincentive to management objectivity.

Amid today's takeover scramble, short-term performance is
needed for survival.

The financial community's stress on very, very short range performance can be ignored only at a company's peril, especially if it
is contemplating equity or debt financing.

It would be a very healthy change if quarterly reports were no
longer required.[5]

Problems with managing for short-term financial objectives arise because operating managers learn that there are
a variety of ways to meet profit and ROI goals. Initially, and
perhaps for many years after profit centers and ROI control
were introduced, managers attempted to achieve good performance by making operating and investment decisions to
develop new and better products, to increase sales, and to
reduce operating costs. These desirable actions were certainly characteristic of the activities undertaken during the
Alfred Sloan years at General Motors, where the profit center form of organization was first implemented.[6] But over
time, it occurred to some managers that during difficult
times, when sales were decreasing, operating costs were in-

creasing, margins were being squeezed, and innovative products were not forthcoming from the company's laboratories, that profits and ROI targets could still be achieved by working a little harder in the finance office. Managers discovered that profits could be "earned" not just by selling more or producing for less, but also by engaging in a variety of nonproductive activities: exploiting accounting conventions, engaging in financial entrepreneurship, and reducing discretionary expenditures.

Historical cost accounting procedures and "generally accepted accounting principles" (GAAP) provide ample opportunities for executives to manage their income and investment measures. As one example, considerable discretion exists for the timing of revenue and expense recognition so as to exhibit steady earnings growth or to meet budgeted income or expense goals for the current period. Occasionally, managers even go beyond what is "generally accepted" to meet budgeted income and expense targets.[7] One-shot opportunities to increase income in the accounting office arise when firms adopt more liberal accounting conventions, for instance, when they switch from accelerated to straight-line depreciation, change from deferral to flow-through for the investment tax credit, lengthen depreciable lives, capitalize previously expensed items, assume higher rates of return on pension fund assets, amortize past and prior pension costs over a longer time period, and switch from completed contract to percentage of completion method for long-term contracts. One-shot earnings boosts can also be created by selling assets whose market values are well in excess of their book values (if the assets are still needed, they frequently can be be leased back to the original owner) or extinguishing liabilities (say, by repurchasing debt at a discount) whose market values are below book values.

GAAP accounting conventions also encourage a financial accounting mentality in many corporate executives. The extensive description in chapters 2–5 of the early history of management accounting practices clearly showed that these practices were developed to serve the operating needs of senior executives. As their organizations became more hierarchical, dispersed, and decentralized, the executives needed financial measures to help them understand their internal operations, to make new product and investment decisions, and to motivate and evaluate the performance of their managers and workers. In contrast, the accounting practices used by most contemporary U.S. companies are mandated by such external reporting authorities as the Financial Accounting Standards Board (FASB), the Securities and Exchange Commission (SEC), and the Internal Revenue Service (IRS). Despite the increased availability of powerful, and steadily less costly, data processing systems, companies typically keep only one set of books (or at most two if tax and financial reporting practices differ). Management accounting practices therefore follow, and become subservient to, financial reporting practices.

Thus, many of a company's investments in its long-term economic health such as R&D, process improvements, advertising and promotion, employee training and skill development, and quality improvements are considered expenses of the period because that is the mandated treatment for financial and tax reporting. If the FASB requires that certain types of leases must be capitalized for external reporting, then those leases, and only those leases, are generally capitalized for internal reporting too. Since no external reporting authority requires an explicit charge for the use of invested capital, companies tend not to burden their profit centers with such a cost of capital either, a practice that helps to explain the lack of widespread acceptance of the residual income modification to the ROI measure (see chapter 7). Instead, many companies assign capital costs to profit centers by attempting to allocate corporate interest expense to divisions. This curious practice makes investments seem more costly when the firm uses a lower cost source of financing (debt instead of equity) and penalizes lines of business (such as a real estate division) that are able to finance much of their operations with debt rather than with corporate equity. Among the reasons given for the practice of allocating interest expense rather than charging all assets with some risk-adjusted cost of capital derived from current market rates is that the sum of the divisional capital charges will "over-recover" the company's actual interest expense and, therefore, the divisional income statements will not sum to the corporate income statement.[8]

Financial accounting practices also lead to bad cost accounting in the allocation of pension costs. All can agree that prior service costs are sunk costs. They represent an obligation of a company for the past service of its employees that no current or future action of the company can affect (except, as some companies have done, to abandon the pension plan entirely and shift the liability to the federal Pension Benefit Guaranty Corporation, an action that will not likely be available to many corporations). The amortization of prior pension service costs must, however, be recognized as a current expense in the company's financial statements. Therefore, many companies allocate prior service costs to their divisions.

In performing the allocation, some basis for allocation must be selected. In one company we examined, the personnel department decided, reasonably enough, that the allocation should be proportional to pension benefits already earned. With this procedure, a plant with an older work force received almost all of its division's prior service costs; several newer plants with much younger workers bore almost none of the burden. Since the workers in the older plant also had more vacation time each year, earned through seniority, the allocated pension cost was spread over a fewer number of labor hours worked than for the newer plants (using a direct labor hour-based cost accounting system). The allocation of the prior period pension expense produced,

by itself, a $4 per hour cost penalty on the older plant rela-
tive to the newer plants. The division reacted to the "cost
differential" by shifting some work from the older plant to
the newer ones. In addition, the products remaining in the
older plant lost market share because their price was raised
in an attempt to earn a satisfactory margin over the plant's
high labor costs. Eventually, the older plant was closed.

Perhaps the plant was closed because the higher actual
costs of its more senior, unionized employees made it non-
competitive with newer, more modern plants. But perhaps
the older plant could have survived and filled a valuable
niche in the division's manufacturing strategy had the company's financial accounting mentality not excessively burdened it by attempting to recover an arbitrarily allocated
sunk cost.

Apparently, the original profit center concept has become distorted. Rather than treat profit centers as entities
linked to produce overall corporate gains, they have become
treated as mini-companies with allocated corporate expenses so that they can be managed as independent financial
entities. This concept, quite different from the one envi-
sioned by Alfred Sloan and Donaldson Brown when they
established General Motors' divisionalized structure, places
corporate priorities on financial, not operating, management. In this view, senior corporate-level executives become
portfolio managers, evaluating the risk-reward tradeoffs of
their operating divisions and making decisions based on
summary financial measures of performance. But they do
not penetrate the divisional structure to make value-creating investments and decisions.

During the past two decades, executives have also
learned how to generate earnings by financial transactions.
Occasionally, executives have found it easier to generate
earnings through creative financial transactions than
through developing innovative products and efficient production processes. The transactions involve creative re-

arrangement of ownership claims through mergers and acquisitions, divestitures and spin-offs, leveraged buy-outs, and sale-leaseback arrangements. They also include creative financing transactions such as off balance sheet financing, use of facilities financed by tax-free municipal borrowing, well-structured leasing activities, discounted debt repurchases, debt swaps, and debt defeasance.

Some of these activities may create value to shareholders; current research is still attempting to sort out the net effect of these financial activities, some of which undo seemingly clever financial transactions accomplished several years earlier. Still, it is hard to believe that a focus on creating wealth by clever financing and rearrangement of ownership claims will help companies survive in the global competition of the 1980s and beyond. Ultimately, wealth must be created by imaginative and intelligent investment in assets and the proper management of them, not by devising novel financing and ownership arrangements for assets.

But perhaps the most damaging dysfunctional behavior induced by a preoccupation with short-term profit center performance is the incentive for senior managers to reduce expenditures on discretionary and intangible investments. When sluggish sales or escalating costs make near-term profit targets hard to achieve, managers often try to prop up short-term earnings by cutting expenditures on R&D, promotion, distribution, quality improvement, applications engineering, human resources, and customer relations—all of which, of course, are vital to a company's long-term performance. The immediate effect of such reductions is to boost reported profitability, but at the expense of sacrificing the company's long-term competitive position.

The opportunity for companies, or their profit centers, to increase reported incomes by sacrificing long-term economic health illustrates a fundamental flaw in the financial accounting model. The flaw compromises the role of short-term profits as a valid and reliable indicator of a company's economic health. A company's economic value is not merely the sum of the values of its tangible assets, whether measured at historic cost, replacement cost, or current market prices. It also includes the value of intangible assets: the stock of innovative products, the knowledge of flexible and high-quality production processes, employee talent and morale, customer loyalty and product awareness, reliable suppliers, efficient distribution network, and the like.

In principle, we could assign values to the stock of each of these intangible assets. Then, when the company decreased its expenditures on these assets, their subsequent decline in value would lower the company's reported income. We do not, however, have methods to value objectively a company's intangible assets. Therefore, reported earnings can not show the company's decline in value when it depletes its stock of intangible assets. It is this defect in the financial accounting model that makes the quarterly or annual income number an inadequate summary of the change in value of the company during the period. In earlier years, when companies gained competitive advantage mainly through economies of scale and low-cost production, the accounting model defect was not significant. But for contemporary organizations, the intangible assets may be the most critical. Therefore, recent overemphasis on achieving superior short-term earnings performance is occurring just at the time when such performance has become a far less valid indicator of changes in the company's long-term competitive position.

Why Are Problems with ROI Appearing Only Now?

It is reasonable to wonder why the problems just described did not emerge earlier. Were Alfred Sloan or Pierre du Pont concerned with their divisional managers curtailing profitable investments in their tangible and intangible resources in order to increase their divisional ROI measure? Probably not.

First, there was apparently less pressure for short-term financial performance in the 1920s and 1930s than existed in the 1970s and 1980s. For example, the pricing formula used in General Motors (see chapter 5) was designed to generate a competitive rate of return over an entire business cycle. The goal was not to show steady year-to-year earnings increases. Years of slack demand, during business contractions, were recognized as normal occurrences and not the signal to contract expenditures on new product development, marketing, or process improvements. Today, pressures from professional investment managers for short-term performance may discourage company managers from making long-term risky investments.

Second, perhaps managers were promoted less often in the smaller organizations of the 1920s and 1930s. Many of the difficulties in profit center evaluations arise from attempting to measure performance over too brief a period, before the long-term adverse consequences from making short-term decisions become apparent. If division managers remained in their jobs for at least five to seven years, there would be less incentive to curtail investments that have longer-term and perhaps difficult to value benefits.

Third, the smaller size of organizations in the twenties may have made more obvious to senior executives when division managers sacrificed long-term value to achieve short-term profit performance. The much larger global organizations of the 1980s, particularly those which take pride in running "by the numbers," may be more vulnerable to short-term optimizing actions by decentralized managers. Thus, the increased size of organizations, without corresponding changes in control and measurement systems, created an opportunity for decentralized managers to take dysfunctional actions.

Fourth, more of the senior management ranks of contemporary organizations are staffed by managers with little
technological or production experience. Earlier in this century, senior managers either were the founders of their organizations or at least had worked their way up through the
operations of the organizations. In the 1980s, more corporate leadership comes from the professional managerial
class, MBAs and CPAs, many of whom are untrained in and
unfamiliar with the technology of the firm's products and
processes. As a consequence, they are less knowledgeable
about how to create value through improved products and
processes and rely more on creating value through finance
and accounting activities, pejoratively referred to by critics
as paper entrepreneurship.[9]

A fifth reason for the decline in value for short-term
divisional profit measures can be attributed to the widespread adoption of executive bonus plans based on accounting measures. General Motors had an accounting-based bonus plan more than sixty-five years ago,[10] but only in the
past twenty to thirty years have accounting-based performance plans become prevalent in U.S. corporations. Although
problems with these plans are well known,[11] they are still
used extensively. Senior executives whose annual and deferred compensation are strongly influenced by reported annual income are surely able to communicate effectively to
their subordinates the importance they place on achieving
annual profit targets.

Sixth, the environment of the 1980s, described in the
next chapter, is sufficiently different from that earlier in the
century so that any management control system, even one
that has served so well for so many years, will likely prove
inadequate to the changed circumstances. Given the radical
changes in the competitive environment, changes in the
global macroeconomic environment, and rapid world-wide
movement of technology and capital, it is unlikely that the
cost accounting and management control systems devised

for the 1925 environment can still be as useful sixty years later.

Summary

The obsolescence of contemporary management accounting systems has likely created significant problems for the managers of large, diversified organizations. In chapters 2 through 5, we traced how management accounting systems evolved to serve the informational needs of managers in ever more complex enterprises: from textile factories in the early nineteenth century through the large multidivisional enterprises that emerged in the 1920s. Throughout this evolution, management accounting procedures played a critical role in providing managers with information about the efficiency and profitability of internal processes. The information enabled managers of large organizations to achieve significant gains from increased size (economies of scale) and increased diversity of operations (economies of scope). Rather than becoming cumbersome and unwieldy with their larger size and scope of operations, these nineteenth- and early twentieth-century enterprises were able to outperform smaller and simpler entities that did not internalize multiple activities within the same organization.

Contemporary cost accounting and management control systems, such as those described in this chapter, are no longer providing accurate signals about the efficiency and profitability of internally managed transactions. Consequently, managers are not getting information to help them compare the desirability of internal versus external transactions. Without the receipt of appropriate cost and profitability information, the ability of the "visible hand" to effectively manage the myriad transactions that occur in a complex hierarchy has been severely compromised.

When senior management no longer receives accurate

information about the efficiency and effectiveness of internal operations, the organization becomes vulnerable to competition from smaller and more focused organizations. Smaller organizations that may be conducting a higher fraction of transactions in the marketplace than within the hierarchy—for example, small steel mills that purchase already processed raw materials, such as scrap, rather than produce steel starting from raw materials—become more efficient than giant enterprises that attempt to manage complex conversion processes with inadequate information. Also, more focused enterprises will compete by concentrating on a narrow product line or range of internally managed activities. The informational needs of enterprises concentrating on a narrow range of activities or products are much less than for those attempting to manage multiple steps in a conversion process or offering full and even unrelated lines of products. Focused organizations will become highly efficient in their narrow product segments or range of productive processes and will outperform diversified organizations that no longer can assess the relative profitability of their varied, frequently unrelated, activities. Whatever scale economies large diversified enterprises attempt to achieve through centralized financing or other administrative activities will be dissipated by their inability to respond to competitive pressures from simpler or more focused organizations. If large, vertically integrated or multidivisional enterprises are to remain successful in the future, they will need to examine whether their management accounting systems can provide relevant signals on their competitive position in the marketplace.

Notes

1. R. S. Kaplan, "Accounting Lag: The Obsolescence of Cost Accounting Systems," in K. Clark, R. H. Hayes, and C. Lorenz, *Technology and Productivity:*

The Uneasy Alliance (Boston: Harvard Business School Press, 1985), 195–226; see also R. S. Kaplan, "Yesterday's Accounting Undermines Production," *Harvard Business Review* (July–August 1984), 95–101.

2. William J. Vatter, *Managerial Accounting* (New York: Prentice-Hall, 1950), 104–105.

3. Especially prominent in their criticisms are R. H. Hayes and W. A. Abernathy, "Managing Our Way to Economic Decline," *Harvard Business Review* (July–August 1980), 67–77; and R. Reich, *The Next American Frontier* (New York: Time Books, 1983).

4. "What's Wrong with Management," *Dun's Business Month* (April 1982).

5. *Ibid.*, 48–52.

6. See Alfred P. Sloan, Jr., *My Years with General Motors* (Garden City, N.Y.: Doubleday, 1963).

7. See the incidents described in "Cooking in Books," *Dun's Business Month* (January 1983), 40–47.

8. Apparently, it was the inability to reconcile divisional incomes, when using a residual income approach, with consolidated corporate income, that led to the demise of residual income at General Electric; see R. F. Vancil, "General Electric Company(B)" Case 9–175–053 (Boston, Harvard Business School, 1972).

9. R. Reich, *The Next American Frontier* (New York: Time Books, 1983).

10. Sloan, *My Years*, chapter 22.

11. D. Meadows, "New Targeting for Executive Pay," *Fortune* (May 4, 1981), 176–184; A. Rappaport, "Executive Incentives vs. Corporate Growth," *Harvard Business Review* (July–August 1978), 81–88; and A. Rappaport, "Selecting Strategies that Create Shareholder Value," *Harvard Business Review* (May–June 1981), 139–149. For a contrary view, arguing that executive bonus plans apparently are consistent with increasing long-term shareholder value, see K. J. Murphy, "Corporate Performance and Managerial Remuneration: An Empirical Analysis," *Journal of Accounting and Economics* (April 1985), 11–42; and K. J. Murphy, "Top Executives Are Worth Every Nickel They Get," *Harvard Business Review* (March–April 1986), 125–132.

CHAPTER 9

The New Global Competition

THE obsolescence of most companies' cost accounting and management control systems is particularly
unfortunate for the global competition of the 1980s. The consequences of inaccurate product costs and poor accounting
systems for process control and performance measurement
were not severe during the 1970s since a combination of high
inflation and a weak dollar sheltered most U.S. manufacturers from foreign competition. High levels of worldwide demand for U.S. products during that decade placed a premium on production throughput. Higher costs and, occasionally, goods of substandard quality could generally be
passed on to customers.

The competitive environment for U.S. manufacturers
completely changed during the first half of the 1980s. First,
disinflation reversed the previous inflationary psychology,
and manufacturers could no longer recover cost increases

through higher prices. At the same time, a sharp increase in the value of the U.S. dollar made foreign produced goods less expensive to U.S. consumers and made U.S. produced goods more expensive to foreign purchasers. In addition to these dramatic changes in the macroeconomic environment, a revolution in the organization and technology of manufacturing operations was leaving laggard U.S. producers in an even more precarious competitive position.

At first, U.S. manufacturers believed that the inroads being made in their traditional markets by foreign, particularly Japanese, manufacturers could be attributed to lower overseas wage costs. Only with some delay did they recognize the onset of a revolution in manufacturing operations. The revolution was triggered by innovative practices developed by Japanese manufacturers during the 1970s and by the availability of new technology that greatly reduced the direct labor content of manufactured goods. Leading the revolution were new practices emphasizing total quality control, just-in-time inventory systems, and computer-integrated-manufacturing systems.

Total Quality Control

Traditionally, U.S. businesses emphasized a form of statistical quality control that specified upper limits of acceptable levels of defective items. Under this philosophy, incoming items from suppliers and outgoing products to customers were inspected and accepted if the estimated defective percentage was below a prespecified limit, the Acceptable Quality Level (AQL). Within factories, the same focus on inspection as a means of obtaining acceptable levels of quality control was followed. The policy of inspecting quality in and passing substandard goods through quality control to increase throughput, while expecting to correct failures with field service personnel if customers complained, led to high levels of inventory, rejects, rework, scrap, and warranty expense—and general confusion throughout the factory floor.

In contrast, Japanese companies and some West European manufacturers in Germany, Switzerland, and Sweden adopted a total quality control philosophy under which the only acceptable quality level was zero defects.[1] While the zero defects goal was never actually obtainable, it provided a target so that a company would never be satisfied with its quality program, even when defects, measured not by percentages but as parts per million, were reduced by substantial amounts year after year.

Many activities had to be done correctly in order to keep reducing part per million defect rates continually. The most important emphasized quality and manufacturability at the design stage. Many manufacturing quality problems arose because of the difficulty of reliably producing a product that had been designed for performance, but with no attention given to its manufacturability. Additional steps included extensive training of all personnel—workers and management—in how to achieve zero defect goals, shifting the responsibility for detecting nonconforming items from quality control inspectors to the persons actually performing the work, continually maintaining equipment and operating machines well within rated limits, and working with suppliers to ensure that every purchased part and raw material was 100 percent free from defects. Companies that implemented zero defect programs with suppliers initially replaced acceptance sampling with 100 percent inspection of incoming items (with return of any batch in which a single defect was detected). Companies soon eliminated all incoming inspection by certifying vendors as qualified to produce defect-free items.

Companies found to their surprise—and in contrast with the prevailing microeconomic wisdom that there had to be an "optimal" percentage of defects to minimize total costs—that total manufacturing costs declined as the incidence of defects decreased. It was less expensive to do whatever was necessary to build a component or product correctly the first time, in conformance with its design specifications, than to use a design and manufacturing process that required defective items to be detected, reworked, scrapped, or fixed in the field. Leading-edge U.S. manufacturers discovered in the 1980s that improved quality provided an important source of competitive advantage.

Just-in-Time Inventory Systems

A second source of manufacturing excellence came from greatly reducing the levels of work-in-process (WIP) inventories. Conventional wisdom in U.S. businesses, business schools, and industrial engineering departments held that inventory could be optimized, a philosophy not unlike searching for the optimal percentage of defects to minimize total costs. Embued with this philosophy, engineers and operations research analysts computed Economic Order Quantities (EOQ) that provided an optimal balance among set-up or ordering costs, storage and holding costs, and stockout costs. Literally thousands of journal articles (including the doctoral dissertation of one of the authors of this book) were written on the mathematics of so-called optimal inventory policies. Inventory theory was studied in all of its complexity—random demand, random lead times, concave or convex (or neither) cost structures, multiple products, hierarchical production processes. You name it, someone wrote a paper on it.

The Japanese did not fall prey to the optimization mentality. They approached the problem from a broader and more fundamental perspective. They were not interested in optimizing the level of inventory; they wanted to get rid of it. In their view, inventory was a form of waste and an admission of failure. It covered up problems and mistakes. Therefore, rather than trying to optimize the level of inventory based on existing conditions, they tried to understand the fundamental forces that led them to hold inventory in the first place.[2]

One force was the need to hold inventory to protect against bad quality. If the machine directly preceding a worker's in the factory breaks down unexpectedly, then the machinist needs to store a batch of items at his machine so that he can keep working in the event the preceding machine goes down. If the next item the machinist pulls from a bin to work on is defective, then he had better have more than one more item in the bin. Otherwise, he will have nothing to work on. Similarly, if a company is not sure about the quality of items obtained from suppliers, it will need to order more than one item at a time. Once the company adopts a total quality program, so that none of the above situations occurs except in highly unusual circumstances, the precautionary motive for holding inventory, to protect against shortages caused by poor quality production, is eliminated and overall inventory levels in the factory can be reduced.

A second source of high WIP inventory levels was the long set-up times on much U.S. equipment. The mathematics of the EOQ formula are driven by high set-up times. If a machine takes four to six hours to change over from one model to the next, a company will likely want to produce more than one item of the model before switching to the next model. The EOQ formula provides a simple means for balancing set-up costs with the costs of holding too much inventory—say, by producing a year's demand for the item so that only one set-up per year is performed for that model. Again, Japanese engineers and managers dispensed with EOQ mathematics by attacking the problem at its source, reducing set-up times. If set-up times could be reduced down to near zero—a goal expressed by measures such as SMED (Single Minute Exchange of Dies) and OTED (One Touch

Exchange of Dies)—then the EOQ would be one or very close to one. In practice, Japanese companies were able to achieve set-up times of three to five minutes in processes that took U.S. manufacturers more than six hours to change over. Most set-up time savings are easy to achieve once one's attention is focused on the problem. But in the post–World War II era, U.S. industrial engineers were directed to commit the bulk of their time to speeding up production processes to reduce cycle time. Japanese industrial engineers, however, spent most of their time working to reduce set-up times.

A third motive for holding inventory arose from uncertainty in delivery times from suppliers. The Japanese manufacturers conquered this source of waste by developing longer-term relationships with suppliers and linking their operations much closer together. Suppliers were given firm production schedules and directed to provide their components in small quantities just at the time the manufacturer needed the component for its production process. Coupled with vendor certification for zero defects, this meant that the supplier's truck could drive directly onto the factory floor and deliver the part when and where it was needed. No indirect labor—receiving, inspection, material handling— or inventory storage was required by the manufacturer. One industrialist visiting the Toyota assembly plant reported that drivers of suppliers' trucks had to insert a card in an automatic gate device to enter the factory, but that the gate would not rise unless the production process was ready for the part being delivered.

This just-in-time (JIT) delivery schedule was also applied vigorously within the factory itself. The goal of zero work-in-process inventory required that no part be produced until the next stage of production was ready to work on it. The just-in-time production philosophy, in essence, pulled products through the factory as they were needed. The JIT pull philosophy was in stark contrast to the traditional factory procedure that attempted to keep every worker and every machine as busy as possible (to maximize the accountant's local efficiency measures of worker output and machine uptime) and to push the output from one stage to the next stage, whether or not the next stage was ready for it and frequently whether or not the produced items being pushed forward met quality standards.

Improved factory layouts also greatly reduced the need to hold and move large quantities of inventory. Grouping machines according to expected sequence of operations, rather than the traditional grouping according to similarity of function, reduced a product's total travel distance (incoming materials to finished goods shipment) from several miles to several hundred yards, an order of magnitude reduction.

The gains from reducing inventory, as from reducing defective production, were enormous. The most obvious saving was the much lower carrying cost from holding inventory. When inventory was reduced from three months of sales to one month, or even much less as has been achieved by many U.S. manufacturers once they adopted the JIT goals, financing costs dropped by comparable amounts. Beyond the obvious financing savings, companies discovered that up to 50 percent of their factory floor space had been used to store in-process inventory. Having eliminated WIP, they found another factory inside their old factory. This permitted planned expansion to be curtailed and allowed for consolidation of previously dispersed facilities.

But even these carrying cost and floor space savings are not the most important savings from JIT systems.[3] Companies discovered the fundamental truth in the Japanese view that inventory hides problems. As companies attempted to reduce inventories, many problems emerged: quality problems, bottlenecks, coordination problems, obsolescence, "shrinkage," and supplier unreliability, among others. In order to keep to the JIT goal, these problems had to be solved. Managers were forced to deal with the problems and fix them instead of attempting to bury or work around them with buffers of inventory. The rationalization of production processes, elimination of waste, and the more visible display of production problems that all follow from the JIT approach permitted great reductions in material losses and great improvements in productivity throughout the factory. Recent studies[4] found that reducing WIP inventory was one of the greatest contributors to increased factory productivity.

Computer-Integrated Manufacturing Systems

Policies to achieve total quality control and just-in-time inventory systems were changes in the way production processes could be organized. These policies could be implemented in any repetitive production process in both manufacturing and nonmanufacturing settings, regardless of the technology being used. For many manufacturing processes, additional capabilities could be realized through expanded use of digital computer production technology—direct numerically controlled machines, robots, computer-aided manufacturing (CAM), and flexible manufacturing systems (FMS). This technology has profound implications for manufacturing processes. At the most obvious level, by substituting machine processing for direct labor processing, it accelerates the decline of direct labor costs as a percentage of total manufacturing costs. It also increases the need for overhead workers such as computer technicians and operators, maintenance personnel, software engineers and programmers. More of a firm's costs become fixed, and direct costs decline as a fraction of total costs. In fact, many of the computer-integrated manufacturing (CIM) costs are not only fixed, they are sunk. Investments in smart machines, in software development, in prototypes and model development all have to be made before production can start.

Computer-controlled manufacturing processes also offer

greatly improved quality and reliability. Companies have found that their output quality has risen substantially after shifting to CIM systems. Some companies invested in such systems just for the improved quality and were less concerned about whatever labor savings were possible.

Computer technology also permits much greater manufacturing flexibility. Increasingly, firms will compete based on economies of scope—the ability to produce a wide variety of products on the same manufacturing equipment—as opposed to economies of scale—spreading fixed factory and divisional costs over a large volume of products, the traditional source of competitive advantage for large U.S. manufacturers. The flexibility capability puts a greater premium on excellence in marketing, engineering, and design rather than on the goals of reducing labor and overhead costs when competing in the low-cost mass production of standardized products.

High-Technology Products:
Short Product Life Cycles

Another contemporary trend is the rapid obsolescence of products. Many products have useful lives of only a few years; the lives of some are one year or less. Many companies compete in these industries not by attempting to be low-cost producers, but by being product innovators. Customers buy the products of these innovative companies because of the value of their unique characteristics. For these companies, the keys to success are continual introduction of high-performance products, timely delivery, customized or niche products, and flexibility to adapt to customer preferences as they gain experience with new products. Producing at low cost is not important because the products are typically sold at high gross margins over their manufacturing costs. Price is determined by value to the customer, not by cost of manufacture. Also, the high gross margins are nec-

essary if the company is to recover its considerable sunk
investment in product and process development. Producing
products in short life cycle industries is virtually the complete antithesis to the mass production of standardized, mature products.

Deregulation: Competition in
Transportation and Service Industries

The impacts of improved quality, lowered waste
through greatly reduced in-process inventory, expanded use
of computer technology, and continual introduction of innovative products are usually illustrated with manufacturing examples, as we have done above. But each of these actions has great relevance for service industries, too. For
example, any organization that deals directly with the consumer—bank, hospital, fast-food chain, hotel, airline, railroad, phone company, or retail store—must be concerned
both with the quality of its service and the manner in which
it is delivered to the customer. Organizations that gain rep-
utations for on-time, reliable, and courteous service will en-
joy a substantial competitive advantage over their rivals.
Reducing the backlog and batch sizes of unprocessed claims,
loan applications, customer requests, and other such in-
process inventory will also lower costs, increase responsive-
ness to customers, and improve service levels. The impact of
computers on the service industries—on airline, hotel, and
rental car reservation systems, for greatly expanded financial services, for extraordinary improvements in telecommunications, and for monitoring of retail sales trends—is
probably more significant than their impact on manufacturing operations. And the ability to continue to offer new services to consumers is vital to service industries whether in
banking, insurance, brokerage, communications, retail and
catalog shopping, or transportation. Therefore, the compet-

itive forces recently unleashed on manufacturing industries are also being keenly felt in nonmanufacturing settings.

Perhaps the major difference between the competitive environment of the manufacturing and service industries is that most service industries do not have foreign-based producers competing with them in the U.S. market. But the vigorous competition promoted by the rapid deregulation movement of the last ten years has more than offset this apparent advantage. Formerly, the managers in service industries, including financial services (banks, brokerage, insurance), transportation (airline, truck, bus, railroad), telecommunications, and health care delivery were sheltered by regulation. Regulators restricted entry by low-cost suppliers and set prices so that overall costs, including a return on invested capital, could be earned. Deregulation forced these service industries to become far more competitive. Organizations that previously were never concerned with the cost and profitability of individual products or product lines had to learn to price competitively and to respond to aggressive initiatives both from within the industry and from new players who previously were not allowed to enter their markets.

Deregulation changed the pricing and profitability picture for the entire industry. One railroad executive remarked,

In a regulated environment, prices are set to cover the costs of the least efficient producer. With deregulation, prices will be established by the most efficient producers. We need to know our costs if we are going to be able to price aggressively, meet our competition, and still make enough money to stay in business.[5]

Economist Elizabeth Bailey, the vice chairman of the Civil Aeronautics Board during the period when it deregulated airlines and formerly head of the Economics Research Group at the Bell Telephone Laboratories, summarized the impact of deregulation on the service industries.

Perhaps the chief benefit of deregulation is that it has increased efficiency substantially. Regulated thinking had the regulators not the consumers as the most important customer. There was little incentive to plan or to pinpoint the sources of markets that were successful and those that were failures, nor to keep costs under control and be responsive to consumer desires. In contrast, deregulation is leading to a substantially more efficient industry, one in which cross-subsidy is absent, a diversity of price/service options are present, and cost-minimizing behavior is prevalent, both in delivery systems and in other operating costs.

These changes are coming about because of fundamental changes in the way firms are conducting business. In every aspect of corporate activity, deeply rooted changes are taking place. Companies are finding that they must be driven by market opportunities and financial needs, not by regulatory considerations. They must calculate their costs on a market-by-market basis, and must learn to base price on cost, competitor's prices and market strategy. Regulatory principles such as value of service, nationwide rate averaging, and so on, cannot survive in a competitive environment. Corporations are seeking to develop products and to market them strategically and to find niches which confer some economic benefit. . . . All in all, a more vibrant, competitive, and innovative spirit emerges from deregulation.[6]

Thus, the deregulation of the transportation and service industries could be expected to increase greatly the demand for excellent cost measurement and management systems. These systems are needed to assess the costs of diverse products and product lines and to control costs for improved efficiency.

Implications for Cost Management Systems

The far more competitive environment in the 1980s has profound implications for cost management systems. Accurate knowledge of product costs, excellent cost control, and coherent performance measurement are more important than they have been in the past. Not every firm finds it desirable to compete by being the low-cost producer, but even those firms that want to play a differentiation strategy by offering special features or services valued by their customers need to know that the price premium they received for their special features and services more than covered their incremental cost to provide these features.[7]

Michael Porter, a leading scholar of corporate strategy, emphasizes the importance of thoroughly understanding costs regardless of the firm's strategy. Given the two basic types of competitive advantage, low cost or differentiation, "the significance of any strength or weakness a firm possesses is ultimately a function of its impact on relative cost or differentiation."[8]

Cost advantage is one of the two types of competitive advantage a firm may possess. Cost is also of vital importance to differentiation strategies because a differentiator must maintain cost proximity to competitors. Unless the resulting price premium exceeds the cost of differentiating, a differentiator will fail to achieve superior performance.[9]

As we have noted, however, the cost accounting and management control systems found in most U.S. companies in the 1980s are of little use for determining product costs, for enhancing cost control, or for encouraging the creation of long-term economic wealth. Our historical review of the development of management accounting systems indicated that the major advances in the design of these systems occurred sixty or more years ago under the influence of the scientific management movement, the growth of multi-activity and divisionalized corporations, and the increased demands for external reporting by tax and regulatory authorities.

The systems designed earlier in the twentieth century worked well for the manufacturing and competitive environment of that time. The systems used extensive recording and reporting of labor costs because labor was the most costly input factor of production. Overhead costs, relatively small compared to labor costs, were allocated based on products' direct labor content. This was a convenient practice. Labor time and labor cost were already being recorded, so no additional information needed to be collected to distribute overhead costs to products in this objective and verifiable manner. And since product diversity was not great in the early years of this century (recall Henry Ford's policy on customer options, "They can have any color they want so long as it's black"), simple average methods of distributing costs to products did not greatly distort relative costs within a product line.

Accounting for inventory was important since the production costs of an accounting period had to be distributed between goods that were sold and goods that still remained in inventory. Cost systems therefore recognized the value added at each stage of the production process by incrementing the WIP cost account after each major processing step, a procedure that generated many transactions for the accounting system to handle.

Finally, the use of periodic profit measures, especially return on investment, for evaluating the short-term economic performance of decentralized managers was sensible for the cost structure of the time. Most of the costs recognized in a period were variable costs that actually represented expenditures made during that period. Relatively few expenses represented either the amortization of expenditures made in prior periods (such as depreciation of capital investments) or expenditures made during the current period that would benefit future periods (R&D, investments in human capital). The distortions introduced by attempting to measure profits in an arbitrarily short period such as a year, a quarter, or a month were thus less severe in the manufacturing environment of the early twentieth century.

Obviously, in the 1980s the new organization and technology of operations and the more competitive environment

caused by deregulation and the emergence of foreign producers undermined the critical assumptions made when
cost systems were designed earlier in this century. Quality
improvements, reduced inventory, more efficient production
processes, and increased automation reduced the direct and
indirect labor content of products and services. Direct labor
is a decreasing fraction of total product costs; 10 percent or
less is typical for many manufacturers. Much of the direct
labor remaining in organizations is more properly thought
of as a fixed rather than a variable cost as companies attempt to offer increased job security to their employees.
Overhead costs are a much higher fraction of total costs and
consequently need to be understood and controlled much
more carefully than in the past. Many companies, in response to their more competitive environment, are expanding the range of products and services they offer, making the
detailed tracing of costs to the diverse outputs more difficult
than before.

As just-in-time inventory policies become more prevalent, the need to keep detailed track of WIP inventory is
reduced.[10] In fact, as WIP inventory flows through a production shop, it does not sit still long enough for accurate records to be maintained. But in any case, with WIP inventory
declining relative to sales, the allocation of period expenses
between goods finished and goods still in process becomes
unimportant. JIT production policies also make traditional
local efficiency measures such as individual worker output
and machine uptime invalid. With JIT, if a worker's output
during a day is lower than expected, it is likely caused by
bottlenecks either before the worker or after the worker;
either situation compels a worker to stop producing. For the
same reason, keeping machines working to produce inventory not yet needed is contradictory to the JIT philosophy.
Firms that adopt a JIT production philosophy, but maintain
their previous efficiency measures, will confuse both workers and managers.

Apart from the major shifts in cost structures away from direct labor and from mostly variable to mostly fixed costs, more of a period's cash expenditures now benefit future periods rather than just the current period. Cash outlays for equipment acquisition, telecommunications and information-processing equipment, software development, research and development for both product and process improvements, improved marketing, distribution, and logistics functions, and such human capital enhancements as employee training and skill building—to name just a few examples—produce long-term benefits to organizations. But the existing financial accounting policies for these long-term investments require that they be completely expensed in the current period or else allocated in some arbitrary fashion to current and future periods. Thus, the organization's profit measurements over short time periods become distorted considerably by the arbitrary expensing of the entity's investments in its future.

The technology for recording, storing, processing, and distributing cost information has radically changed since the early twentieth century. Manual operations are obsolete and virtually nonexistent. With digital technology, continuous records of actual operations are possible. For computer-controlled manufacturing operations, the data required to direct machine processing can be retained as a continuous record of actual machine time and performance. Products can be labeled with machine readable bar codes, making automatic, continual tracking of processing feasible. Inexpensive computing and powerful, user-friendly software programs provide greatly expanded capabilities for tracing costs to products using disaggregate cost pools, multiple costing rates, and diverse measures of activity and cost drivers.

The challenge for today's competitive environment is to develop new and more flexible approaches to the design of effective cost accounting, management control, and performance measurement systems.

Notes

1. Many articles have documented the commitment of Japanese and European manufacturers to total quality control. Among them are W. J. Abernathy, K. B. Clark, and A. M. Kantrow, "The New Industrial Competition," *Harvard Business Review* (September–October 1981), 68–81; R. H. Hayes, "Why Japanese Factories Work," *Harvard Business Review* (July–August 1981), 56–66; J. Limprecht and R. H. Hayes, "Germany's World Class Manufacturers," *Harvard Business Review* (November–December 1982), 137–145; D. Garvin, "Quality on the Line," *Harvard Business Review* (September–October 1983), 64–75; and D. Garvin, "Japanese Quality Management," *Columbia Journal of World Business* (Fall 1984), 3–12.

2. The development of just-in-time inventory systems is discussed in R. J. Schonberger, *Japanese Manufacturing Techniques* (New York: Free Press, 1982); R. Hall, *Zero Inventories* (Homewood, Ill.: Dow Jones-Irwin, 1983); and A. T. Sadhwani, M. H. Sarhan, and D. Kirigoda, "Just-in-Time: An Inventory System Whose Time Has Come," *Management Accounting* (December 1985), 36–44.

3. See R. C. Walleigh, "What's Your Excuse for Not Using JIT?" *Harvard Business Review* (March–April 1986), 38–54.

4. R. H. Hayes and K. B. Clark, "Exploring the Sources of Productivity Differences at the Factory Level," chapter 4 in the book they edited, *The Uneasy Alliance: Managing the Productivity-Technology Dilemma*, (Boston: Harvard Business School Press, 1985), 151–188, and B. Chew, "Productivity and Change: Understanding Productivity at the Factory Level," Harvard Business School Working Paper (Boston, 1986).

5. George Craig, vice president, Marketing, Union Pacific System, in private correspondence with one of the authors.

6. Elizabeth Bailey, "Price and Productivity, Change Following Deregulation: The U.S. Experience," Carnegie-Mellon University Working Paper (Pittsburgh, 1985).

7. These ideas, linking cost measurement to the firm's strategy, are well explicated in Michael E. Porter, *Competitive Advantage* (New York: Free Press, 1985), 11–16, 62–118, 127–130.

8. *Ibid.*, 11.

9. *Ibid.*, 62.

10. Rick Hunt, Linda Garrett, and C. Mike Merz, "Direct Labor Cost Not Always Relevant at H-P," *Management Accounting* (February 1985), 56–60; and James Patell, "Adapting a Cost Accounting System to Just-in-Time Manufacturing: The H-P Personal Office Computer Division," in William Bruns and Robert S. Kaplan, eds., *Accounting and Management: Field Study Perspectives* (Boston: Harvard Business School Press, 1987).

CHAPTER 10

New Systems for Process Control and Product Costing

THE intellectual basis for the management accounting systems in most of today's organizations has been made obsolete by contemporary trends in global competition, by a revolution in the organization and technology of manufacturing, and by deregulation. Innovative organizations are now developing and experimenting with new approaches to measuring and controlling costs and evaluating the performance of decentralized managers. Ultimately, good solutions will be produced from these efforts and will be transferred to other organizations. At present, we can only speculate on what these future solutions will look like. But certain trends do seem clear and can be expected to be part of any future management accounting system.

Let us focus initially on cost measurement and cost management systems, postponing a discussion of profit and performance measurement systems for the final chapter. Let us also return to basics by asking what functions an adequate cost system should perform. We can think of four different functions for a cost system:[1]

1. Allocate costs for periodic financial statements
2. Facilitate process control
3. Compute product costs
4. Support special studies

The first of these objectives, to accumulate period expenditures and then to divide them between cost of goods sold and inventory in an objective, consistent, and verifiable manner, has driven the practice of cost accounting throughout this century (see chapter 6). To a large extent, the overemphasis on cost allocation to produce periodic income statements and balance sheets explains the irrelevance of today's cost systems for managerial decisions. We will, therefore, ignore this objective for now and reconsider it in the final chapter in the context of a broader discussion on periodic performance measurement.

The fourth objective emphasizes the role of cost data for ad hoc special studies such as capacity expansion, equipment replacement, and major contractions of product lines and facilities. By definition, it is hard to know in advance what data will be most relevant for a special study. Designing a cost system for special studies is thus not an overtly operational goal. We can hope, however, that whatever cost system we do design will produce and retain data relevant for special studies. Historical, disaggregate data should be retained in an easily accessible form to facilitate such studies when they arise.

The focus of our attention, then, will be the two objectives we know must be met by all good cost systems: to facilitate process control and to compute product costs.

Process Control

Process control must be accomplished at the level of the organization where the process occurs. There cannot be just one process or cost control system. A system that facilitates process control at the machine level will be different from a system for measuring and controlling costs at a research laboratory or in an overhead support department. Thus, the first step in designing a process control system is to specify the organizational unit, the cost center, that will be the object of the system.

Having specified the cost center, the next step attempts to determine the activity measures that cause cost variation to occur. As we saw in chapter 8, the most common activity measure has been direct labor hours. For some cost centers, the number of direct labor hours worked will continue to be an important determinant of cost variation. But there could be many such cost drivers within a given cost center, or the cost drivers could differ across cost centers. For instance, machine hours may be relevant for highly automated departments, number of orders received or processed for the receiving department, number or some physical measure (pounds, gallons, square meters) of orders shipped for the shipping department, number of set-ups and pounds of material moved for an indirect labor department. Our goal should be to do the best we can in explaining the short-term variation in costs within each cost center.

This goal forces us to be quite specific about what we mean by "short term." The definition will vary by cost center. It must be determined by understanding the time period during which we can expect effective process control to occur. In departments producing many items per day, the per-unit material, labor, machine time, and utility consumption could be controllable daily, hourly, or even more frequently. In such situations, where the relation between outputs produced and inputs consumed is well specified by the underlying scientific or engineering laws governing the process or by extensive experience with a stable production process, the cost control system should build on the production control system, likely already in existence. Cost control system designers will need to leave their offices and work closely at the production process to learn what information can be captured and reported back to production supervisors to enhance their process and cost control activities. This could lead to daily or even more frequent cost control reports.

For departments such as a research laboratory or central staff or for a department assembling a huge machine—a task that will take months to accomplish—hourly or daily cost control is nonsensical. Thus, for each cost center, we must make a judgment about the periodicity of a measurable unit of work. For operations turning out multiple parts per second, it is not helpful to have a monthly cost control report that will be delivered in the middle of the subsequent month. But daily or weekly cost reports can only be confusing for a department producing output only once a month or requiring several months to complete a measurable unit of work.

In summary, each cost center needs:

1. A clear definition of its boundaries,
2. An estimate of the time period to accomplish measurable units of output, and
3. An understanding of the cost drivers that explain variation in costs (if any) with variation in the activity level in the cost center.

When we have accomplished these three tasks, we can prepare a flexible budget for the cost center. That is, for a period of interest (which could be hourly for a production center, monthly or semiannually for a department staffed with knowledge workers), we can produce an estimate of expected costs for the cost center and how the costs will vary depending on the actual levels of activity occurring in or accomplished by the cost center. At the completion of the period for which the flexible budget was prepared, we measure the costs actually incurred and the level of activity (the actual measures of the cost drivers) in the cost center. We compare actual to budgeted and investigate any significant variances.

Great advances in cost control are possible with current production technology. For any computer-controlled process or any information-processing production task, digital data are needed to perform the operation. These same data can then be captured to learn what was done, when it was done, how long it took, and what was produced. Unlike the situation faced by the engineers of the scientific management movement, who had to collect performance data with the proverbial stopwatch and clipboard, today's production data are part of the production process. Cost systems need only record and process these data in order to produce a virtually continuous record of actual output and resource consumption. With digitally controlled production processes, variance reports could be produced for production intervals measured in milliseconds. The new technology has reduced the cost of collecting, recording, processing, and displaying production performance by many orders of magnitude. Contemporary process control systems must take advantage of this breakthrough in information-processing costs.

One question that arises is the role for allocations from outside the cost center in such a control system. For purposes of process and cost control, allocating costs not directly affected by activity levels in the cost center has no apparent value. If the costs are not controllable by the cost center, they should not be included in the report specifically designed to facilitate process control within the cost center.

In addition, in a good process control system, only those costs that are both traceable to actions taken in the cost center and can be measured at the cost center level should be assigned to the cost center. For example, cost center demands made on a utility department for energy, such as kilowatt hours or steam, that can be metered at the cost center level should be part of the costs assigned to the cost center. But if local metering does not exist, cost control is not enhanced by allocating utility expense to cost centers even though cost centers may consume substantial amounts of energy. Other examples of assignable costs include set-up personnel used in the cost center, demands on materials handlers, use of quality control personnel, and repairs and maintenance. But again, if we can not trace the costs and measure actual cost center consumption of these resources, process control is not enhanced by allocating them.

The demand for allocations of nontraceable costs to cost centers likely arose from the financial reporting requirement that such costs be included in inventory valuation and thus, be allocated to products. Since the only way to link common plant or corporate level costs to products in the two-stage allocation process was through a cost center burden rate, common costs had to be first allocated to cost centers. Once we recognize that product costing can and should be accomplished independently from process control, the need to allocate nontraceable costs to cost centers disappears. About the only plausible reason for allocating nontraceable costs occurs when senior managers need to enlist the support of cost center managers to monitor the growth of plant and corporate overhead costs. But this allocation can be done for informational purposes and hardly seems relevant for evaluating the performance of cost center managers in their local process control activities, their main area of responsibility.

Short-Term Product Costs

Understanding short-term variable costs is helpful for many short-term decisions such as fine tuning the desired product mix in light of current operating and market conditions, accepting or rejecting special orders, or bidding on small jobs to cover incremental costs. The system outlined above for cost control would not be adequate for short-run product decisions since it does not identify all short-run variable costs. In particular, it excludes variable but nontraceable costs (such as locally unmetered utilities). Therefore, the cost control system must be supplemented with reasonable estimates of incremental, but currently unmeasured, product costs. In addition to the estimates of products' variable indirect or overhead costs, the short-term cost system should also reveal the products' physical demands on the organizations' scarce or capacity resources. Even for short-term product mix and incremental pricing decisions, it is important to know not just incremental out-of-pocket expenses, but also the amounts of any resource used by current or proposed products. Otherwise, products may be priced to cover their incremental, but not their opportunity, costs. That is, they will be using valuable capacity of the organization which could have been used, alternatively, to produce products that have higher margins per unit of scarce resource consumed.

Despite the emphasis of most management accounting courses on computing relevant costs for short-term product decisions, there is a danger in using short-term variable costs for most decisions on product pricing, product introduction, product abandonment, order acceptance, product mix, and make versus buy. These decisions turn out to involve the commitment of the firm's capacity resources and should be made in light of the long-term, not the short-term, variability of costs. The failure to recognize the long-term nature of most product-related decisions has prevented cost accounting students, teachers, and practitioners from understanding the causes of the rapid growth in the so-called "fixed costs" of the firm.

Long-Term Product Costs

The most important goal for a product cost system is to estimate the long-run costs of producing each product, each salable output, in the company's product line. This goal must be sharply distinguished from the traditional cost accounting notion of product costing (as described in chapters 3 and 6). Traditional product costing allocates all factory costs to products for purposes of valuing inventory and cost of goods sold. This traditional role has led to cost systems, of the type described in chapter 8, that perform allocations on a simple and easily measured basis—usually direct labor or dollars—but that introduce all manner of cross subsidies and distortions when the resulting allocations are believed by managers to bear some resemblance to actual product costs.

A good product cost system measures the long-run costs of each product. Conventional notions of fixed and variable costs are ignored because, for purposes of product cost analysis, the time period is long enough to warrant treatment of virtually all costs as variable. In effect, we have to reverse the trend of thinking that has led us to direct costing concepts. For many products, the direct costs have become a small fraction of the total cost to produce and deliver the product to the customer. The cost categories that have increased fastest in recent years have been factory overhead costs, the costs of design, development, and applications engineers, and costs incurred outside the factory for marketing, selling, distribution, and service. As argued in the preceding chapter, these costs are mostly fixed with respect to the level of output; indeed, in many cases, they are sunk since the expenditures must be made before production begins.

That many of the most significant product costs are called fixed or sunk signifies the poverty of current cost accounting thinking. All costs are the consequences of managerial decisions at some time. While some cost categories may not vary currently, based on the quantity of current production output, that does not mean that they are not controllable or caused by product-related decisions made every day. These so-called fixed costs have been the most variable. They are the costs that have increased the most during the past several decades, as a percentage of total manufacturing costs.[2] The goal of a good product cost system should be to make more obvious, more transparent, how costs currently considered to be fixed or sunk actually do vary with decisions made about product output, product mix, and product diversity.

We can start our analysis with factory overhead departments. Examples of such departments are set-up, quality control, manufacturing engineering, receiving, shipping, production scheduling, and inventory control. Current thinking about fixed and variable cost distinctions would classify most of the costs of these departments as fixed. That is, if one month we produced 20 percent more or 20 percent less of each product, there would not be much change in the costs incurred in any of these departments.

But something, not just total physical volume of products, explains the growth and current size of each of the departments. Assuming that the current size and costs of the overhead departments are defensible, given their function and mission, our task is to identify the cost drivers for these departments. What factors occupy the time and attention of the people in overhead departments? Perhaps the best question to ask the head of each department is why there are eight people (or whatever the actual number is) in this department and not just one. What demands are placed on the department that cause the task to be more than one person could handle? If the answer turns out to be sheer physical volume of outputs, we can safely assume the cost is variable in the traditional sense; more or less output implies more or less costs in the department. For many overhead departments, however, we have found that the demands imposed by producing 100,000 units of the same product are very different from the demands imposed by producing ten units each of 10,000 different models or products. The latter situation, even though it could represent the same physical volume of production, requires more scheduling and set-ups; more items of inventory to be ordered, received, inspected, stored, kept track of, and moved about; and more orders to be shipped.

By investigating in detail the demands placed on factory overhead departments, we will likely learn that cost drivers are more than just physical volume of production. Among the cost drivers could be number of set-ups, hours of set-ups, number of orders placed, number of orders received, number of customer orders, number of shipments made, quantity of material ordered, number of parts, components, and sub-assemblies in final products, amount of inventory, number of inspections, and number of engineering change orders (ECOs). We are attempting to ask, What causes overhead? What creates work or imposes demands on overhead support departments? Why are there ten people in this department and not one or two? The goal is not to embarrass the managers of support departments or to intimidate them into shrinking their staff. The goal is to learn why the staff exists at its current level, and what keeps them busy. Perhaps the best clue that any cost category is variable, not fixed, is to observe if there is more than one person or one machine in the department covered by the category. If the cost of this category does not vary with something, why is more than one unit needed to handle the work in this department or category?

Two researchers of contemporary manufacturing processes, Jeff Miller and Tom Vollmann, have identified a "hidden factory" where factory overhead costs occur.[3] The factory is "hidden" because existing cost accounting systems concentrate on direct labor and materials and hide the costs of overhead departments by simplistic allocations based on labor or materials. To make this hidden factory visible, we need to start understanding the causes of overhead costs, a goal that virtually all existing systems fail miserably to achieve. The primary cost drivers for manufacturing overhead are not physical volume of production, but transactions—transactions involving exchange of materials or exchange of information. Miller and Vollmann define four types of transactions that drive overhead costs.

1. Logistical transactions: to order, execute, and confirm materials movement. Personnel busy with logistical transactions include indirect shop floor workers as well as people engaged in receiving, expediting, shipping, data entry, EDP, and accounting.
2. Balancing transactions: to match the supply of material, labor, and machines with demand. Purchasing, materials planning, production control, forecasting, and scheduling people perform balancing transactions.
3. Quality transactions: to validate that production is in conformance with specifications. People in quality control, indirect engineering, and procurement perform quality transactions.
4. Change transactions: to update manufacturing information. Manufacturing, industrial, and quality engineers involved with ECOs, schedules, routings, standards, specifications, and bills of materials perform change transactions.[4]

Miller and Vollmann advocate a variety of mechanisms to eliminate transactions and thereby reduce overhead costs: just-in-time inventory systems, design changes to reduce component count in final products, stability (reduced number of ECOs), and automation.

These are all desirable actions, as we discussed in chapter 9. To develop long-term product cost information, how-

ever, we need only understand and adopt the "costs of transactions" philosophy that Miller and Vollmann advocate. The
process starts by pinpointing, through interviews, the cost
drivers for each factory overhead department. Once we understand what causes overhead, we can attempt to trace the
overhead costs to products.

The cost tracing process starts not at the product level,
but at the component level. For many production processes,
the product does not appear until the final assembly stage.
We must work with the basic unit of production at each
stage, which will usually be raw material or purchased components and subassemblies. For every individual component
or subassembly, we attempt to estimate its demands on the
factory cost drivers, that is, number of set-ups, number of
orders, number of inspections, number of material movements, amount of labor and machine time, and so on.

We can then sum across all components for an estimate
of the total number of transactions of each type. Once we
have identified the total costs that are driven by each type
of transaction, simple division will provide the cost per
transaction of each type. In an important sense, this process
is exactly analogous to the first stage of the two-stage allocation process described in chapter 8. But rather than trace
overhead costs to cost centers, as is done in the typical cost
system described in chapter 8, this procedure decomposes
overhead costs into homogeneous cost pools, homogeneous
in that cost variations in any given pool can be explained by
a single cost driver.[5] The outcome of the first-stage process
is a large set of cost pools, each of which has a cost per unit
of cost driver, for example, cost per set-up, cost per inspection, cost per labor hour in a particular department, cost per
material dollar, or cost per machine hour in a particular
department.

To start the process for estimating the long-term cost of
each component or subassembly, we obtain the number of
each cost driver used by that component or subassembly in

a given period; specifically, we measure or estimate for each component the number of direct labor and/or machine hours in each cost center, the number and perhaps duration of set-ups, number of inspections, quantity of material dollars consumed, etc. These quantities are then multiplied by the unit cost of each driver (determined in the first-stage process described in the preceding paragraph) and summed to arrive at the fully traced cost for each component and subassembly. This cost, which corresponds to developing product cost information at the second stage of the two-stage process, includes both easily developed labor, materials, and machine costs as well as the share of factory overhead costs caused by the production of this component. With this information, the product costs are obtained easily by imploding (summing) all component and subassembly costs back into the final product.

Obviously, this process is not precise. We will not be able to obtain product cost information with the five significant digits reported by conventional systems, as in the example shown in chapter 8. Nevertheless, we will have done the best we can to understand the demands made by each product on the factory's resources, and we may well have gotten the first digit in our product cost estimate correct, an accuracy goal rarely achieved by existing cost accounting systems.

An important implication of the "cost of transactions," or overhead cost attribution, approach is that all overhead costs should be considered variable. If we decide to narrow our product line by dropping products that we now see are very costly for our factory to produce, we must reduce the size of some support departments and perhaps sell off some currently unneeded equipment in order to realize the cost savings. What we have gained from the process is a knowledge of where we should expect the cost savings to occur and a ballpark estimate of how much the savings should be.

The outcome of such a product cost tracing study can be surprising.[6] The procedure was applied to the diverse product line of a plant with $10 million in sales. For this product line, 23 percent of the products accounted for 85 percent of total dollar sales, a figure that is probably typical for many product lines. More surprising, however, was the finding that these 23 percent of the products produced 400 percent of the plant's profits (after also assigning a capital charge to the fixed assets and inventory used by each product). The remaining 77 percent lost money; they did not cover the cost of all overhead resources used for their production, including the investment in fixed assets and inventory. The revaluation in product costs was enormous. Previously, the direct-labor-based conventional accounting system showed profit margins in excess of 40 percent, with low-volume customized products priced to achieve 45 to 50 percent margins. The strategic cost analysis that attributed overhead costs to products based on both transactions and volume revealed that some of these low-volume products actually had gross margins of − 400 percent. Products that had been previously thought to have been the most profitable were actually bleeding the division to death through the heavy demands they were making on the plant's support departments.

Perhaps the firm needed to keep the 77 percent of the products shown to be unprofitable so that it could be a full-line producer and be able to generate the high sales of its high-margin products. Or perhaps it did not realize that 77 percent of its products were losing money because its cost system, which allocated overhead costs based on direct labor hours, was shifting costs from the small-volume, frequently set-up products to the high-volume, long-running, mature products. The cost system was concealing the high profits actually being earned by these latter products.

Were we to learn that a high fraction of products are losing money, eliminating all unprofitable products and shrinking the organization would be only one of many possible responses. We could reprice currently unprofitable products to try to recover in the marketplace the higher costs of producing these products. For low-volume orders, we could try to charge a supplementary fixed fee to cover the transactions costs of handling small orders. Or we could try to lower the cost of producing low-volume products; it might be possible to redesign them so that greater use is made of common rather than unique components or to use fewer components in the final product. We could try to work with the customer to reduce some of the costly features in the product, such as short lead times for low-volume products, or to encourage consumers of low-volume products to switch to other products that do the same job. There are many actions we can contemplate or take once we understand the problem. The challenge is to begin to understand our costs. At present, the costs of the "hidden factory" are either hidden or, worse, shifted so that profitable products appear unprofitable and unprofitable products appear to be profitable.

The role of transactions in generating costs was recognized a quarter century ago in a brilliantly insightful article by Peter Drucker. Drucker observed:

While 90% of the results are being produced by the first 10% of events, 90% of the costs are being increased by the remaining and result-less 90% of events.

Economic events are, by and large, directly proportionate to revenue, while costs are directly proportionate to *number of transactions*.

Furthermore, . . . efforts will allocate themselves to the 90% of events that produce practically no results. . . . In fact, the most expensive and potentially productive resources (i.e., highly trained people) will misallocate themselves the worst.[7]

Drucker noticed that corporate accounting systems prevent managers from seeing the costs of operating a full-line production facility:

Now the only way the accountant can allocate costs is in a way that is proportionate to volume rather than proportionate to the number of transactions. Thus $1 million in volume produced in one order—or in one product—carries the same cost as $1 million in volume production by 1 million individual orders or by 50 different production runs. . . . *The accountant is concerned with the cost per unit of output rather than with the costs of a product.*[8] (emphasis added)

Drucker warned of the dysfunctional consequences from following a full-line marketing strategy with cost systems that do not accurately trace costs of individual products:

Most large companies typically end up with thousands of items in their product line—and all too frequently fewer than 20 really "sell." However, these 20 items or less have to contribute revenues to carry the costs of the 9,999 nonsellers.[9]

In an extraordinarily prescient observation, remarkable for having been written more than twenty years ago, he concluded:

Indeed, the basic problem of U.S. competitive strength in the world economy today may well be product clutter. If properly costed, the main lines in most of our industries will prove to be fully competitive despite our high wage rates and our high tax burden. But we fritter away our competitive advantage in the volume products by subsidizing an enormous array of "specialities," of which only a few recover their true costs. . . . The competitive advantage of the Japanese (in the steel, aluminum, and electronics industries) rests on little more than the Japanese concentration on a few models in one line—as against the uncontrolled plethora of barely differentiated models in the U.S. manufacturers' lines.[10]

The new role for estimating the long-run variable costs of products is also consistent with the role for management accounting systems articulated forty years ago by William Vatter (discussed in chapter 7). Vatter emphasized that the accounting system is most valuable to management not when it answers questions, but when it raises them.

From the managerial viewpoint, the accountant should be the source of questions for management to answer . . . in the broader sense of asking the questions that management is curious enough in its own right to want answered. . . .

Accounting for management is not management, and it should not be thought of as such. But accounting can be made to serve managerial purposes . . . and it can help management to do a better job than could be done without it.[11]

Present accounting systems, however, conceal problems or signal problems where none exists, such as when mature, high-volume products are made to appear too costly because many of the costs of newly introduced, low-volume products are shifted onto them.

Our proposal to trace or attribute more accurately overhead costs to products is analogous to the philosophy used by Japanese engineers to understand better the consequence of long set-up times.[12] The traditional American approach for both overhead allocation and batch sizes has been a short-term perspective optimized with respect to current conditions. For inventory, Economic Order Quantities, based on current set-up times, were computed. In cost accounting, costs that did not vary with physical volume were labeled as "fixed" costs. Concepts such as direct costing, breakeven analysis, and flexible budgets were devised that did not explain or attack what caused the fixed costs in the first place. Just as the Japanese engineers changed the rules of the game by working to reduce and eliminate set-up times, we need to eliminate the mentality that fixed costs are necessary for production, but are not influenced by our product and production decisions. Once we accept that virtually all product costs are variable over some reasonable time period, then it becomes necessary to do whatever we can to understand the sources of all overhead costs and to trace them to the activities that drive these costs. We must abandon conventional rules that either ignore fixed costs (the direct cost approach) or allocate them on an arbitrary, usually dysfunctional, basis (the full cost approach).

As a corollary of this philosophy, we can start to understand why attempts to stem the increase in overhead costs frequently fail. Such attempts usually start with a mandate from senior management that overhead costs be reduced, usually by some arbitrary percentage. After, say, 10 percent or 20 percent of support personnel have been removed, the remaining managers and personnel soon discover that they can not perform all the functions being demanded of them. The cost reduction effort has failed because the symptom of the problem, growth in support personnel, has been attacked, but the fundamental causes remain. The plant is still being asked to produce the same diversity and complexity of outputs that generated the demand for support personnel. Sounder ways to reduce overhead costs might be to simplify the production process to eliminate costly transactions or to pare the product line of some low-volume products that generate a disproportionate demand for overhead support. A product cost system that made the costs of product diversity and complexity more transparent to management would also make it more obvious which actions would likely be successful in reducing overhead costs.

Costs Outside the Factory

So far, we have been as guilty as conventional product cost systems in focusing narrowly on costs incurred only in the factory. Manufacturing costs may be important, but they are only a portion of the total costs of producing a product and delivering it to a customer. Many costs are incurred "below the line" (the gross margin line), particularly marketing, distribution, and service expenses. Traditional accounting practice, based on a line-item financial income statement, combines these costs into aggregate functional categories, and many cost systems mirror this functional approach. What is missing is an understanding of the costs of reaching and servicing particular types of buyers and the cost of using different distribution channels.

Michael Porter emphasizes the importance of understanding costs incurred outside the factory.

A business unit usually produces a number of different product varieties and sells them to a number of different buyers. It may also employ a number of different distribution channels. Any of these differences may give rise to segments in which the behavior of costs in the value chain may be different. Unless the firm recognizes differences in cost behavior among segments, there is a significant danger that incorrect or average-cost pricing will provide openings for competitors. Thus cost analysis at the segment level must often supplement analysis at the business unit level.[13]

The cross subsidies and product cost distortions that occur when factory costs are not traced accurately to products also occur when the costs of using different distribution channels or of selling to different types of buyers are not traced to products. Evaluating product cost and profitability based solely on factory costs can provide inaccurate estimates of relative profitability.

We can only speculate as to why cost accounting teaching and practice have ignored marketing and distribution costs for the past half century. But as with many other failures of contemporary cost accounting systems, the causes can likely be attributed to a financial reporting story somewhere in the distant past. Until the 1930s, cost accounting textbooks devoted considerable space and attention to distribution costs; today's books, in contrast, virtually ignore the subject. We believe that as the financial accounting role became dominant during the 1930s, marketing and distribution expenses came to be considered costs of the period and not of the product. Therefore, they were expensed on the income statement each period and not allocated, as were factory overhead costs, between inventory and cost of goods sold. For financial and tax reporting statements, marketing and distribution costs were not traced and allocated to products.

Again, in principle, nothing prevented managers fifty years ago from attributing, for internal purposes, marketing and distribution costs to products even though these costs were being expensed as a lump sum for financial and tax purposes. But given the costs, at that time, of operating multiple accounting systems, the benefits from a more accurate product costing procedure may not have exceeded the costs. Several decades later, however, the cost of information technology was reduced by many orders of magnitude, and the diversity of marketing channels had increased. But because the treatment of marketing and distribution expenses as period, rather than product, costs had become so ingrained, few companies attempted to understand better the costs of their diverse distribution activities.

For example, in one business we studied,[14] a division thought that its product line sold to Original Equipment Manufacturers (OEM) was less profitable than product lines sold to distributors and wholesalers because the gross margins on its OEM line were much lower. Only after performing a study that broke out total distribution costs into the cost of supplying and servicing each channel did it realize that the OEM business was as profitable as all the other lines. Before doing the study, the division managers had failed to realize how inexpensive it was to sell and distribute to OEM accounts relative to all the other channels it was using. Conversely, business previously thought to be quite profitable turned out to be only marginally so because the cost of reaching customers through the channel exceeded the price premium obtained from this class of customer. Therefore, when products are sold to different classes of buyers—industrial, commercial, institutional, government—the costs of reaching different classes should be traced to the products. Similarly, the costs of different distribution channels—

distributors, retail, wholesale, brokers, direct mail, OEM, export—need to be understood and traced to the products sold through each of these channels.

The tracing of selling, distribution, and service costs to individual product lines and products may not be easy. It could involve an exercise similar to that described for tracing factory overhead costs to products: interviewing marketing and sales people to learn how their time and effort are allocated across buyer segments and distribution channels. But such an exercise will at least give the company a rough estimate of the cost drivers of its marketing, sales, and distribution efforts and how these costs vary by channel and product line. Even a rough estimate will be a dramatic improvement over current systems that do not identify the specific costs of different segments and channels and, hence, do not trace the costs to the specific products sold in these segments and channels.[15]

Companies have to know the total cost of acquiring resources—material, capital, people, and technology—plus the cost of transforming these resources into final products and services, of delivering their outputs to customers, and of servicing them. As Alexander Hamilton Church intimated over eighty years ago, a good product cost system will accumulate costs, by product and product line, across the entire value chain so that the company will know its total cost of producing each good and service.[16] Collecting costs into traditional financial accounting categories, like labor, material, overhead, selling, distribution, and administrative, will conceal the underlying cost structure of products. It will lead firms to make critical decisions such as price and distribution based on averaged costs that incorporate cross subsidies and distortions. Misguided decisions leave the company vulnerable to attacks by focused competitors or by competitors who know their costs well. These competitors can price aggressively in high-volume segments where the company has priced its output too high because of inaccurate information from its cost system.

Process Control and Product
Costing Systems: A Summary

Current cost accounting systems attempt to satisfy three goals: to allocate certain period costs to products so that financial statements can be prepared monthly, quarterly, and annually; to provide process control information to cost center managers; and to provide product cost estimates to product and business managers. Typically, only a single cost system is used for these three quite different goals. Because financial accounting considerations have been dominant, only the first of the three goals is accomplished well. The cost allocations used for the periodic financial and tax statements usually receive clean opinions from external auditors and tax authorities. The system designed to satisfy external reporting requirements, however, does not facilitate process control within cost centers and leads to inaccurate and distorted individual product costs.

It would be desirable to have a single system satisfy all three cost accounting objectives. But given the low cost and high power of information-processing technology, this should not be a necessary design criterion. Of more importance is to perform each function well. If initially this objective requires separate systems for financial reporting, process control, and product costing, the benefits of performing each of these important functions well should outweigh the costs of developing and operating three different systems.

One reason for suspecting that separate systems are needed is the different time frame for the activities. Cost systems to aid process control must have reporting cycles specific to the process being controlled—hourly, daily, weekly, even semiannually—for the information to be of most use to cost center managers. Financial reporting systems must follow the cycle of mandated external reports— quarterly and annually. And product cost information requires even a longer time horizon. Because long-run variable costs are the most relevant for estimating product costs, they are still useful even if only computed annually. Given the very different reporting periods that these purposes entail, from hourly to annually or longer, it seems unlikely that a single cost system can be asked to perform all three functions.

Process control and product costing systems will also have dramatically different roles for cost allocations. When attempting to provide prompt feedback to responsibility center managers, the process control information should report on activities directly under the control of the manager: the outputs produced and the resources consumed within the responsibility center. Allocating costs from outside the center or spreading costs that have been measured at the plant level will not help the manager to correct a problem or learn more about the process under his or her control. Therefore, the process control system should employ a minimum of allocations. Also, fixed and variable costs—relative to the reporting time period (hourly, daily, monthly)—should be segregated and the factors that cause costs to vary within the reporting period—labor time, machine hours, set-ups, materials processed—should be understood and measured.

The product costing system, in contrast, with its goal of tracing virtually all costs to products, will require extensive allocations especially to attribute indirect, overhead, and marketing costs. In service organizations, there may be no direct, traceable product costs. All the costs may represent resources that cannot be measured directly with the provision of a unit of service. But the amount of resources required, in aggregate, and established over time will be a function of the number, diversity, and volume of products produced. The product costing system will attempt to trace these long-run costs to individual products and, thus, by its very nature, will require extensive subjective judgments and allocations. This suggests yet another difference between process control and product cost systems: process control information will be objective and measurable; product costs will be subjective and the result of an allocation procedure.

In between these extremes, the cost information for financial reporting will require some allocations but need not be accurate at the individual product level. It will trace some costs to products but indirect costs can be allocated on almost any arbitrary basis, as long as it is consistent from year to year. Also, not all product costs are allocated to products for financial reporting. Marketing, distribution, and general administrative costs are considered period costs for financial reporting, whereas the product cost system will attempt to attribute the magnitude of these non-factory costs to individual product lines.

Even the audience for the outputs from the three systems will be different. Production supervisors, plant managers, and the operations staff will be most interested in the process control system. Marketing and product managers, business managers, and senior general managers will be most interested in the product cost system as they attempt to make product decisions and assess the profitability of their various products and product lines. Finally, the primary audience for the financial reporting system will be outside investors and creditors and the senior executives of the corporation who interact with these outside constituencies.

In summary, the three functions of process control, product costing, and financial reporting have different time periods for reporting, different categories of fixed and variable cost, differing degrees of traceability and allocation, different sets of relevant costs, and different audiences. While all three systems may process information from a common, integrated data base, it seems unlikely that a single system can be designed, at least in the near future, to serve these three diverse functions. Rather than undertake an extensive effort to design a single comprehensive system, it may be desirable to start by designing separate systems that perform each function well and in an efficient manner. Over time, as we gain more experience with the three systems, methods for linking them may become more obvious than they are today.

Notes

1. The multiple functions for a cost system were described by John Dearden in "Profit-Planning Accounting for Small Firms," *Harvard Business Review* (March-April 1963), 66–76; and in his book, *Cost and Budget Analysis* (Englewood Cliffs, N.J.: Prentice-Hall, 1967), 1. Many of the problems caused by using aggregate overhead rates (as discussed in chapter 8) were diagnosed by Dearden in these two references.

2. See Exhibit 1 in Jeffrey G. Miller and Thomas E. Vollmann, "The Hidden Factory," *Harvard Business Review* (September-October 1985), 143.

3. *Ibid.*

4. Miller and Vollmann, 143–146.

5. This point was developed by Robin Cooper.

6. The procedure for tracing support department costs to products via transactions was developed and implemented by William Boone when he was director of strategic planning at the Scovill Corporation. The process is described in detail in Robin Cooper, "Schrader Bellows," 9–186–272 (Boston: Harvard Business School, 1986).

7. Peter Drucker, "Managing for Business Effectiveness," *Harvard Business Review* (May-June 1963), 54–55.

8. *Ibid.*, 55–56.

9. *Ibid.*, 56.

10. *Ibid.*, 56.

11. William J. Vatter, *Managerial Accounting* (New York: Prentice-Hall, 1950), 509–510.

12. Recall our discussion of just-in-time inventory systems in chapter 9.

13. Michael E. Porter, *Competitive Advantage* (New York: Free Press, 1985), 93.

14. This marketing cost analysis was also conceived and implemented by William Boone at Scovill (see note 6).

15. The analysis can be extended further to all levels of the firm, including the attribution of corporate headquarters overhead to products. See H. Thomas Johnson, "Managing Diversity and Strategic Overhead Cost: Weyerhauser Company, 1972–1986," in William Bruns and Robert S. Kaplan, eds., *Accounting and Management: Field Study Perspectives* (Boston: Harvard Business School Press, 1987).

16. This point is developed in detail in chapters 2–4 of Porter, *Competitive Advantage*, 33–163.

CHAPTER 11

Performance Measurement Systems for the Future

THIS book documents the subversion of management accounting systems. Their original purpose of providing information to facilitate cost control and performance measurement in hierarchical organizations has been transformed to one of compiling costs for periodic financial statements. In chapter 8, we indicated the shortcomings of existing cost accounting systems, and in chapter 10, we described opportunities for new initiatives for process control and product costing systems. Given that existing systems are not helpful for process control or for computing individual product costs, we have argued that compiling cost information for periodic financial statements is the only plausible rationale for the systems we observe in practice.

But the role of short-term financial performance measurement has itself been undermined by rapid changes in technology, shortened product life cycles, and innovations in the organization of production operations. Short-term financial measures have become invalid indicators of the recent performance of the enterprise. The reduction of direct labor content in final products, the increased capital intensity of production processes, and the great contribution to a firm's success provided by its stock of knowledge[1] and intangible resources[2] all combine to make it impossible to obtain a valid measure of short-term profits. Attempts to match revenues with costs during arbitrarily short periods will cause current period costs to include large allocations of expenditures made in prior periods as well as expenditures made in the current period, but whose benefits will be realized mainly in future periods.

The Meaninglessness of Short-Term Profits: An Example

To see this phenomenon at work in an actual situation, consider the profit measurement of a company producing software for personal computers. The revenues of the current period are easy to measure as sales to distributors and customers. The variable costs of sales are also easy to measure—the cost of a floppy disc and a manual. Variable costs might sum to about $5, probably less than the dealer discount for prompt payment. Gross margins are thus extremely high. Some period expenses will be required for advertising, promotion, and administration, but the bulk of period "expenses" are the amortization of development expenses for the current product line (if not already written off) plus the expenses of developing future generations of products. Obviously, the timing of expense recognition for the development of current and future products, the lifeblood of the business, will be extremely arbitrary and subjective. As a consequence, the measurement of profit for any short period—certainly a quarter, perhaps even a year—will not be a valid measure of changes in the economic wealth of the enterprise.

For any particular software product, the profitability over the lifetime of the product will be managerially relevant and relatively easy to measure. In the early periods, we start by accumulating the development costs for the product. After the product has been commercialized, we measure sales less variable costs and the traceable marketing and administrative expenses. At the end of the product's useful life, we subtract the initial cash outlays for development expenses from the net cash receipts during the years the product was sold to determine the cumulative profitability (or loss) from this product. In this way, we can learn its overall profit or loss. But attempting to allocate this overall product profit to short time periods within the product's life cycle will be arbitrary and virtually meaningless.

The nature of the business is characterized by large initial cash outlays followed by periods of large net cash receipts (if successful) where variable costs are a trivial fraction of sales. In this environment, it makes sense to budget and to compute expenditures, receipts, and, ultimately, profits for each product, or project, in the company. What does not make sense is to arbitrarily allocate cash outlays from one period to another in a vain attempt to measure periodic profit. At any one time, the firm is a collection of projects, some of which are in the investment stage and some in the harvest stage. Subtracting the cash being spent on investment projects from the cash being received from projects in the harvest stage will produce a number, but not a number that can be interpreted as the firm's "income" of the period.

Firms with short life cycle products, characterized by large initial cash outlays followed by large net cash receipts, appear similar to the Venetian caravans we described in the opening chapter. We argued there that it was not meaningful to attempt to allocate the profits of an entire voyage or expedition to arbitrarily short time intervals during the voyage. Neither is it meaningful today to attempt to allocate the life cycle profits of a product to arbitrarily short intervals within that life cycle, whether a month, a quarter, or a year. An alternative scheme for measuring periodic financial performance would record the cash invested in each product or project and, when it is commercialized, measure the rate at which the total cash investment is being recovered, given current rates of selling, selling prices, and production costs.[3] Such a procedure articulates with the life cycle budgeting practices for products and projects and does not introduce the arbitrariness of short-term periodic profit measures.

But our arguing against the allocation of project profitability to short periods within the life of the project does not imply that we believe it fruitless to attempt to obtain valuable indicators of short-term progress. Certainly, cash flow is important, and we would want to know the pattern and structure of a company's cash receipts and expenditures. The rate of net cash recovery on previous investments, as just described, would also be a valuable indicator. But knowing sources, uses, and patterns of cash investment and recovery is very different from working hard every month and every quarter to produce complete income statements and balance sheets, complete with amortizations, capitalizations, and many other accruals.

The Importance of Nonfinancial Indicators

More important than attempting to measure monthly or quarterly profits is measuring and reporting a variety of nonfinancial indicators. The indicators should be based on the company's strategy and include key measures of manufacturing, marketing, and R&D success. For example, a company emphasizing quality could measure internal failure indicators—scrap, rework, part-per-million defect rates, unscheduled machine downtime—and external failure indicators—customer complaints, warranty expenses, and service calls. Companies wishing to become lower-cost producers will want to develop productivity measures to show trends in their ability to produce more with less. In the short run, higher profits could be due more to price recovery—prices for outputs rising faster than the costs of inputs—than to productivity improvements. In the longer run, however, low-cost producers must succeed by productivity gains, not just by exploiting short-term favorable pricing situations that will likely be available to their competitors, too.

Many firms are striving to achieve the just-in-time production and delivery systems we described in chapter 9. Measures that support this objective include average set-up times,[4] throughput times, lead times, and average number of days production in inventory. Other measures of success in a more responsive manufacturing system are average distance traveled by products in the factory and percentage of delivery commitments met each period.

Companies attempting to improve their design and process flexibility will want to measure total number of parts per product, percentage common versus percentage unique parts in products, and the number of subassembly or bill of materials levels. Increasingly, companies are recognizing that the greatest leverage to reducing product costs occurs at the design stage. Simplification of design and reduction in number of unique parts in a final product will do more to reduce total product costs than heroic efforts at process improvement and automation once a poorly designed product reaches production. One of the most successful realizations of design simplification benefits was the IBM Proprinter, introduced in 1985.

The machine was "designed for automation" ... with 60 parts, against 150 for comparable printers when IBM began designing the product two years ago. One molded-plastic side frame took the place of 20 other parts. Motors twist and lock in place, eliminating four screws, four nuts, and four washers. . . . The fewer parts there are, the more reliable the product and the smaller the inventory-management job.[5]

Existing cost and performance measurement systems fail to recognize the high costs of poor product designs and the great benefits from the parts reduction that can occur when "design for manufacturability" becomes an engineering department goal.

Companies whose competitive advantage comes from a continuing flow of innovative and high-performance products will want to measure the total launch time for new products, the achievement of product and process development milestones, key characteristics (accuracy, speed, reliability) of new products, and customer satisfaction with the features and characteristics of newly introduced products.

Many companies claim to derive value from their employees, but few make the effort to measure their progress in enhancing employee value. Measures such as absenteeism, turnover, recruiting success, morale, skills, and promotability would seem to be relevant for evaluating trends in the organization's human resources. A number of companies have placed safety indicators near the top of their list of short-term performance factors. These indicators can include number of consecutive days without an injury or accident and number of workdays lost due to accidents.

Not all of these indicators will be relevant to any single firm or organizational subunit. No firm or manager can concentrate on improving performance on fifteen measures at once. At any given time, there must be a few objectives that the firm and its divisions want to achieve. But reaching a particular level of reported quarterly profits is unlikely to be among the few near-term objectives whose achievement will help the firm maintain its trajectory for long-term profitability. Management accountants, designing and maintaining the firm's performance measurement system, must be aware of the evolution of the organization's key strategic factors. The accountants are not responsible for choosing the organization's key performance factors, but they can work with operating managers to devise measures for the factors and then collect and report periodically on the values for these measures.

Thus, the new production environment will not only require entirely new process control and product cost measurement systems, as discussed in chapter 10. It will also force managers to reduce their current emphasis on short-term profitability measures, such as earnings and return on investment. Short-term financial measures will have to be replaced by a variety of nonfinancial indicators that provide better targets and predictors for the firm's long-term profitability goals.

In an important sense, a call for more extensive use of nonfinancial indicators is a call for a return to the operations-based measures that were the origin of management accounting systems. The initial goal of management accounting systems in nineteenth-century textile firms and railroads was to provide information on the operating efficiency of these organizations. Measures such as conversion cost per yard or pound and the cost per gross ton-mile provided easy-to-understand targets for operations managers and valuable product cost information for business managers. These measures were designed to help management, not to prepare financial statements. The need to expand summary measures beyond those used to measure the efficiency of conversion reflects the greater complexity of product and process technology in contemporary organizations. But the principle remains the same: to devise short-term performance measures that are consistent with the firm's strategy and its product and process technologies. We need to recognize the inadequacy of any single financial measure, whether earnings per share, net income growth, or ROI, to summarize the economic performance of the enterprise during short periods.

Conclusions

The obsolescence of management accounting systems has not occurred overnight. The systems, whose intellectual roots can be traced to events sixty to one hundred years ago, worked well for the times in which they were designed. We have speculated that the dominance of financial accounting procedures, both in education and in practice, has inhibited the dynamic adjustment of management accounting systems to the realities of the contemporary environment. These realities, including remarkable expansions of information technology, a more virulent global competition, shortened life cycle of products, and innovations in the organization and technology of operations, have all contributed to the new demands and new opportunities for corporate management accounting systems. Despite the enormous increase in information-processing capabilities, however, most organizations still use a single system to generate their financial and management accounting reports. Even within the management accounting system, the value of having specialized systems for short-term process control, for periodic performance measurement, and for product costing has generally not been exploited.

If organizations' management accounting systems fail to provide useful signals for measuring the efficiency of processes and profitability of products, the ability of senior executives to manage their large enterprises will diminish. They will become vulnerable to inroads made by smaller or more focused competitors. Large organizations attempting to manage multiple and diverse activities with inadequate management accounting systems will find it difficult to capture the economies of scale and scope that otherwise would arise from internalizing multiple activities within a single entity.

Poor management accounting systems, by themselves, will not lead to organizational failure. Nor will excellent management accounting systems assure success. But they certainly can contribute to the decline or survival of organizations. As diversified organizations attempt to compete against smaller and more focused entities, the need will be high for excellent systems to guide capital investment, provide goals for decentralized managers, coordinate operations, judge the efficiency of internal processes, and evaluate the profitability of product offerings.

Thus, we are at a time of unparalleled opportunity. The need is great, the technology exists, and the possibilities are uninhibited by existing practice. Nor is the task particularly difficult or complex. We are not trying to split the atom, perform genetic recombination, or explore the solar system. All that may be required is to return to basics, to ask what makes sense and what is important for the organization: What information is needed for management planning and control functions? Rather than attempt to extract such information from a system designed primarily to satisfy external reporting and auditing requirements, we should design systems consistent with the technology of the organization, its product strategy, and its organizational structure. By working closely with design and process engineers, operations managers, and product and business managers, management accountants will undoubtedly be able to design systems that effectively serve the goals of these diverse constituencies.

Designers of early management accounting systems in textile mills, in railroads, in primary steel and steel-fabricating companies, and in the vertically integrated and multidivisional enterprises of the early twentieth century developed systems that supported their organizations' goals.

The management accounting systems were seen as necessary components for managing the increased scale and scope of operations as the organizations internalized activities that formerly were conducted by smaller firms through market-mediated exchanges. For too many firms today, however, the management accounting system is seen as a system designed and run by accountants to satisfy the informational needs of accountants. This is clearly wrong. Accountants should not have the exclusive franchise to design management accounting systems. To paraphrase an old saying, the task is simply too important to be left to accountants. The active involvement of engineers and operating managers will be essential when designing new management accounting systems.

Contemporary trends in competition, in technology, and in management demand major changes in the way organizations measure and manage costs and in the way they measure short- and long-term performance. Failure to make the modifications will inhibit the ability of firms to be effective and efficient global competitors.

Notes

1. A firm's knowledge stock could include its know-how and "know-why" of production processes that permit zero defect, just-in-time, and flexible production (as described in chapter 9) and it would also include the firm's superior performance characteristics.

2. The organization's intangible resources could be composed of highly skilled, dedicated, and motivated employees; its brand-loyal customers; and its long-term suppliers.

3. The use of cash flow and cash rate recovery for periodic performance measurement has been articulated in two articles by Yuji Ijiri: "Cash-Flow Accounting and Its Structure," *Journal of Accounting, Auditing and Finance* (Summer 1978), 331–348; and "Recovery Rate and Cash Flow Accounting," *Financial Executive* (March 1980), 54–60.

4. In addition to measuring actual set-up times, related performance measures used as targets by some firms include "single minute exchange of

dies" (SMED)—the exchange of tools in under ten minutes—and "one touch exchange of dies" (OTED).

5. John Marcom, Jr., "Slimming Down: IBM Is Automating, Simplifying Products to Beat Asian Rivals," *The Wall Street Journal* (April 14, 1986), 1, 10.

Index